How to Get the Best Legal Help for Your Business

(at the lowest possible cost)

Mead Hedglon
Practices law in Oklahoma City
and assists businesses in managing
legal matters

McGraw-Hill, Inc.
New York   St. Louis   San Francisco   Auckland   Bogotá
Caracas   Lisbon   London   Madrid
Mexico   Milan   Montreal   New Delhi   Paris
San Juan   São Paulo   Singapore
Sydney   Tokyo   Toronto

Library of Congress Cataloging-in-Publication Data

Hedglon, Mead J.
  How to get the best legal help for your business (at the lowest possible cost) / Mead J. Hedglon.
    p.   cm.
  Includes index.
  ISBN 0-07-027783-4   —ISBN 0-07-027786-9 (pbk.)
  1. Attorney and client—United States. 2. Lawyers—United States.
3. Business enterprises—United States. I. Title.
KF311.H43   1992
340'.023'73—dc20   91-43154
                                                                                         CIP

Copyright © 1992 by McGraw-Hill, Inc. All rights reserved. Printed in the United States of America. Except as permitted under the United States Copyright Act of 1976, no part of this publication may be reproduced or distributed in any form or by any means, or stored in a data base or retrieval system, without the prior written permission of the publisher.

1 2 3 4 5 6 7 8 9 0 DOC/DOC 9 8 7 6 5 4 3 2

ISBN 0-07-027783-4
ISBN 0-07-027786-9 {PBK}

Trademarks

Dialog is a registered servicemark of Dialog Information Services, Inc.

Lexis is a registered trademark of Mead Data Central, Inc.

Martindale-Hubbell is a registered trademark of Martindale-Hubbell, a division of Reed Publishing Company

Westlaw is a registered trademark of West Publishing Company

The sponsoring editor for this book was David Conti, the editing supervisor was Caroline Levine, and the production supervisor was Suzanne W. Babeuf. It was set in Baskerville by McGraw-Hill's Professional Book Group composition unit.

Printed and bound by R. R. Donnelley & Sons Company.

This publication is designed to provide accurate and authoritative information in regard to the subject matter covered. It is sold with the understanding that the publisher is not engaged in rendering legal, accounting or other professional service. If legal advice or other expert assistance is required, the services of a competent professional person should be sought.
      —*from the declaration of principles jointly adopted by a committee of the American Bar Association and a committee of publishers*

For Leda

Contents

Preface   vii

1. Do You Really Need a Lawyer for This...?   1
2. What Lawyers Fit Your Needs   15
3. Establishing a Regular Outside Counsel for Your Company   28
4. Getting a Trial Attorney When and Where You Need One   48
5. Getting the Right Stuff from Your Outside Lawyers   74
6. Hiring In-House Laywers   91
7. What to Expect from In-House Lawyers, and How to Get It   111
8. Why Lawyers Act the Way They Do   126
9. When Employees and Attorneys Bump Heads   141
10. What to Do 'til the Lawyer Gets There: First Steps When You Are Sued   152
11. How Litigation Really Works   167
12. What Happens When You Finally Get to the Courthouse   183
13. Getting off the Litigation Merry-go-Round: Alternative Dispute Resolution   200
14. Budgets: Control of Costs and More   213
15. How to Read Your Lawyer's Bill   230

16. Systems That Keep You in Touch with Your
    Attorney and Your Case   245
17. When and How to Fire Your Attorney   256
18. Evaluating Results   266
19. Planning for the Twenty-First Century   281

Glossary   286
Index   292

Preface

The number of lawyers will increase to more than 1 million by the beginning of the twenty-first century. The impact of legal matters on business operations will likewise increase. You can gain a competitive edge by effective and efficient handling of legal matters. This book will show you how.

Anyone who makes business decisions, or aspires to, needs to know how to work with the law and with lawyers. A small business cannot absorb expensive mistakes, and legal services are very expensive. The larger business needs to control not only the dollar costs of resolving legal matters, but also the distraction, delay, and disruption caused by the intrusion of legal issues into business affairs.

This book emphasizes lawsuits for the same reason that CPAs emphasize taxes: Each involves the direct application of the state's power to you or your business. In litigation there are choices you can make that will improve the overall results. Similar choices will help you use legal services to solve or avoid problems without resort to the courts. But it won't happen by accident: You have to manage your business's legal matters.

A trial attorney's view of business litigation is strikingly different from yours. What you, the client, see as expense, is income to the attorney. For the attorney, success happens in the courtroom; the client must achieve success in the real world.

Like two giant draft horses, when you and your attorney are pointed in the same direction, harnessed together, and moving in unison, much more can be accomplished than by your individual efforts. Communication gives direction. Linking fees to value harnesses you together. Systematic control coordinates your efforts.

This book will guide you through the decisions that only you can make. Is a lawyer needed? What kind? How should you choose a lawyer? Is the lawyer performing satisfactorily? What should you do with legal papers? How should you tell the lawyer what you need and can afford? How do you know if you are getting what is needed? When and how should you fire a lawyer? How can you evaluate results?

There are books available that tell you how to do-it-yourself. If you have the time, you might be able to complete some routine legal procedures. There are also excellent texts and treatises of the type lawyers buy, always a little out of date because the law evolves constantly. A one-volume text can give nothing more than superficial guidance on broad general principles. Finally, lawyer-bashing books are amusing, but they won't help you make real decisions. This book will tell you, the client, how to get the best results from your lawyers.

There are 50 sets of state laws and a vast amount of federal law, all being continuously refined or changed by the courts and legislatures. The illustrations and examples of law in this book reflect what the law was at some unique time and place. Do not rely on any statement of the law published in a book for guidance in a particular situation. Nothing in this book should be taken as advice as to what the law is.

If you need to put this book to work immediately—say, because you have just been served with legal papers—read Chap. 10 first, then read Chap. 4. Otherwise, read this book straight through. Then put it on your bookshelf; when you need to do a legal task, take it down and use it as a step-by-step guide.

This book is designed to make it easy to delegate each task. For example, if you need to have your regular outside counsel select a trial attorney in a distant city, give her this book and direct her to proceed as described in Chap. 4.

Throughout this book, when a personal pronoun is used to refer to the lawyer who represents you, the feminine form is used. Law practice is becoming gender neutral. Women constitute about half of new lawyers, and are becoming judges at a rapid pace. A prejudice that a half-century ago limited women to family and probate practice has long since disappeared. Those who retain the prejudice today see it turned against them.

The purpose of the forms in this book is to illustrate. If you wish to use them, read them carefully and adapt them to your particular situation. Lawyers have traditionally used form books as a place to start—a checklist—in creating documents that fit a client's needs precisely. You should do as much for yourself.

Each chapter focuses on meeting some need you will encounter in managing legal matters. When you put these ideas to work, you may find the "Procedures" that follow each chapter useful in laying out the steps to be taken or items to be considered. Like the lawyer's form books, these procedures are a starting place.

The focus of this book is on obtaining an acceptable outcome in any legal matter at a reasonable cost. Lawyers have come to believe that clients will pay more for more effort. A wise client pays for effort that has value.

Mead Hedglon

1
Do You Really Need a Lawyer for This...?

Ron and George had a deal. Ron would provide the software and the programming expertise, and George would purchase and install the hardware at his business. They would develop the system jointly. When it was ready, they would license its use worldwide. George's lawyer eagerly offered to look at the deal and prepare the documents. The lawyer offered to reduce his hourly rate, however, George turned him down. George did not want to spend even a few hundred dollars for legal help.

The lawsuit came a few years later. Ownership of the system, which now contained all the records of George's business, was in dispute. The fees of George's new attorney might cause the business to go under. How could George have known at the beginning that he really did need legal help? How can you know when you need legal help?

An experienced general practitioner of the law, not protecting herself against malpractice and not trying to justify a fee, looks at several aspects of what can be done for you. Primarily, there is the question of how far your particular situation has progressed. When the facts of a situation are being established, you benefit from the technical skill provided by a *lawyer*. After the main facts have occurred, you may need an *attorney* to argue about what they mean. Before the situation develops, the advice of *counsel* might enable you to avoid the entire problem.

Regardless of what the factual circumstances call for, you may not be willing to accept the most advantageous type of legal service. Other ways for you to obtain the same benefits as are offered by the legal profession, and the amount of money at stake, must also be considered. Weighting these points can guide you accurately in deciding whether or not to incur legal fees.

At the beginning, George needed advice about whether the deal was workable. Unfortunately, George had not placed enough trust and confidence in a counsel to accept such advice. Later, already locked into a dispute, George was compelled to rely on an attorney to protect his interests. George's difficulties would have been easier to handle if a lawyer had drafted a contract that covered the important points and accurately reflected the intentions of the parties.

You can analyze any business situation to determine when you need legal help, what kind you need, and how to get the most benefit from it.

The Lawyer as Technician

The question of whether or not you need a lawyer is really a question of what a lawyer can do for you in a particular situation. What lawyers do for clients is get the facts right. Knowing the law, lawyers know which facts are important and how to prove those facts to obtain a desired legal outcome. You need to recognize situations where getting the facts right has important legal consequences.

Getting the Facts Right

There are true facts. There are facts everybody knows. There are facts you think you know. There are irrelevant facts. And there are facts that are not facts yet. Lawsuits are said to be decided on their facts. The lawyer's job is to make sure you can prove the right facts. The lawyer studies the law to learn which facts determine the outcome of a matter, and also what will suffice as proof of those facts.

The image of a lawyer hunched over a table surrounded by open books and piles of paper, although accurate, does not tell you what the lawyer is doing for you. An example where it is easier to see what lawyers do is the investigation of a spectacular casualty, such as an oil refinery fire.

After the fire is out, there are many needs for information. The sales department wants to know how much product has been lost and if they will need to supply customers from other sources. The production department wants to know what has to be repaired or replaced to get back into operation. The engineering department wants to know what improvements and revisions can be accomplished in the reconstruction. The insurance department wants to know what the value of the loss is so that a claim can be filed. Management wants to know what happened, who is to blame, and what needs to be done to prevent repetition. Most such information will be taken on faith and used for business decisions.

The lawyer picking though the smoking debris is looking for proof, not information. The lawyer's objective is to find and preserve evidence that will support a legal theory that has yet to be developed. In the refinery fire instance, the lawyer developed evidence by interviewing witnesses, taking photographs, and studying records. Subsequent study of the evidence and the law led to two legal theories. Either a hose had separated from its brass fitting (possible product liability) or a worker had failed to secure the clamps connecting the hose (possible negligence). The hose had wire coiled inside as reinforcement. After the fire burned the hose away, the wire was exposed. The brass fittings were gone, melted. At the lawyer's direction, everything at the fire site was carefully photographed to preserve the evidence. Examination of those photos showed melted brass soaked into the ground at the end of the reinforcing wire, indicating that the hose had not separated from the fitting. The preserved evidence "proved" that neglect in securing the clamps caused the loss.

A lawyer preparing a contract is doing the same things. The main facts are the intentions of the parties to the contract. The lawyer may interview his own client, and sometimes the other party, to find out exactly what is intended. The contract is fashioned to express accurately and precisely the intentions of the parties.

A well-drafted contract is like photographs of a fire site. If a dispute does develop at a later time, the parties can study the contract for guidance. If the lawyer did a good job, the contract will include provisions which, like the photos of the wire ending in melted brass, will prove how the parties intended to resolve such a dispute.

The essence of the lawyer's work is in getting the facts right so that the intended legal result is accomplished. A lawyer representing a buyer of real estate investigates the facts of the land records to be sure that the buyer receives good title to the property. A bank's lawyer, documenting a loan secured by a lien on real estate, establishes the interests of the parties for possible use in a later foreclosure. Or a lawyer might direct a purchasing agent to write down the phone numbers, times, and dates of calls placed in an effort to obtain replacement goods for a contract not fulfilled, for later use in proving damages.

What Is a Lawyer?

As used here, the term *lawyer* means a person who has qualified as an officer of the court, knows the law, and practices law as an occupation.

Lawyers are trained to execute legal procedures. A lawyer may be employed as a mere scrivener. A *scrivener* is someone who is concerned only with the writing of a contract, and who has no input into what is agreed to. A lawyer may be employed to do legal research, searching in a library for the law and reporting his findings in a memorandum. In litigation, a lawyer may be employed to review documents to identify which are significant or to extract all the facts from a witness in a deposition. The lawyer's focus is on the facts and what the facts mean under the law.

The lawyer can be thought of as standing behind you, fashioning and shaping the instruments which serve your purposes, much as a medieval armorer remained in the castle making weapons for his king. Although a lawyer must meet professional standards of competence and ethics, she acts as you direct and not on her own initiative.

Alternatives to Lawyers

Getting the facts right is the basic task of many workers. They complete the vast majority of transactions with no direct or apparent involvement of lawyers. Nearly all transactions are routine for at least some of the parties involved, with well-understood facts and consequences. The expertise of people who routinely handle even the most complex transactions is usually sufficient to detect discrepancies and recognize the need for help from a lawyer.

Lawyers have a traditional role in some routine transactions which are wrapped in legal mystique. Buying real estate, perfecting security interests, and forming corporations are typical of ordinary matters that fall within a legal sphere of influence. There are other ways to get such jobs done. In many states, for example, real estate deals are commonly closed by title insurance companies. If everything about your deal fits the normal pattern, the absence of a lawyer should make no difference. If your deal does not fit the pattern, however, you may find that it cannot be completed, or that it has unexpected—and undesirable—consequences.

A dangerous way to rely on common patterns is to use ready-made forms which appear to be standard. The problem is that the forms can be used by people who do not know how to fill them out, and who are unaware of their ignorance. An example is a commonly used banking form entitled "Participation Certificate." Printed and sold by a well-established stationery firm, it was used by many institutions to buy or sell interests in loans. Such transactions, called *loan participations*, are intricate. What is interesting is that the printed form has a blank space with the notation, "due date." Inserting the maturity date of the underlying loan provides some information but has no effect on the rights of the parties. Filling in any earlier date suggests that the buyer has a right to require the seller to buy back the interest, a consequence that is not consistent with the common understanding of participations.

There are nonlegal sources of expertise for nonroutine transactions. Guidance in complying with various governmental regulations is available from the staffs of enforcement agencies, such as the Internal Revenue Service, the Environmental Protection Agency, the Occupational Safety and Health Administration, and their state counterparts. Of course, anything you disclose can be used in an enforcement action against you.

Some vendors, such as banks and collection agencies, may offer to help you set up procedures to improve coordination with the services they offer. However, their systems are designed to serve their needs, not yours.

When Lawyers Won't Help

Sometimes a lawyer isn't much help. Any business, however small, can get caught up in a complex, multiparty deal. A common example is industrial financing funded by municipal bond issues. The prospect of employing a few local people may induce the county industrial development authority to offer you a long-term loan to expand your plant. The deal sounds good when explained by the "experts," who will collect huge fees and commissions when the deal closes. As the closing date approaches, a 3-in stack of "bond documents," along with a 2-in stack of "loan documents," are presented for your review. You can and should read the documents, and perhaps have your lawyer explain them to you. However, if the terms will not be changed—that is, if it is a "take-it-or-leave-it" proposition which you have decided to take, the lawyer, in that role, has little to offer.

Similarly, you may have already committed to a deal before signing the contract. For example, you might purchase furniture and equipment for a restaurant, arrange for provisions, and commit to a 1-year contract for a Yellow Pages ad before signing a lease. At that point, all a lawyer can do is read the lease and tell you what it says.

Having a lawyer read over complicated documents is no substitute for gaining your own working understanding of what they mean to your business. The lawyer's advice that the papers are "OK" is no substitute for your own intuition and judgment about the entire deal.

You may be tempted to strike a deal with someone and leave the details to the lawyers. But the details are the margin of survival in most deals. A lawyer's focus on the law and facts may give you a valid, binding contract that does not serve your interests. In the end, the details are always the client's responsibility.

How Important Is Lawyer's Work?

A lawyer's work is directed at controlling the risks in a deal. Some deals are so small as to negate the payment of any amount of fee. Other deals are so large as to make any reasonable fee insignificant. A typical lease illustrates some ordinary business risks. A 5-year lease at $2000 per month is a $120,000 commitment, plus the cost of improvements, plus the costs of moving. What happens if highway construction cuts off access to the shopping center? Could your cash flow sustain the costs of relocation if the landlord fails to provide necessary maintenance? Could your cash flow cover the entire cost of maintenance of the common area under a triple net lease if all the other tenants default?

In conclusion, if you don't know all of the facts (including intentions), why they might be important, or how to prove them, you need a lawyer.

The Attorney as Advocate

The attorney's way of helping a client is entirely different than the lawyer's. An attorney applies knowledge about the law to shift power in your favor, dealing with the facts as they are already established.

Shifting Power

Attorneys invoke the power of the state to enforce your rights—specifically, rights which are being denied or ignored by other parties to a transaction. Usually, disputes about rights are settled by the parties without state intervention. This is acceptable when the parties have fairly balanced power in the transaction. For example, a seller has the power to ship substandard goods. The buyer has the power to withhold payment. These kind of differences, perhaps based on misunderstandings or differences of opinion, are worked out between the parties because each has sufficient power to force some accommodation of their point of view.

When there is a great difference in the power of the parties, the rights of the weaker party are easily ignored by the unscrupulous. A person who has sustained a loss may assert a claim under an insurance policy against his own casualty insurance company. The claimant has the power to write letters and fill out claim forms. The insurer has the power to pay or not to pay. If there is a difference of opinion about whether the loss is covered, the insurer may exercise its power, withhold payment, and ignore the claimant's rights.

Alone, the claimant can do nothing. However, by suing the insurance company, the claimant can bring the power of the state to bear on the insurance company. The validity of the claim will be determined by the state acting through the courts, and the rights of the parties will be enforced by the sheriff.

A strong, solvent company can find itself in the situation of the insurance claimant. Even a weak debtor can simply not pay. Even a powerful company may need the power of the state to collect from an unscrupulous debtor.

The state's power is frequently called upon because of genuine differences about what the facts are and about what rights flow from the true facts. The parties would find a mutually acceptable solution if they had essentially equal power. One party, unable to gain an acceptable accommodation from the other, calls upon the law. The first step is to bring in an attorney. The presence of an attorney in a dispute is an implied threat to bring the matter before a court.

You have to decide if introducing that kind of power will help you. If your power is much less than your opponent's, then perhaps you will be better off with the power of the court being brought to bear. On the other hand, if your ability to influence events is sufficient or increasing, introducing a whole new source of power is pointless.

The analysis of the relative power of the parties should include everyone effected by the transaction, not just the direct participants. Define all of the relationships. Consider what is transpiring between the parties and the choices that each has. List all threats, demands, and complaints. Consider the personalities involved. Who is stupid, smart, flexible, stubborn, emotional, calm, loyal, persuasive? Will you lose an advantage over a weak character if everyone hires attorneys? How are things changing with the passage of time? What is happening in your business environment? Inflation, a rising or declining trend in the real estate market, war in the regions that supply raw materials, or advancing technology may affect the relative strengths of the parties.

If you conclude that your rights, too valuable to simply surrender, are being ignored because you lack the power to have them honored, hire an attorney. If your adversary hires an attorney to enforce claims against you, hire an attorney.

What Is an Attorney?

An attorney is more than a lawyer. An attorney is a lawyer who has been empowered by a client to act on the client's behalf. Of course the attorney must know the law, but his key talents are persuasive. Effective attorneys are quick, able to "think on their feet" and improvise while in the midst of encounters with the adversary.

In preparation, an attorney must gain a thorough understanding of your situation, needs, and desires. You must be satisfied with your attorney, because everything said by your attorney in open court is absolutely binding on you. In order to perform effectively, your attorney must be free to act without interference or distraction from you. You must turn over complete control to the attorney during confrontation. Client control of how a case or negotiation is to be conducted limits the lawyer to the role of a technician. When you turn over control, the attorney's focus can be entirely on the adversary.

Your attorney can be thought of as standing in front of you, shielding you from your adversary and facing the problem, perhaps wielding instruments fashioned by a lawyer. The romantic terms "champion" and "hired gun" refer to the attorney's role, fighting for clients.

Alternatives to Attorneys

When you are engaged in a lawsuit, you need an attorney. There are no practical alternatives. When you are served with legal papers, especially a summons and complaint, the court is exerting its power over you. Once subject to the court's jurisdiction, you are governed by the court's rules. Ordinarily, the court's rule is that a corporation can be represented in court only by a duly licensed attorney at law. More important, the rules impose deadlines and requirements which must be met or rights are forfeited. Prudence requires that you have the benefit of an attorney's knowledge. Similar rules apply when before other tribunals, including elected or appointed boards (zoning, for example) and administrative agencies.

There is a strong temptation to save attorneys' fees when a case is in a small claims court, when the opposing party seems ready to settle directly with you, or when you are not really a direct defendant, as when an employee's wages are garnished. The difficulty is that when the court is involved, the requirements of the rules must be strictly followed. Even if you settle, unless the proper procedure is followed, the case may remain in the court records to haunt you in some future credit check or as a lien on your property. By the time you discover this, the other party may be long gone.

Attorneys shift power by calling on the power of the law and also by effective advocacy. Many complicated business disputes are routinely settled by nonattorneys with special expertise in applying the law. For example, shipping claims, governed by a complex of federal law, regulations, and filed tariffs, are handled by tariff clerks and audit bureaus with essentially no involvement of lawyers. Similarly, pipelines settle surface damages on their rights of way, and receiving departments return nonconforming goods. Such routine dispute solving reflects the character and honor of the industries and individuals.

Power is also shifted by the largest group of advocates, salespeople. The salesperson represents his or her company every day, applying persuasion before disputes take form and positions harden.

When Attorneys Won't Help

The power of the law to enforce your rights is limited. You may win a lawsuit with your customer, and in the victory lose the customer. You may win a lawsuit against an adversary who is willing to frustrate any effort to collect money by seeking relief in the bankruptcy court. Asbestosis claimants learned that lesson. You may win control of a corporation only to find its assets drained and its customers alienated. The people you sue do not have to do business with you. That is raw economic power, rarely affected by the law.

If you win a lawsuit, what happens when the attorneys are done? The problem does not remain in the courts forever, although it will seem to. Eventually the court's judgment must be implemented in the real world. What relationships will be damaged or destroyed in the process of the attorney's work? Are these long-term relationships that might have continuing value?

In some industries it is common for attorneys to take the lead in negotiating on behalf of their clients. Without such an established pattern, introducing an attorney automatically escalates any dispute into a conflict. Bringing in your attorney suggests that you don't think your rights are being respected and implies a threat to resort to the law.

How Important Is the Attorney's Work?

The defense of claims is potentially significant on two levels. If you lose, you may lose the entire amount of the claim asserted against you. In some situations there is exposure to punitive damages, but ordinarily the value of the claim is what is at risk in the case. That is easy to evaluate. The second level of risk has to do with precedent. If you lose a case that proceeds to judgment, especially if there is an appellate opinion written, the notoriety may attract more, similar claims. On the other side, in asserting claims on your behalf, when there is no counterclaim, all that is at risk is the value of the claim.

In conclusion, whenever you must call upon the power of the state to enforce your legal rights, or an adversary hires an attorney to assert claims against you, you need to hire an attorney.

The Counsel as Advisor

The greatest benefit obtainable from legal services comes from good counsel. Advice sought and accepted before commitments are made helps you avoid problems and concentrate on the most fruitful endeavors.

Avoiding Hidden Traps

On the day of your grand opening, the city inspector shows up and wants to see your "business license," and you don't know what he is talking about. Or an oil-drilling crew arrives in the middle of the golf course site you have developed and claims the right to use as much of the surface as is reasonable and necessary to drill and operate a well. Either surprise, the rule you never heard of or the rule that is not what you expect, is unpleasant. Trained to be skeptical and often in adversarial situations, counselors at law are sensitive to subtle clues about hidden traps. The questions they ask may make you uncomfortable. Trying to find something wrong with a deal seems like a negative approach. That is why promoters and brokers refer to counsel as "deal killers."

Clients often receive counsel without asking for it. An experienced proprietary school operator decided to open a new school in a state where he had not previously operated. He hired local counsel to form a corporation in the new state. The counselor insisted on a complete explanation of how the business would work. The discussion of capital requirements made it obvious that the school site would be leased. A state license requirement was the reason for forming a local corporation. Counsel pointed out that without the state license the leased site would be unusable, and also that processing the license application would take some months. The advice was to delay the effective date of a lease. The client had not asked for help with either the lease or the state license, and was not happy to get the advice. As it turned out, however, the client's savings in lease payments during the licensing delay were substantial. Entering strange territory is a good reason to seek counsel.

Anytime you consider an unfamiliar type of transaction, there is a chance that specific words will have unexpected meanings not found in the dictionary. In the early 1980s, for instance, executives of savings-and-loan associations, expert at making loans secured by single-family dwellings, were rushing into the high-return commercial loan market. The savings-and-loan people were embarrassed by their ignorance of such terms as "takeout commitment," "participation," "due diligence," and "standby letter of credit." Taken in by some corrupted brethren, they assumed that whatever those words meant, it was "OK." As it turned out, those words did not have the expected meanings. A counselor, having forgotten some of the things she learned in law school, may have to ask what those strange words mean, so she can tell you what she learns from the answer.

Ordinary social familiarity does not give you much insight into how individuals will act in a business deal that has gone sour. You may know your brother-in-law or a golf buddy pretty well. But until your relationship involves the loss of their personal money, you don't know much about them as business partners. The only way to know how good your business relationships are is to work through a few money problems. In a deal with anybody—long-time acquaintance or complete stranger—counsel may suggest an elaborate written document that expressly covers almost everything. By this means, two things are accomplished. Negotiating a picky and detailed contract tests everyone's character. When it is done, you can rely on the document more and the individual's personal merit less. Where you and the other party have been able to work out problems in the past, such a complicated document is not needed. The difference is in the basis of trust, not the complexity of the deal. Counsel can guide you in making deals with strangers and familiar people in strange roles.

What Is a Counsel?

A counsel is a lawyer with a client who listens. The term suggests broad experience and wisdom. There are few counselors. There are few clients who seek or accept advice. The use of the term *counselor* or *counsel* suggests that the client is accepting the advice that is needed, not just what the client wants to hear. In a product-liability situation, for example, a lawyer will tell you what the law is, and an attorney will defend the cases, but a counselor will tell you if you need to recall the product.

The basis of good counsel is in-depth background knowledge of you and your business. Counsel moves on her own initiative to understand your needs, and acts on those needs by identifying and explaining to you the best solutions. This calls for the highest level of trust and confidence on your part. The advice is accepted by being given due consideration, whether or not it is followed. When you are willing to accept advice, the focus of the counselor is on you.

The counselor might be thought of as standing beside you. With the lawyer behind you fashioning instruments and the attorney before you confronting the enemy, the counselor whispers in your ear, saying what must be said about the decisions you must make.

Alternatives to Counsel

Avoiding hidden traps is the basic work of business executives. Accountants, bankers, insurance brokers, publicists, and other business advisors have much to offer in this regard. Don't overlook trade associations, which often have expertise gained in lobbying efforts. As a prudent businessperson, you routinely gather available information and weigh it before making decisions. Of course, asking the questions that will turn up problems may reveal plans and ideas that you would prefer to keep confidential.

You may be reluctant to pay for counsel. After all, the exercise of that kind of judgment would seem to be your job. Although pulling together all of the information available from other sources for your counsel will make her more effective and efficient, saving time and focusing her effort on the most likely trouble spots, the fee may seem redundant. Keep in mind that all of those alternative sources of information are looking out for their interests, not yours. When balancing counsel fees against unknown risks, remember that free advice is usually worth what you pay for it.

When Counsel Won't Help

The relationship between you and your counsel is not established simply by paying a single fee and visiting for an hour in a dry, dusty law office. The advice and guidance must be tried and found useful, and withstand the test of time before it will be trusted. The necessary quality of advice will be forthcoming only after counsel has had the opportunity to observe you under stress, and to watch the industry go through whatever cycles or other economic phenomena affect it. This implies a mutual commitment over a long period of time. There is a danger that counsel's impartiality and objectivity will be prejudiced. There is a second danger that you will come to rely on counsel for advice to the exclusion of others with greater expertise.

How Important Is Counsel's Work?

The advice of counsel is about the opportunities and risks you take or avoid. What is your worst business nightmare? Consider this: You innovate a new product or service and market it regionally. With a combination of hard work, talent, and luck, you find the market and begin to grow. A national marketing company expresses an interest. You are on your way. Then you get a letter demanding that you stop infringing a preexisting, registered trademark used in interstate commerce for many years on an inferior product only remotely similar in use to your brainchild. Counsel might have recommended a trademark search when you were picking a name for your product. Your entire business is at stake! No counsel can eliminate business risk, but good counsel makes it possible for you to evaluate the risks to take and the ones to avoid.

Summary

When you ask yourself if you need to spend money on legal services, think of how you would want an employee to work out that question on your behalf. After each chapter is a one-page procedure. Following these procedures step by step ensures consideration of the key points of each chapter. Whether you delegate a specific task or do it yourself, having the procedure as a ready reference puts each in the context of the overall objective.

In deciding if you need to pay a lawyer, first consider how far events have progressed as an indication of what kind of legal service is needed. When everything is in the future, advice of counsel is appropriate. When the facts are being shaped by events happening in the present, a lawyer's knowledge of the law is applicable. When the main facts have already happened, an attorney's advocacy may be required. The world is never static. Some new facts continue to develop in any matter. Therefore, a single individual may provide some of all three kinds of services in any given matter. For example, an attorney's advice to settle a case is clearly counsel. Nonetheless, one type of service will dominate.

If the matter is not routine, a lawyer will get the facts right. If the power of the state is being invoked to enforce legal rights, an attorney can act as your advocate. Counsel will be beneficial when encountering unknown places, transactions, or people. With fair consideration of the alternatives, and the limits of legal help, the need can be assessed accurately. After that it is just a matter of getting what you need and controlling the cost, the subject matters of the rest of this book.

How far have the facts developed?		
Situation	*Example*	*Need*
Facts being developed	Drafting a contract to establish the facts of the parties' intentions	Technical expertise to know what facts are needed and how to show them, a lawyer
Facts already established by past events.	Materials that don't meet specifications, or the occurrence of an accident	Advocacy to put existing facts in the best light, an attorney
Facts which will limit choice to be made have not yet been established	Whether to sell through company stores, franchisees or dealers	Advice to avoid hidden traps and consider legal aspects, counsel

If your need is met by a lawyer, consider:

Alternative sources	The use of forms, standard procedures, service agencies, especially for "routine matters"
Potential impact	Some deals are "take-it-or-leave-it" propositions
Amount at stake	What are the practical limitations and obligations imposed

If your need is met by an attorney, consider:

Alternative sources	Salesmanship solves many problems, but litigation requires an attorney
Potential impact	How to sell a customer you've sued
Amount at stake	Cost of concessions to settle

If your need is met by counsel, consider:

Alternative sources	Banker, CPA, or trade group
Potential impact	Your willingness to pay for advice
Amount at state	Worst-case outcome

Procedure: Deciding whether to incur legal fees.

2
What Lawyers Fit Your Needs?

The best source of information to use in planning to meet your legal services needs is the stack of bills your lawyers have sent you in the past year. Those bills at least define the needs that have been addressed in the past. The bills, analyzed with your background knowledge, will show you what legal services are used, by whom, and where. That information, tabulated and summarized to create a legal access chart, will be a guide you can use to provide for ready access to legal services that will efficiently meet the needs of your business.

The raw material for this analysis is the actual legal bills. You will be marking the bills up and sorting specific items into categories, so a complete set of photocopies is a convenience. You need to work with a copy of the original bill, not an accounting record, so that you can focus on the details. This analysis can be done manually, or, if you are adept at using it, with a spreadsheet on a personal computer.

Total Legal Outlay

An internationally renowned engineering and consulting firm added up a year's worth of legal bills from its principal outside law firm and discovered, to their surprise, that the law firm charged them more in one year than any other single outside vendor.

The first thing to do with your legal bills is add them up. Don't bother to separate out charges for disbursements and expenses; you are looking for the total cost of legal services. There is no need to figure out when the services were rendered; the billing dates are close enough for this analysis of a year's outlays.

The total of the legal bills is only part of the story. Add the total salaries of any in-house lawyers. Don't include employees who, although licensed as lawyers, are not employed primarily for the practice of law. Divide the total salaries by 0.6 to get an assumed cost. In law firms, overhead, exclusive of professionals' salaries, should run from 38 to 42 percent of revenue regardless of firm size. Using this percentage for your in-house lawyers avoids any peculiarities of your internal cost accounting system and is close enough for this analysis.

A portion of your indemnity insurance premiums goes for the legal costs of defending claims. Insurance premiums can be divided into insurer's marketing expense (commissions), profit, risk-spreading cost (the gamble), and claims costs. Your insurer may be willing to tell you the actual percentage of your premiums that it expects to spend for the defense of claims. If not, figure about one-third of the premiums, even if you have no pending claims. Your indemnity policies, which pay damage claims made by others against you, may include: general liability, premises liability, directors and officers, errors and omissions, environmental, garage keepers, automobile, completed operations, products liability, malpractice, or others. Your insurance broker or agent can give you the total premiums.

A portion of trade association dues can often be attributed to legal services—for example, a lawyer lobbyist. Fees of collection agencies or property managers may include payments to lawyers for collections or evictions. Advertising expense may include legal fees for network clearance. Lenders often pass legal fees directly to borrowers. The value of awareness of such indirect legal expenses is that you may be able to control or avoid them.

The cost of general information about the law and legal matters—subscriptions to newsletters, for example—should not be included. Tax advice from your accountants should not be included.

Your legal outlay is the total of these items: legal fees, in-house lawyer salaries and overhead, part of insurance premiums, and indirect legal fees. This total does not provide for opportunities missed, collections unmade, and cases lost. Also not provided for are the nondollar costs that attend all legal troubles, especially litigation: distraction, disruption, defamation, disclosure, and delay. Compare your legal outlay to your pretax profits to see the potential benefit of careful management of your legal matters.

A new business, or one that has not used legal services, will not have a history of legal expense to analyze. Some projections will suffice for the new business. In starting a new business, your primary legal needs are for counsel, generally for basic planning and avoidance of problems, and some technical help in forming the business entity. A new business engaged directly in a law-related service (title insurance and technology licensing are examples) might employ in-house lawyers immediately, but the owners and managers of most new businesses will use independent lawyers. Such start-up services are an opportunity to establish a regular outside counsel.

In an established company, the fact that no legal services are used means that there are no legal problems, or that legal problems are being handled without involving lawyers, or that the burden of legal problems is being borne by some other part of the company. For example, the cost of out-of-specification materials received from vendors may show up in scrap or rework costs. You might avoid the problem by spending more on receiving inspections. Or you might satisfy an unhappy customer by replacing defective goods you have shipped. Just where that burden ends up is a cost accounting question that is beyond the scope of this book. However, many costly situations can be handled legally. The cost might be avoided with precise specifications and warranties in purchase orders, or shifted to whomever caused it by "vouching in" under the Uniform Commercial Code. An astute manager will apply the most effective resources, including legal, to control total costs.

Charting Expenditures

Regardless of your particular circumstances, developing a legal access chart for your company will provide a tool for analyzing what kind of lawyers you need in various situations.

Preliminary Considerations

Sort out and discard the items over which you exercise no control, generally the legal services that you do not pay for directly. That includes the portion of insurance premiums attributed to defense costs if you have no pending cases. However, an attorney, hired by an insurer to defend you, owes you undivided loyalty. You can and should have substantial interaction with insurance defense counsel, and you should feel free to ask for an estimate of the fees charged to defend you. An accurate approximation of insured defense costs is sufficient, and should be included in the analysis.

Sort out the bills paid for highly specialized legal work. These are one-of-a-kind jobs that are not likely to be repeated. Examples are: a trademark search for use in choosing a company name; termination of sponsorship of an employee benefit plan; or registration of a security. The selection of specialists for such work should always be made ad hoc, that is, for the particular matter at hand.

Also, sort out the bills paid for legal services provided in distant locations. A distant location is any place too far away from your main office to reach within an hour or two. As a practical matter, you will want to hire a lawyer on the scene. Choosing lawyers at a particular location, like hiring specialists, is an ad-hoc process. Mark the ad-hoc bills as you sort.

Type of Services

The different roles of "counsel" as advisor, "attorney" as advocate, and "lawyer" as technician were described in Chap. 1. These are not sharp distinctions; an individual may serve in all three roles in a single matter. As a client, you dictate the role to be filled by what you ask for. Drafting an ordinary contract, closing a real estate deal, or completing a routine foreclosure are work in the lawyer role. Litigation and negotiation are mostly done in the attorney role. Rendering advice to decision makers is the essence of the role of counsel. As the client, you know which role you wanted filled.

Review each bill and decide what kind of services you were seeking. You will have to think about what you wanted at the time the service was rendered. You also need to study the detailed description of what was done. Based on what you wanted and what was done, you should apportion each bill among the three roles, lawyer, attorney, and counsel. At best, what you will get is an approximation, so don't struggle with particular items. Mark the dollar amount apportioned to each role on the bill.

Who Are the Users?

Even in a small company, where the boss can keep track of the legal work by looking in his checkbook, it is worth the effort to note which operations incur legal expense. Each item of legal expense should be charged to the person, or their department (credit, purchasing, personnel), that needed the legal help to get their job done. It may help in keeping track of these items to write a two- or three-word description of what the legal work related to on the bill. In a small company, an accounts receivable clerk or a bookkeeper may bring a past-due account to the boss's attention, with the CEO making the decision to get legal help. The attorney may work directly with the clerk to collect the account. The bill should be charged to the collection function. The purpose of this part of the analysis is to discover who needs access to lawyers. Again, the easy way to do this is to mark up the copies of the invoices.

Tabulating the Data

The foregoing steps should provide you with a pile of bills, each marked with the amount of money apportioned to the roles of lawyer, attorney, or counsel, one or two words about what the work was for, and who needed the work done. You can put that data on a spreadsheet that follows the form of Fig. 2-1. For a small company, this can be done manually on a large sheet of paper.

Bills for legal services in a narrow specialty or a distant location, needing ad-hoc attention, should be tabulated separately if there are many of them.

List the actual users of legal services, in the order of their rank within the company, in the left column. This is really a vertical organization chart. Using titles instead of people's names keeps the focus on the purpose of the legal services. The ranked users should be grouped into at least two, but no more than five or six, levels. The data from each invoice, to whom charged, for what, and amount attributed to each role (lawyer, attorney, or counsel), is entered on the spreadsheet. The dollar amounts in each column are subtotaled for each management level.

Figure 2-1 illustrates a simple tabulation for a small company, but it is not an example, the amounts and ratios are not typical of anything, and it should not be used for comparison. Your company's data will be unique. The tabulated data from the legal bills provides an overview of what kind of legal services the company is using and who is using them. As always, some managers will be unhappy with the cost allocations and rankings. To get away from continuing criticism of the detail, and to make the data easier to use as a management tool, put the subtotals on a chart in the form illustrated by Fig. 2-2, the legal access chart, by transferring the subtotals for each level of management.

For your business, you can expect to see a concentration of counsel services at the higher levels of management and lawyer services at the lower levels. Most money spent for ad-hoc services will probably be for representation by attorneys. Note in the example that the amount spent by the sales manager and credit manager on lawyer work, $111,145, is enough to cover the estimated position cost of an in-house lawyer as developed below.

Cost of Legal Services

The American Bar Association (ABA) surveyed its members regarding their incomes in 1989. Since the ABA annual dues, after the first year, are a couple of hundred dollars, the bottom end of the profession is not reflected. The average lawyer's income for the preceding year (1988) was claimed to be $117,800 and the median to be $76,600. Lawyers in firms with less than five members averaged $90,900, while those in firms with more than 50 lawyers averaged $131,800. At the time of the ABA survey, Congress was attempting to raise the salaries of federal

Who uses legal service	What for	How much is spent		
		Lawyer	Attorney	Counsel
Chief executive officer	Set up company	$ 500		$1,500
	Jones proposal			600
	Trade Secrets			200
	Bond financing			2,700
	No-compete clause			300
	Name change	750		1,100
Executive management subtotal		$ 1,250		$6,400
Plant manager	Factory lease	$ 2,000		
	Permit, waste	450		300
	Press failure			275
	Roe claim		775	
	Waste removal	175		
Credit manager	Collect debt		1,200	
	Perfect security interests	38,400		
	Credit documents	37,900		
Sales manager	Dealer contract	3,200		
	Employment agreement	975		
	Shipping claims	185		
	Doe claim		4,750	
	Trademark			300
	Store leases	27,650		
	Mart lease	210		
Operating management subtotal		$111,145	$ 6,725	$ 875
Indirect legal expense:				
Insurance premium			17,000	
Association dues			400	200
Total legal expense		$112,395	$24,125	$7,475

Figure 2-1. A tabulation of data from legal bills.

What Lawyers Fit Your Needs?

	Lawyer	Attorney	Counsel
Executive management			
Annual expenditure			
(subtotal from Fig. 2-1)	$ 1,250	$	$ 6,400
Estimated position cost	$107,100	$142,800	$214,200
Positions available	Nil	Nil	Nil
Ad-hoc annual expenditure	$	$	$
Operating management			
Annual expenditure			
(subtotal from Fig. 2-1)	$111,145	$ 6,725	$ 875
Estimated position cost	$107,100	$142,800	$214,200
Positions available	1.04	0.04	Nil
Ad-hoc annual expenditure	$	$	$

Figure 2-2. The legal access chart summarizes and simplifies the data from the legal bills.

district court judges to about $125,000. As a practical matter, a lawyer of good reputation and standing in the community would like to earn about what a federal judge should be paid. To generate the necessary revenue, about $210,000, a diligent counselor, charging clients for about 1500 hours per year, needs to bill at an hourly rate of about $140. Billing more hours will cut into the time needed for running the business and keeping up to date with new developments.

The top New York City law firms pay new graduates $85,000. The salaries of some state court judges and the median incomes of Illinois lawyers are in the mid-$50,000. To have a sense of what is fair and reasonable, you need to consider the skill and experience of the individual and the local market.

The roles of lawyer, attorney, and counselor call for different levels of experience and different kinds of skills. A new lawyer from an average law school can perform only the most rudimentary tasks. With 5 years of experience, most lawyers are able to do a technically competent job. Lawyers who are able to gain the trust and confidence of clients move on to the role of attorney, learn new persuasive skills, and in about 5 years more will be journeymen advocates. The wisdom and experience needed to attract clients seeking advice generally takes even longer. The increasing experience levels are reflected in correspondingly higher hourly rates.

The extremes, overpaid New York associates and underpaid state court judges, can be ignored in figuring out what lawyers need to earn. Most lawyers are affected by the same economic forces that affect the starting pay of school teachers in public school systems. Over the past couple of decades, and across the country, the ratios of teachers' salaries to lawyers' earnings has remained pretty much the same.

To estimate the cost of filling a legal position in your community, call your local school board and obtain the base salary offered for new school teachers. One suburban school district in the Southwest paid new teachers, without advanced degree or specialty, $17,850, for the school year 1990–1991.

The gross revenue needed to support a business's legal counsel is about 13 times the salary of a new school teacher—in that Southwestern community, about $232,050. To be well paid, an attorney need to generate about nine times a teacher's salary, or $160,650 in our example location. An experienced lawyer would need revenue about six times the teacher's salary, or about $107,100 in that place. Convert these gross revenues to net compensation by multiplying by 0.6. A new lawyer usually makes less than twice what a new teacher makes.

The actual earnings of individual lawyers will vary widely from these figures. Some work much harder than others. Partners in law firms, in addition to what they earn by providing services, share in profits made on the work done by associates. Efficiency and effectiveness of marketing are often reflected in hourly rates. Those attorneys who accept the risk of contingent fees are sometimes handsomely rewarded. Despite the individual differences, these figures calculated from teacher salaries will approximate gross fees and net incomes of lawyers whose practices are set up to respond to the needs of businesses.

Interpreting the Legal Access Chart

This tedious task of assembling information from your legal bills will build a simple but powerful management tool in the form of Fig. 2-2, the legal access chart. The legal access chart defines the legal needs of the business in terms of the skill level required, lawyer, attorney, or counsel, and the level of management to which the services should be delivered. The information from past legal bills shows what has been done. The actual experience of any successful business is a good indicator of what should be done.

You may want to provide for more legal help, based on new developments or an evaluation of past results. Add estimates of the fees for those additional services to the legal access chart, at the appropriate role (lawyer, attorney, counsel) and level of management. Again, separate those which will be hired ad hoc.

The obvious needs of a start-up situation suggest counsel working with top management. In a mature company, the greater need is often for lawyers to work with operating management. For example, the credit manager needs a lawyer's help to perfect security interests, or the personnel department needs an attorney's help to defend workers' compensation claims. The legal access chart points out the value and impact of legal services at the operating level of the company, where most problems start.

The legal access chart can be used to determine how many lawyers, attorneys, and counselors would be required to meet your needs if you were to concentrate the work in the smallest number of individuals possible. The specialty and distant-location services (ad hoc) must be kept separate because they cannot be concentrated in a few individuals. Insert the estimated position costs calculated with the local new teacher's salary multiplied as stated above. Divide the annual expenditures tabulated for each type of service and for each level of management in your business by the estimated position costs. The example in Fig. 2-2 illustrates expenditures 1.04 times the cost of one lawyer position serving operating management.

Many companies do not spend enough on legal services to fully support any single position. You might combine the lawyer and attorney expenditures to make up one counsel position. An experienced and skillful counsel will be able to handle any of the tasks characterized as lawyer work. Of course, it does not work the other way. A person at the salary level of a lawyer will not ordinarily have the stature and influence needed to fill the role of counsel. What this means as a practical matter is that you may fill in-house lawyer roles while still relying on outside sources for counsel.

Every client is important to a solo practitioner who mostly represents individuals in their personal legal needs. Every client has the potential to be, or to refer, a personal injury case with a one-third contingent fee. How significant is your business to a law firm? Very significant if your fees are supporting one or more positions. Your potential as a source of referrals to a law firm with a business practice is practically nil, especially if you are from out of town, or consulting the firm for specialty services. Generally, the importance of the revenues you provide depends on the size of the firm. Revenue equal to half a year's teacher salary is quite important to a solo practitioner.

Meeting the Needs

Legal services are obtained three ways: by selecting attorneys on an ad-hoc basis, to handle a particular matter; by establishing a regular outside counsel, to deal with matters routinely, and by hiring in-house lawyers. You may use any or all of these approaches at any time.

Ad Hoc

Occasionally, every company uses the ad-hoc approach because attorneys are needed at the scene of litigation or attorneys with special skills are required. Ad hoc is just a short way to say that you are getting legal help with a particular matter. You may not have enough legal business to maintain any ongoing relationship with a lawyer or a law firm. Many businesses do not spend any money on lawyers for years at a stretch. Perhaps the lawyer you have used in the past is no longer available, or was unsatisfactory. The selection of a trial attorney is a typical situation for the ad-hoc approach, but the same method is used whenever you need a particular attorney for a specific matter.

Selecting an attorney to meet each specific situation as it arises has the advantage of flexibility. Finding exactly the expertise that applies to your unique problem should provide excellent results. However, the ad-hoc approach requires a greater investment of time and effort in the selection process and closer supervision of the work.

Establishing Regular Outside Counsel

The most effective and efficient legal service is counsel. Good lawyers draft good papers and brave attorneys will fight adversaries to the last drop of your blood, but it takes good counsel to keep you out of trouble. Counsel's awareness of your affairs will enable her to notice what is important to you, to find hidden traps, and sometimes to discover hidden opportunities. Such good counsel is necessarily founded on knowledge and experience.

Establishing and nurturing a counsel relationship requires more than just going back to whoever has handled your last matter. Maintenance of the relationship requires regular, fee-generating contacts. Otherwise, the lawyer's knowledge of your situation will go stale.

There is a potential cost advantage in having your legal work done by a regular outside counsel, or by her associates. Most of the cost of legal services is determined by the time expended. Every time you engage a new lawyer, that person must be educated in the peculiarities of your industry and your company. That education cost is reflected both in the legal bills, at her hourly rate, and in your time explaining things. When your regular counsel is familiar with all of your legal matters, the education time is shortened even when the work is done by an associate lawyer.

With a regular outside counsel in whom you have confidence, you may be able to delegate more authority to your own subordinates. For example, if your marketing manager leases store locations, having him work with outside counsel may relieve you of concerns about his negotiating skills. You may feel more able to take a vacation, knowing that your second-in-command has ready access to legal help in an emergency.

Lack of flexibility in choosing lawyers may leave you with representation that lacks the skills and interests needed to find new solutions to new problems. The use of a single law firm may tempt you to abdicate your responsibility to manage your legal matters. A long relationship may lead to complacency or excess profit taking by the law firm. These are the kinds of problems associated with any decision to "sole source."

In-House Lawyers

As you look at the amount you spend on legal services, you may begin to think about in-house lawyers. When the legal access chart indicates that you can support one or more lawyers, it calls for the kind of "make-or-buy" decision you have with any component of your product or service.

There is an expectation that the use of in-house counsel will result in cost savings. The marketing cost of a law firm, about 20 percent, is avoided. The overhead burden, particularly for office space, may be less. The special knowledge of in-house personnel may make them more efficient and effective, but to realize that benefit, continuous outside training is required along with other costs of maintaining professional competence.

In-house lawyers may have less than 100 percent utilization. If nonlegal duties are assigned to a lawyer, to fill in, the privilege of communications between the client and that attorney will be confused and perhaps destroyed. An actual cost savings requires a sufficient volume of work to keep an in-house lawyer occupied about two-thirds of the time.

It takes a strong personality to build a company. Can you, as an entrepreneurial CEO, accept advice from an employee? Company builders often feel that the business acumen and judgment of anyone who works for them is inferior to their own. Indeed, outside counsel whom you like and respect may refuse full-time employment simply because they do not want to have a "boss." Good lawyers are not servile. A counselor who tells you what she thinks you want to hear is worthless. Legal advice, which always incorporates judgments, has the most value when it is not what you "want" to hear. Will you have enough respect for an employee to respect judgments that are at variance with your own?

In-house attorneys have a difficult time conducting litigation on behalf of their employers. A trial attorney has a strong obligation to be responsive to the demands of the court. The court's requirements may conflict with what is expected of employees. Court business takes precedence over company matters, for example, staff meetings. When trying cases, secretaries are needed in the evenings or early mornings. For the attorney, the trial work is itself very demanding and has little to do with the conduct of the business. It is not "productive" in the usual business sense. Other employees see attorneys as a source of demands and burdens, a nuisance. An attorney's opportunities for advancement within the company are limited. A strong commitment from the organization is absolutely required to achieve success with in-house trial attorneys.

The role of lawyer may be more compatible with the limitations of in-house employment. An in-house lawyer's easy accessibility and familiarity with your business translates into the competitive advantage of quick, efficient execution of legal procedures and contract drafting. Most of the work of an in-house lawyer is generated by routine matters that do not involve executive management. The supervision of in-house lawyers must be structured to ensure loyalty to the client-company, and not the person immediately above them on the organization chart.

The legal access chart which you derive from your past legal bills defines the legal services needed by the business in terms of the roles of lawyer, attorney, and counsel. You should select individuals qualified to fill those roles and permit them to do so.

What Lawyers Fit Your Needs?

1. Establish your total legal outlay.

   Include for an established company:

   Amounts paid to law firms
   Compensation and overhead of in-house lawyers
   Claims cost portion of insurance policy
   Indirect legal services paid through

   Trade association
   Advertising agency
   Property manager
   Lender
   Collection agency
   Other service vendor

   Estimate for unmet or hidden needs, including:
   Uncollected accounts
   Product lost to out-of-specification materials
   Other losses from enforced legal rights

   Project for a new business:

   Partnership agreement or incorporation
   Financial documentation for lender or shareholders
   Contracts for location, equipment, supplies, etc.
   Protection of patents, trademarks, and copyrights
   Employee contacts and benefits
   Other anticipated legal expenses

2. Allocate each legal outlay to need for either lawyer, attorney, or counsel services.

3. Allocate each (lawyer, attorney, or counsel) service to the level of management requiring it.

4. Tabulate the amounts allocated to each type of legal service at each level of management using a spreadsheet following the form of Fig. 2-1.

5. Enter the subtotals for each type of service and level of management on the legal access chart, Fig. 2-2.

6. Compare the amount paid for each type of service provided to each level of management with the estimated cost of a full-time professional.

7. Decide for each need at each level of management if the need is best met by regular outside counsel, ad-hoc attorneys, or an in-house lawyer.

Procedure: Determining sources of legal services.

3
Establishing a Regular Outside Counsel for Your Company

The most important thing about legal counsel is finding the right one. Often, lawyers are avoided because they charge too much, accomplish little, and you cannot tell if they know what they are doing. With the right counsel, you gain reliable access to sound legal advice. The objective in retaining regular outside counsel is to gain her expertise in avoiding excessive charges, wasted effort, and poor quality.

Your particular needs as a client determine who might be your best choice as counsel. The recent experience of a Japanese chemical company illustrates a unique match of needs and qualities. This chemical company had purchased mineral rights, and constructed facilities, to extract iodine at a site located in a rural county in the United States. The operation involved pumping brine out of the ground, removing the iodine, and pumping the brine back into the underground reservoir. The rights to pump the brine, which flowed freely underground, became the subject of a dispute with the owners of the adjoining surface.

The Japanese firm had hired a reputable and capable law firm, located in the state capital. The dispute about the right to pump brine became a difficult lawsuit. The legal bills mounted and no progress was apparent. None of the lawyers spoke Japanese, and none of the Japanese employees of the chemical company spoke English. The attorney and client communicated through the individual who had been the broker in the original deal. It was to his advantage to shift responsibility for all problems to the law firm. The Japanese firm, caught up in cultural conflict and unfamiliar with local political and social pressures, could not understand or use the advice being given.

Living in that same state capital was a lawyer, a solo practitioner, who had served with the U.S. forces in Japan and married a Japanese woman. He did not have influential contacts, a fancy office, or a reputation as a great trial attorney. He had not made much money as a lawyer, did not dress well, did not have a phone in his car. Because his wife was Japanese, however, he was invited to a reception for the owner of the Japanese company, where he learned in casual conversation of the company's legal problems. His ability to speak Japanese made his advice accessible to the company.

This solo practitioner had ordinary intelligence and political astuteness. His ability to understand the client and make his advice understandable to the client made him the right counsel. At the request of the Japanese company owner, he began to make some inquiries. On his recommendation, the former firm was replaced by a trial attorney from the county where the extraction plant was located. The case was quickly settled on amicable terms. The solo practitioner became and remains the Japanese company's regular outside counsel.

Advice can prevent a situation from developing into a problem only if you get it early. The objective of having regular counsel is to minimize the obstacles to getting such early advice. The cost of keeping counsel on standby may not directly increase sales or cut costs. The main benefit is that your decisions are better. A second benefit is that counsel will help you do a better job of buying all other legal services.

Why Have a Regular Outside Counsel?

Any business, and particularly your business, has a core activity that creates revenue. However much you might like to concentrate on that productive activity, other considerations intrude. The government regulates your relations with your employees, the disposal of your waste, how long you keep your records, and then taxes everything. Vendors don't ship and customers don't pay, the landlord defers maintenance, and the banker demands that your spouse sign the note. You will handle almost all of this yourself, but sometimes you will want to know the legal rights and remedies you are bargaining with. Having an established relationship with counsel, you can call her at any time, and, without having to explain every detail, get attention, advice, and, if necessary, action. The net effect should be to leave you more time to be productive.

When you have prepared a legal access chart, as described in Chap. 2, you can see what you are spending for legal advice, counsel, given to the top management. Is the amount you actually spend only a small part of what would be needed to support a professional working full-time? On the other hand, is the amount enough that you think it worthwhile business? If the answer to both questions is "Yes," you should have a regular outside counsel even if you have some in-house lawyers and want to use a variety of attorneys for specific matters.

Financial institutions, insurance companies, talent agencies, technology license brokers, and similar companies which deal primarily in legal rights, may be able to justify counsel in-house, even at the start-up stage. That is the exception to the rule that, for most companies, counsel is obtained from an individual who is independent.

The Benefit of Creativity and Imagination

A regular outside counsel can become a specialist in your business. Every business has unique arrangements and patterns. For example, in a wholesale optical laboratory, the bulk of the frames and lenses that are processed may come from a single supplier. The supplier will set a credit limit based on history. In hard times, or when expanding, the lab operator may use all of the credit available from the bank. The bank will have filed a blanket lien. In a cash-flow squeeze, counsel's knowledge of the business may help the operator negotiate a higher credit limit with the supplier, by showing how a "purchase money security interest" can take priority over a blanket lien.

Similarly, a franchised service required the operator to purchase equipment from the franchisor and pay a royalty based on gross revenues. The franchisor took a security interest in the equipment and controlled the use of the company name. As technology developed, the same service could be provided with generic equipment for about the same cost. Counsel recognized that the real value of the business was in the long-term customer contracts and not the system and equipment furnished by the franchisor. The franchisor had provided forms for customer contracts. By substituting a new contract form which named only the operator and described the equipment and services in generic terms, the franchisor's stranglehold was broken. When it was time to renegotiate the franchise agreement, the operator's control of the customer contracts enabled him to get a better deal.

The value of general knowledge about your business and the capabilities of you and your employees is not its relevance to any particular legal matter. Such knowledge, applied with your counsel's creativity and imagination, generates unexpected solutions to problems which may have no obvious legal implications. For example, any time you have to negotiate, counsel can find points for agreement or contention, to use to keep the process going.

Saving Time and Money

On those occasions when you need legal advice to handle a specific question, having regular counsel will save you time at every stage. You need not lose time figuring out whom to call. You will make contact more quickly, and with less "phone tag" by knowing when and where reach to your counsel. The response need not be delayed while she figures out how she will be paid, and makes sure she has no conflict of interest. Knowing who you are, counsel won't need to spend time getting your name and address right. These routine points easily eat up days. Once counsel starts working on your matter, the factual background she already has will help her to focus on the critical issues. Knowing your business, and your habits, she will know what priority to give the work.

A subtle benefit of a regular relationship is that counsel collects more fees in the long term by giving good value. Consider the typical job of forming a corporation. A fee of $500 gets you a name check, some forms filled out, a set of preprinted by-laws, and advice to see your CPA about a Subchapter S election. That kind of mindless paper processing is unimportant compared to the coming together of people, ideas, and capital. Regular counsel, or someone hoping to become regular counsel, might take time to inquire into your hopes and plans, looking beyond the immediate billing opportunity.

The Qualities of an Ideal Outside Counsel

Any outside counsel must perform satisfactorily, a subject discussed in Chap. 5. In choosing counsel, you must look beyond ability. You are looking for a person who is motivated by an interest in business generally and your business in particular.

Most lawyers are interested in their business, which is providing legal services, and most will be interested in selling their services to you. Any duly licensed lawyer can hold himself out as a "corporate lawyer" or "contracts lawyer," and many do so in the hope of attracting business. The few counselors who will serve you best are individuals with an interest in how business really works, that is, in how products are made, how quality is controlled, how marketing happens, and the like. This interest goes beyond just making money.

Genuine interest manifests itself in questions about how your business works. This is a person who is happy to take a plant tour. This is a person who asks questions that are none of her business, just to satisfy her curiosity. This is a person who sends you clippings and suggestions about potential opportunities. She will be happy to read your annual report, sales materials, and press releases, as well as the trade press of your industry. Time permitting, she will attend conventions, trade shows, or your sales meeting. The motivation for doing these things is intellectual satisfaction, not just sending you a bill. When you find counsel who has the interest, you encourage it by paying for advice when you can use it.

The ability to work well with others is based in confidence and self-assurance. Business and business law become ever more complex, and special expertise is needed even in ordinary matters. Taxes, for example, affect everything. The source of tax expertise may be your CPA, your in-house accountant, or a lawyer who specializes in tax matters. Your counsel can send you to the best specialists only if she is confident that the merit of her own services will bring you back in the future.

You will be getting into a kind of mentor relationship with your counsel. It is probably easier to do that with a person you perceive as senior to yourself. Age for lawyers is measured both from date of birth and from date of admission to the practice of law. It is essential that your counsel have sufficient experience and stature to command your respect and confidence. Without that respect and confidence, you will not weigh his advice properly.

Tact and diplomacy are essential elements of counsel's personality, because you are going to permit this person to influence you. One reason to have counsel is to avoid unprofitable confrontations, so look for coolness and unflappability under pressure. Sometimes businesspeople like to brag about how aggressive and nasty "their" lawyer is, and there is sometimes reason to hire bluster and toughness, but counsel's demeanor will be reflected in your actions.

You, as client, must live with the consequences of your decisions, and you have the right and responsibility to make those decisions. Counsel's responsibility is to advise you impartially, sometimes telling you things you do not want to hear. Mutual respect is essential if the relationship is to survive a frank exchange of views.

You will accept counsel only from someone you like and trust. Words such as loyalty, honesty, candor, respect, admiration, confidence, and intelligence all describe the kind of character that counsel must have to be effective. They are good words, but you have to decide what they mean. In the end, acceptance of a particular individual as your counsel is subjective.

Where Will You Find the Right Counsel?

As unimportant as it may seem in an era of instant communications, physical location is a primary consideration in selecting regular outside counsel. It is a matter of access. One lesson from the federal effort to clean up the savings-and-loan mess is that long-distance legal counsel does not work. New institutions, created as receptacles of the assets of defunct institutions, are required to obtain all legal services from centrally located law firms. The new institutions have no corporate history; everything is being done for the first time. To deliver the kind of legal advice and guidance needed, the lawyers have to travel. The burden of the travel costs, including the time charges and the dilution of effort, is sufficient to discourage consultation. The failure to get the kind and amount of legal help needed is a principal reason for the failure of the new institutions to liquidate assets quickly and efficiently.

You want to be able to visit your counsel, or have her come to you, without making a major excursion of it. The fax and the modem cannot convey the subtle messages of body language. If you are in a small town, look first in that town. The big-city guys do not have any monopoly on brains or wits. If you are in the suburbs, look first for someone on your side of town. Law firms tend to locate their offices near the courthouse. That is for the convenience and efficiency of the trial attorneys. Counsel, on the other hand, need to be close to clients. In terms of having ready access to counsel, proximity to the courthouse is no advantage to you unless your own offices are also nearby.

Despite what the Internal Revenue Service thinks, having lunch with your counsel is a good way to exchange ideas and opinions. If you cannot meet your counsel for lunch without disrupting your day, you are too far away. When counsel visits your place of business, she can observe much that you would never explain. Is work piling up? Are employees idle? Is the office tense? Or happy? Physicians are trained to rely on observation when examining a patient. Counsel examining a business client similarly needs to observe the client.

Law Firm Size

The choice between a large, powerful, well-connected law firm and a solo practitioner cannot be made by weighing the claim "bigger is better" against the reality that legal services are custom-crafted by individuals. Firm size should be considered in choosing counsel. For discussion, firms can be categorized arbitrarily as mega-firms, big firms, mid-size firms, small firms, and solo practitioners.

The Mega-Firms

A mega-firm is characterized by having more than 300 lawyers, offices in the major U.S. cities and in Europe and the Pacific rim, and at least some of the largest international banks or multinational manufacturers as clients. The largest law firm has more than 1600 lawyers and offices in more than 40 countries. Such firms hire the top graduates of the best-known law schools. The talent and resources they offer may exceed any reasonable needs of ordinary business clients with ordinary business matters.

The newer mega-firms are the product of mergers of big firms and rapid growth. They have no long-term experience of managing such large organizations in what is essentially a cottage industry. Whatever the talents of the individual lawyers, the organization structures are untested. Having multiple offices is not relevant to your need for counsel, and presents internal management problems. On balance, the management weakness of mega-firms negates any advantages they might have as a source of counsel for your company.

The Big Firms

The big firms are characterized by a change in the management dynamic that occurs when the firm begins to hire associates that have not been met by all of the partners. This may happen in firms as small as 30 lawyers with as few as 15 partners. The big firm holds itself out as a full-service firm, prepared to meet all of your business needs. Therefore, it may have an office in Washington or may tout itself as "bicoastal." The long-term commitment to pay overhead drives a continuous marketing effort. The staff may include a publicist and marketing director in addition to an administrator. Large firms will have management committees and recruitment programs, and will be dominated by accounting functions required to realize all time expended as time billed. Large firms hire law firm management consultants. Such firms tend to have an anchor client, and may not be able to survive if they lose the big client. Most large firms are formally divided into departments or working groups. The departments may reflect the local economy, e.g., oil and gas, talent contracts, or admiralty, or may be divided by areas of law, e.g., tax, securities, or litigation.

The big law firms offer high-quality legal talent, supported by the best libraries, databases, communications, and staff available. Among the excellent practitioners in such law firms there are many whose personal abilities could fully satisfy your need for counsel. Unfortunately, generating the money to pay for this magnificent capability limits the ability to actually serve in the role of counsel.

The wide range of talent available within the firm is beneficial only if exactly what you need can be found there. In a large firm your counselor may be limited to the resources within the firm in meeting your needs.

Ordinarily, fees are based on hours expended. For the most part, you will want to compensate your counsel in an amount related directly to the services she has personally rendered. In a big firm, partners' income comes mostly from profits on fees generated by associates. Even if the partner worked full-time for you on a year-around basis, her hourly-based fees would not cover the compensation she expects. Partners in big firms are rewarded for maximizing client's legal bills. Your legal access chart indicates if you have enough attorney and lawyer work to support a counsel in a big law firm. In a large firm in a large city, a least $100,000 in billings each year are needed to compensate a partner for being your counsel. If you are not the source of enough routine and profitable legal work, the partner will try to hand you off to an associate or junior partner. That will free up the partner's time to go hustle more profitable clients.

Associates and junior partners may have plenty of talent, and may be interested in your business, but you should reject them as counsel. Associates do not work for you, they work for the firm. You cannot promote them or give them a raise. Their employer, the firm, will evaluate them mostly on the basis of hours billed. Associates cannot command the firms resources, or place them at your disposal in a crisis. Associates cannot reduce the bill for time charged by a partner or other associate.

Associates, Rainmakers, and "the Rule of Three"

A stale joke makes a point about associate billings. An associate of a major firm, having died at the age of 29, arrived at the Pearly Gates. Asked how he felt about reaching Heaven, he told St. Peter that he was pleased, but he would have liked to have spent more time living. St. Peter at first seemed puzzled and then the explanation came. Based on the number of the hours the associate had billed in his short lifetime, it appeared that he was an old man.

To avoid having their income limited by the hours available and market rates, partners in law firms rely on leverage. "Rainmakers" get the work in, associates do it. Excellent lawyers may become "rainmakers." Well dressed, with many contacts and impressive credentials, they go out to meet and greet prospective contacts. They are salespeople. That effort keeps them busy. Their native ability as counselors is not available to you. You may reach them to discuss your crises, but all you will get is soothing noises until you can be turned over to one of the worker-lawyers.

Associate billings are expected to follow the "rule of three." That is, associates are expected to bill to clients an amount equal to three times their compensation. One-third of their billings will go to overhead. One-third is their salary. The balance is profit to the firm, to be distributed to the partners. To achieve this, the development of new associates must be accelerated to bring them to the point where their hours are fully billable within weeks after graduation. That is why salaries for some elite new graduates reached $85,000 in 1989.

In the more commonplace law firms, with ordinary law school graduates, starting salaries range from $25,000 to $40,000. The rule of three requires billings of $75,000 to $120,000 per year. The pressure to bill time creates several kinds of problems. Partners need to find work for the associates. The associates have little time to devote to building client relationships that will turn them into "rainmakers" in their own right. A survey responded to by 155 law firms indicates that, after giving lip service to quality of work, billable hours is the key criterion for evaluating associate performance. New business development is what counts most for senior partners.

The Mid-Size Firm

The mid-size law firms, usually with about 10 to 30 lawyers, are generally managed by a consensus of the partners. The taking of binding votes leads to hard feelings. The casual and informal decision-making process is slow and unwieldy. The partners will frequently discuss improving the management, but will be reluctant to submit to a real management structure. They may have an office administrator to attend to details, but delegate very little authority to that person. An individual partner who seems like a good match as your counsel will probably have sufficient power to shape the firm to meet your needs.

A mid-size firm ordinarily has the depth and facilities to support your counsel adequately. If your counsel is unavailable, a partner should be able to fill in. The library, conference rooms, computers, and communications equipment will be adequate for any ordinary business matters. As with big firms, associates are not in a position to be satisfactory as counsel.

Your counsel's loyalty to the mid-size firm may prevent her from going outside the firm to obtain needed expertise. Mid-size firms generally see themselves as "full service," meaning that you use the trial attorney they have. The term "boutique" is sometimes used to describe mid-size firms which specialize, operating like a department in a large firm. Insurance defense, municipal law, and probate are typical nonbusiness specialties. Common business-oriented specialties include tax, oil and gas, patent and trademark, securities, and bankruptcy. If your counsel practices in such a specialty firm, she is more likely to refer your matters to other kinds of experts when appropriate.

The Small Firm

The small firm, of three to nine lawyers, may not even be a common enterprise for the practice of law. Many small firms are just office sharing arrangements. The partners share expenses, but each keeps the bulk of the fees she individually collects. The few decisions are made by consensus or a dominant individual. Partners will generally back each other up if the practices overlap. The library will be small, covering only state law. The support staff and facilities may be minimal, but the lawyers will know how to get large copying jobs, fax service, and even extensive research done outside the office.

If you find a compatible counsel in a small firm, you can be confident that she will know about meeting payrolls, filing the 940 and 941 tax returns, and the importance of collecting from customers. Lack of partnership status is of less concern, since the firm contributes little to the services being performed. Similarly, concentration of a firm's practice in a nonbusiness area such as matrimonial or criminal law is no impediment if the individual is interested in your business.

The Solo Practitioner

Solo practitioners are real lawyers, living by their wits. They can conduct their business with nothing more than a roll of quarters and a phone booth. Their library may be in the courthouse. Their letterhead may be a macro in the word processor. Some solo practitioners, usually by concentrating on a limited type of practice, earn large sums of money. Some solo practitioners, as the term is used here, may employ other lawyers as associates, and have elaborate offices and support staffs. These true entrepreneurs readily identify with small-business operators.

A solo must have street smarts and business sense to survive. If you pay one to counsel you, she will readily refer you to whatever specialists you may need. More often, though, she will seek nonlegal solutions, because solos know what really happens in the courthouse. The key question to ask a solo practitioner is whether she is interested in your business, not just in having your business.

The disadvantage of using solo practitioners is that they need lots of clients to survive. If you take up an excessive amount of her time, she may neglect the marketing of her practice to others. She may become dependent on your business, which will impair her ability to be candid.

The size of the law firm is less important than the capabilities and accessibility of the individual you choose as counsel. Some may argue that large firms attract more capable people. Others will suggest that the complexity and costs of larger organizations impairs accessibility.

Finding the Right Individual

Having settled on the desirability of having regular counsel, and with a sense of what qualities that person will have, you can begin your search.

Accessibility suggests that you start close to home. Your analysis of total out-of-pocket legal costs will suggest some limits on the size of the law firm in which your ideal counsel is likely to practice. You will be able to find a satisfactory individual by applying basic sales techniques, prospecting and qualifying. The market for legal services is inefficient. Buyers and sellers have difficulty finding each other, displaying and inspecting what is offered, and establishing price or value. Using prospecting and qualifying techniques will gain you a measure of control.

Prospecting for Candidates

The conventional wisdom is that you find good lawyers by their word-of-mouth reputation in the community. Your banker, CPA, suppliers, and trade association personnel may be willing to share opinions about the local legal talent. The basis of such opinions is usually obscure. The fact that someone is a low-handicap golfer or on the board of a charitable organization will contribute little to your thinking. Actually, the "community" knows nothing about what you need as a counsel. Limiting your search to the pool of well-known lawyers simply excludes most of the real talent that is available. Good reputation is not much help, but don't disregard the warning of a bad reputation.

Ask for referrals, with skepticism. Keep in mind that the people you are asking are precisely the people you will be seeking advice about. Your banker's lawyer, for example, has a direct conflict of interest. Referrals are an indication of which lawyers have "contacts." Contacts may be useful in specific instances. Counsel's role is broader. She should be able to make the right contacts for various specific matters as they arise. Many county bar associations have a referral service. They will give you a couple of names from a list of lawyers who have signed up and agreed to a fixed-price initial conference. Lawyers pay, in addition to dues, a nominal fee to get on the list and sometimes a small additional fee for each referral. By specifying that you want referral to lawyers located nearby, with some experience, and a business law practice, you should find some worthwhile prospects.

With a view to the importance of accessibility, look in your own office complex or building. You may meet prospective counsel in various social or community activities, but keep in mind that they are likely to share your prejudices and blind spots. You may be acquainted with lawyers employed as judges, in-house counsel, or in a narrow specialty, who will suggest some candidates, but be sure they are sending you to people they consider well qualified, and not just doing favors for their friends.

There are some things that will not help you in this inefficient market. Advertising by lawyers is now permitted. The U.S. Supreme Court has decided that consumers have a right to information. The advertising in the Yellow Pages and on television is generally aimed at consumers of criminal, divorce, bankruptcy, and personal injury-related legal services. Broadcast advertising is expensive and justified only by a mass market. You will not find the information you need in such advertising. A claim that a practice is "concentrated" in contracts, corporations, or business law may reflect only wishful thinking. A practice "concentrated" in 10 or 15 fields probably has expertise in none. Although there are some accrediting organizations of long standing and with meaningful standards, most certificates seem to be mere marketing devices.

Promotion devices used by law firms that want your business include newsletters, brochures, and firm resumes. Some law firms merely add their logo to newsletters purchased ready to go. Of more value are newsletters produced within the law firm. A more dignified form of self-promotion is speaking at seminars sponsored by trade and professional organizations. One way in which lawyers keep track of who is an expert is through brochures that advertise seminars for lawyers.

If you exhaust these avenues without success, consider having an open house. Some companies do this during the holiday season, or to celebrate an anniversary. Invite your banker, suppliers, insurance agent, and CPA. Set up a tour of your factory, or display examples of your most creative work. Invite all the lawyers who have offices within a reasonable distance; make up the list from the phone book. Have your guests sign a book indicating their affiliation. Those who show up are interested in having your business. Those who ask questions are interested in your business. There is nothing magical about finding good prospective counsel. Those who work in the legal community find quickly that some lawyers are difficult to work with, most are reasonable, and a few are very compatible. It is largely a question of personalities. Any competent lawyer is a prospect. Of eight or ten accessible lawyers you get to know, you should find one or more who would be successful as your counsel. In choosing counsel you are merely sorting out those with whom you are most compatible.

Qualifying Prospects

Qualify prospective counsel by interviewing her in her office. Telephone the individual lawyer you have identified as a prospect to make an appointment. If you cannot reach her by phone, she should be rejected as not accessible. When you reach the lawyer, ask for an appointment at a mutually convenient time. Let the lawyer set a time when she is sure she will be available. Tell her that you want to discuss possible representation, and that you are not seeking any specific legal advice. There should be an express understanding that there will be no fee paid, unless one is required by a referral organization.

Since the lawyer has chosen the time, she should show respect for you by being on time. Before settling into a discussion, put yourself in control by asking for an office tour. Most lawyers like to show off their offices. While you are looking around, notice whether or not it is an efficient workplace. Is the lighting and ventilation adequate? Is it clean and orderly? Are the people busy, idle, friendly, surly, appropriately dressed? Does the lawyer introduce you? Lavishness, a symbol of success in personal injury or criminal defense firms, is merely overhead in law firms that handle business matters.

Then, let the lawyer take the lead. Where does the interview go? You want an opportunity to describe your business. Cover how and when you started, what recent developments are important, and the kinds of legal questions you anticipate. Listen to the lawyer's questions. Does she inquire about why you might need counsel, and how legal issues fit into your business as a whole? Are possible conflicts with existing clients discussed? Is she sensitive to tax and cost considerations? Does she seem interested in helping you get the most effective and efficient legal help possible? Does the lawyer listen to you?

Keep in mind that in this interview you and the lawyer are two businesspersons sharing views to decide if working together will be mutually beneficial. You need to know what her practice objectives are. Does she really want a business practice, or does she prefer doing mortgage foreclosures, divorces, personal injury, or whatever else comes up? What kinds of business clients does she presently have? Will she give you some references? What is her personal story? Does she have the broad experience and courthouse exposure that will provide a sound foundation for dealing with your matters? Ignore bragging about court victories, but look for stories about how clients have been helped. Is this a person who will find hidden traps in business transactions? Does she want your business enough to spend some time on this conversation?

If the rapport is there, press on to the terms on which representation might be available. Ask about the billing and time-keeping system, and other charges for copies, postage, and telephone. How are time records used in setting fees, and who can make adjustments? Now that you are getting to the heart of the matter, how much this will cost, does she back away from the hard issues, or explain them fully? You do not need a counsel who makes you feel good by avoiding the tough questions.

Test Closings

If you can afford the expense, having prospective counsel handle minor matters is a good way to test your choice. You may have a lease to be looked at, a corporation or partnership to be formed, or a license application to be filed. It might be something you could handle yourself. If your prospective counsel points that out, and offers to show you how, you are working with the right person.

Working through a legal problem with counsel will show you if your search has accomplished its objective. Responsiveness and prompt attention are a large part of accessibility. Her interest in your business will be reflected by the quality of the work and attention to detail. If the nature of the work is such that it can be handled more efficiently by an associate, look for her continuing involvement in assuring that your needs are satisfied. Does counsel strive to give full value, with advice that is practical and useful? Is the fee commensurate with the value? Cost is the acid test of accessibility.

The final test is for candor. Is this counsel going to tell you when you are wrong? If you don't know, because she has not done so already, take the next hare-brained scheme you get to her. Tell her you like it. Lie! If she tells you, in the face of your enthusiasm, that it's a dumb idea, you've found your counsel. That is candor.

Fortunately, you do not have to do this all at once. The rewards of a strong counsel relationship come only from a sustained effort to find the right person. When you do find the right person, formalize the relationship.

The Retainer Agreement

You look to your counsel for pragmatic advice about the legal aspects of business situations. Counsel should run her business as well as you run yours. That comes down to having a clear agreement on the price for her services, in writing. This is what lawyers call a *retainer agreement* or an *engagement letter*.

The object of the fee arrangement is to set up a fair scheme for compensating counsel. You are limited only by your creativity in finding ways to determine an appropriate fee for counsel. Retainers paid annually or monthly to cover ordinary consultations have fallen from favor as time-keeping systems have tracked costs more accurately. A discounted hourly rate with a monthly minimum and maximum will cover phone calls and routine work, if there is a consistent work flow. Volume discounts, reduced rates for work done beyond a specified amount, will help keep billings down. Flat rates for routine tasks make costs predictable. If you beat down the fees, eventually the quality of the service will suffer. If you are really tough, your counsel may just go out of business. On the other hand, uncontrolled fees will drift upward without any relation to value.

Be wary of bartered fees. Lawyers are audit targets for the Internal Revenue Service, so any gift of samples to counsel should be motivated solely by the need to make her familiar with the product.

Figure 3-1 is a sample retainer agreement which you can adapt to your needs. It incorporates some features explained in later chapters. Counsel needs to know who the client is and who is authorized to speak

Figure 3-1. A form of retainer letter for regular outside counsel.

YOUR COMPANY LETTERHEAD

Current Date

Jane Counsel
Law Firm Name
Street Address
P.O. Box
City, State, Zip Code

Re: Legal Services

Dear Ms. Counsel:

XYZ Company has authorized and directed me to confirm the arrangements by which you will provide legal counsel to the company.

The scope of your counsel will be determined by our requirements as they develop. You may anticipate receiving requests for advice from the undersigned, John Doe, or Mary Roe. Further, if neither I nor any other authorized officer is available, you are hereby authorized, but not required, to take action which is, in your judgment, required to avoid a default or waiver of rights by the company, subject to ratification of that action at the earliest possible opportunity.

We will compensate you for your services by paying, on your invoice, fees determined by the time expended at an hourly rate of $125. You have agreed to prepare detailed invoices, based on contemporaneous records, reporting what you have done, the date you did it, the time expended in tenths of an hour, the matter it related to, and identifying by initials the person actually doing the work. In addition, we agree to reimburse you for your actual out-of-pocket expenses incurred on our behalf, including photocopies, long-distance telephone, electronic database access, and travel expenses.

Please forward your invoices monthly. We will remit payment in full within 5 business days of receipt, subject to review and audit, taking a 1 percent discount on fees only.

Please advise the undersigned in writing before starting any project for which you estimate that your fee will exceed $500 in any month or $1500 in total. Ordinarily, projects of this or greater magnitude should be invoiced separately.

(Minimum/maximum option)
We agree that you may charge us for a minimum of 2 hours each month, whether or not the time is actually used, and you have advised that you will discount your fees 10 percent for the first 5 hours each month.

Figure 3.1. (*Continued*)

(Volume discount option)
You have agreed to discount fees charged for hours in excess of 50 hours per month by 10 percent.

(Flat-rate option)
You have agreed to handle each forcible detainer at the Hidden Valley Apartment Complex for $175.00 plus disbursements through execution of a writ of assistance, plus taxable costs. Your fee for collection of judgments for past-due rents, in such actions, shall be 20 percent of the amount collected, net of court costs.

You have been individually chosen for your personal qualities to act as counsel to the company. We understand that for reasons of efficiency or availability you may from time to time utilize other lawyers in your firm to assist you; however, we expect you to personally supervise such work done for us. From time to time we may require the services of persons having special capabilities and seek your assistance in making such arrangements. In those situations, we expect that you will fully disclose any relationship you may have with such persons.

The files you maintain on the company's matters are to be and remain the property of the company. You have agreed to assert no lien on the company's files and to deliver them on demand. Any copies made for your own use shall be at your own expense.

From time to time we will routinely send you copies of press releases, catalogs, and other material published by the company. These are merely for your information and not intended to generate a professional response. However, when we submit materials to you for legal evaluation prior to publication, we anticipate being charged for time expended in review and evaluation.

We rely upon you to seek such expertise or assistance as may be required. Experts or specialists retained on our behalf shall contract directly with us under your supervision.

Please report any instance of obstruction or lack of cooperation by any employee immediately, so that misunderstanding of our goals and objectives can be clarified by the undersigned.

We look forward to having the benefit of your advice and counsel in the years ahead. If this proposal is acceptable to you, please sign where indicated below and return the original to us.

XYZ Company

by_____
Fred XYZ, President

for the client. The letterhead may identify the client. The full names of corporate subsidiaries and trade names should be specified, so that conflicts of interest can be avoided. The letter should be signed by the officer designated by the board of directors to handle legal matters. Other persons who are authorized to contact counsel for various kinds of assistance should also be named. Even in a one-person company, the back-up person who opens your mail while you are on vacation may need to send legal papers. This form of retainer letter authorizes counsel to act in such situations.

You are establishing a regular outside counsel so that you will have ready access to advice. Limiting the scope of the work covered by the basic arrangement will help control costs. As particular needs become apparent, the necessity of a supplemental retainer letter will make you aware that additional costs are being incurred. In one instance, a regular outside counsel's associate was asked to write a memo on what steps should be taken to collect a judgment. When the memo arrived, it was merely a summary of the statutes, but it was accompanied by a bill for over $4000. Cost should always be identified before projects are started.

Regular outside counsel is selected for her individual characteristics, and she should provide the required services personally. However, she may be more efficient, and quicker to respond, if she utilizes the services of other lawyers. For example, you may need to know immediately how to be sure you get paid on an emergency, no-bid contract to repair government property. This is a complicated research project on a narrow issue. Because you need the answer this morning, she may assign the research to someone who is available and has access to the particular state's law.

The basis for determining the amount of the fee should be clear. In reality, simple multiplication of the hourly rate by the time expended only calculates cost. Most lawyers like to preserve some flexibility to adjust the fee upward for very good results. Clients want to write off time that had no beneficial effect. For the services of counsel, the hourly rate is a compromise that discounts such variables. That rate should be specified, along with the hourly rates of any persons on whom counsel expects to call for assistance.

The billing and payment procedures show how and when you will meet your obligation to pay fees, and also establish the reporting system that will enable you to maintain control of your legal matters. Monthly billing is normal. It is reasonable for counsel to send you a nominal bill for remaining on standby, even in months when nothing happens: You may need to know that nothing happened.

Detailed bills, showing what work was done, the date and time expended, and who did the work, can be prepared on standard software. Lawyers are always concerned about collecting their fees. Often they ask for an advance deposit. That is a one-sided way to control credit risk. It is better to agree to pay the full amount billed within 5 business days, perhaps taking a discount, reserving the right to review the bill later.

Provision should be made for out-of-pocket expenses. Although routine copying, postage, and telephone bills seem like ordinary overhead, in the law business they can become significant for some matters. Many law firms require entry of the client account number to gain access to the postage meter, copy machine, or long-distance phone line. What is important is that the charges be low enough to eliminate any profit incentive for their use.

Your counsel has an absolute duty of loyalty to you. Particularly in a small firm, she may regularly refer work to lawyers and attorneys in other offices. Clearly, a direct cash payment to her by the receiving lawyer is a problem. In industry it would be called a "kickback." Among "professionals," referral relationships with specialists are common. In every case where legal work is referred to another law firm, the receiving law firm should be hired and paid directly by your company. Generally, loyalty follows payment. You may compensate your counsel on referred matters by paying her directly for acting in a supervisory role.

Nothing Lasts Forever

After all this effort, you will feel relief when you have established a satisfactory relationship with outside counsel. Mutual loyalty and understanding will enable you to obtain sound advice and help your business over the long term. Some limitations will keep the relationship healthy for you.

Eventually, a decline in physical or mental health, or a change of direction in life, or other event, will cause the paths of you and your counsel to diverge. Your counsel may not grow with your business, or may take your business for granted. As your need for ready access to legal help develops, perhaps at different locations or in narrow specialties, you may want to cultivate other outside counsel. There is no reason to limit yourself to just one regular outside counsel.

The term "general counsel" means different things to different people. In some jurisdictions it means an attorney who is authorized to speak for the client on any subject. In this age of instant communications, there is no need to name an outside lawyer as "general counsel." It creates problems in ending the relationship. How do you tell the world that somebody is no longer your "general counsel" without damaging their reputation? There is no graceful way to do so. A law firm may urge that it be named "general counsel" in an effort to control all the legal business of the company, including out-of-town and specialty work. Avoid the use of the term "general counsel."

There are two problems when counsel is on the board of directors. The attorney–client privilege, discussed in Chap. 8, is diluted and may be destroyed. Worse, it is a conflict of interest. A director who is a lawyer and a member of a law firm selling services to the company is engaged in self-dealing. How are you going to seek out the best trial attorneys when your counsel is on the board touting his firm? If you decide to have counsel attend board meetings, keep her confidential reports and advice separate from the regular minutes.

Conclusion

With a substantial investment of time and effort, you can find counsel able and willing to respond to your needs. The focus of the effort is on your needs, and the relationship you establish with your counsel. In the next chapter, the problem of finding the right attorney to handle a particular case is addressed.

1. Consider personal qualities needed in your counsel:

    Interest in you and your business
    Confidence and self-assurance
    Experience and stature
    Personality and demeanor
    Compatibility

2. Consider impact of location on accessibility.

3. Match law firm size to your business requirements:

    Mega-firms' capabilities may not be relevant to counseling.
    Big firms require substantial fees to sustain counsel.
    Small firms may keep work that is better sent elsewhere.
    Solo practitioners lack depth and backup.

4. Search for prospective counsel:

    Inquire in your business community.
    Ignore advertising.
    Note speakers at seminars, luncheons, etc.
    Invite all local practitioners to an open house.

5. Interview prospects at their offices and note:

    Prospect's desire for your business
    Efficiency of prospect's office operations
    Sensitivity of prospect to your cost concerns

6. Use prospect for a sample matter and note:

    Promptness
    Quality of work:
        Thorough
        Error free
        Complete
        Accurate
    Cost effectiveness
    Candor

7. Retain regular outside counsel, using retainer letter, Fig. 3-1.

    Provide an explicit method for determining fees.
    Identify alternative contact persons.
    Specify the billing and payment procedures.

8. Remain open to the possibility of finding additional regular outside counsel as business grows and new problems develop.

Procedure: Establishing regular outside counsel.

4
Getting a Trial Attorney When and Where You Need One

You are sued, or some other major legal question comes up, and you don't have an attorney. Perhaps you don't have an established "regular outside counsel," or the lawsuit is on the other side of the country, or the case is outside your regular counsel's expertise. Now what? Now you hire an ad-hoc trial attorney.

Selecting and hiring trial attorneys is difficult and risky. By the time you find out that you hired the wrong trial attorney, you may have lost the case. In-house lawyers can be closely supervised and their work reviewed. The advice of regular outside counsel can be rejected. A trial attorney acts on your behalf. There is little opportunity to recover from a trial attorney's mistakes. Yet, to do you any good, the trial attorney must act quickly and decisively. The persuasive skills that are so useful in the courtroom are also used to attract clients and keep their confidence. Altogether, you are going to have to trust this person.

You meet this challenge by evaluating the matter which you need help with, identifying candidates and choosing one, and retaining her. When looking for regular outside counsel, you focused on your needs as a client. When looking for a trial attorney, look first at the needs of the case. Then search for attorneys who can satisfy those needs. From that list, select the attorney who is most able to craft the evidence into a persuasive presentation of your case, and use a formal retainer letter as a blueprint for a trusting relationship and effective use of your resources. The procedure laid out in this chapter will help you find an attorney, anywhere in the United States, who can give you the representation you need, within the tight deadlines imposed by litigation.

Time Pressure

There is always a tight deadline when you need a trial attorney. If you are going to be the plaintiff, the facts are developing and you need guidance from the trial attorney about what to do or say. If you are a defendant, there is a deadline for your response. When you need to respond to a lawsuit, look at the papers. Chapter 10 describes how to find or calculate the date for response. If it is 20 days after service, count from the first day anyone (not just you or your employees) received the papers after they were first sent by the adverse party. Traditionally it was easy to get extensions of time, but in recent years extensions have been hard to come by. The trial attorney will need some time to investigate and prepare the responsive papers. Focus on that time limit. Start as soon as feasible after you know where the lawsuit is pending. Check the calendar, and your watch, and get going. This procedure should take 5 business days or less from first notice of the lawsuit to having the attorney working for you under a signed agreement.

Delegate the Search

Time and good judgment are needed to find the right trial attorney. You may not have the time. The interplay of personalities, essential to the role of regular outside counsel, is less significant with trial attorneys. This is a task you may need to delegate because of the intense effort required. A manager with administrative talent and an aggressive, inquisitive personality can handle it, as can your regular outside counsel or an in-house lawyer.

Lacking an in-house person, you may want to use your regular outside counsel to find you a trial attorney. It won't be cheap. It takes time to find a good trial attorney, more so because your counsel will be acutely aware of the danger of making a mistake. Counsel will want to avoid the risk by handling the case herself, an argument for big, multioffice firms, or minimize the risk by hiring the biggest, most expensive firm in town. If you are going to delegate this task, insist that the procedure in this chapter be followed to the letter, and every step documented.

The actual choice of attorney must be made by you, even if you are following a recommendation. The retainer letter should be on your letterhead and signed by a company officer. Never allow an outside counsel to get between you and your trial attorney. Trial attorneys are simple souls who need to understand clearly who is the client and who is paying the bill.

Artistic Advocacy and the Journeyman

You need to get the "right" trial attorney, but that is not necessarily the "best" trial attorney. The appellate judges and the law school professors will tell you that the outcome of a case is determined by applying the law to the facts. The law comes out of reports of past decisions, and the facts are simply the truth. The lawyer generally cannot change the law, and he never can change the facts. In the real world, the trial attorney does make a difference. Effective advocacy is an art in which the relevant provable facts are used to paint a picture which fits a pattern viewed favorably by the law. It is the art of persuasion.

The key to winning is understanding what is relevant. A grasp of the general law, and close analysis of the law applicable to the particular case, is required to determine relevance. The fact that a person has halitosis has no relevance in determining if he drove a car negligently. The smell of alcohol on his breath gives a different result. Understanding of the law develops from long study and experience. While lack of experience can be partly overcome by study and research, it is not necessary to do exhaustive research on every point of law that comes up. An experienced trial attorney makes judgments about what aspects of the law should determine how the case comes out and applies the effort to those points.

Imagination and creativity are required to prove some facts. Not every true fact can be proven directly. Some true facts are merely states of mind. Intention is an example. Artistic trial attorneys create ways to prove the facts. If a man says that he intends to remain in a warm room and not go out into the cold, the fact of the statement is evidence of his intent. If at the same time he can be shown to have been pulling on a warm coat and gathering up gloves, hat, and scarf, proof of those observations tends to establish a different intent. Experience with juries teaches a trial attorney what kinds of proof work.

One of the pioneers of the plaintiffs' personal injury bar is the source of two examples. In one instance, the injured plaintiff was required to wear a prosthesis, an artificial limb, as a result of the claimed injury. The plaintiff had adjusted well to his situation, and looked pretty good. The trial attorney, throughout the trial, left a package wrapped in butcher paper on the table in the courtroom. (This was before meat came in foam trays with plastic wrappers.) At the magic moment in the trial (timing is everything), the package was unwrapped, revealing the prosthesis that the plaintiff had to wear for the rest of his life. The use of butcher paper evoked in the jury the imagery of meat, bone, and blood, subtle proof of the plaintiff's loss.

This same great trial attorney also teaches a lesson in explicit descriptions. The deceased had been injured in a collision between his vehicle and the rear wheels of an oncoming semi-trailer. The accident happened on a curve in the roadway. The truck driver testified, credibly, that he had not crossed the centerline. Plaintiff could not prove that the car had not crossed the centerline of the road. The construction of an exact scale model of the roadway and vehicles demonstrated what happened. Due to an error in the design of the road, the rear wheels of the trailer would necessarily cross the centerline when the truck was driven carefully and correctly around the curve. The state paid damages for the negligent design of the road.

Such examples of attention-grabbing techniques are somewhat dated. What was a new idea in the 1950s is old hat today. Graphics, computer simulations, and videotape demonstrations are within the grasp of most who would be trial attorneys. Sophisticated techniques and courtroom "presence," the ability to keep track of jury, witness, judge, and adversary while making a dramatic presentation with words and body language, although tremendously important, come into play only after the long, tedious preparation process. Even then, many judges neutralize histrionic talent, requiring attorneys to obtain permission before moving from the podium. During the preparation process, most cases—95 percent in federal courts—are settled.

The abilities to develop a winning theme for the case, to execute a program of discovery to establish evidence supporting the theme, and to do so at a reasonable cost, are what you need from a litigator. The great orator, impressive, persuasive, will actually assign your case to an associate for preparation. Business cases don't have the dramatic elements that sway juries, or build reputations. The real challenge is to keep the jurors awake. You need a journeyman craftsman, not an actor.

What Your Case Needs

The choice of a trial attorney depends on the task at hand. The personal chemistry between attorney and client is less important, and perhaps a distraction. The ability to marshal resources is much more important. The process begins with an analysis of the case. Figure 4-1, a trial attorney selection checklist, is a worksheet to use in developing a list of candidates. The "profile" portion of the checklist will help you

Trial Attorney Selection Checklist

Case name:

                            Deadline:_____

Court, file:

Profile

Location: State/Federal

                         Small town   Big town

Adversary: Birth year:
            Admission year:
            Firm size:

Type of case:

	Larger firms	*Smaller firms*
In-house support capability	Substantial	Minimal
Responsiveness required	Casual	Urgent
Discovery burden	Routine	Complex
Legal intricacy	Ordinary	Sophisticated
Sharpness of fact disputes	Sharp	Vague
Spending limits	Loose	Tight

Candidate Sources

Referrals

Directories

Five Candidates

Name   *Firm*   *Phone*
1.
2.
3.
4.
5.

Figure 4-1. The trial attorney selection checklist assembles information for use in selecting a trial attorney.

keep track of variables as you study the case. Most of these variables fall in a range between extremes, not absolutes. As arranged on Fig. 4-1, the left side favors smaller firms, the right side favors larger firms, within the range of firms from which you will make your selection.

Location

The technical legal term for the proper location for a lawsuit is *venue*. Venue is usually proper if the case is filed in a defendant's home territory. Selecting venue is a tricky, technical question that is best left to trial attorneys. You need the help of a trial attorney in the city where the case is, or in the nearest large city within the same county. If you have been sued, Chap. 10 details how to locate the court where the case is pending. If you need to file the suit in a state court, you may need an atlas to find the county seat. For state court cases, you will look for a trial lawyer at the county seat or in the largest city in the same county.

The federal courts sometimes have jurisdiction over cases involving citizens of different states or cases involving federal laws. If that might be a possibility, you should also note the city where the federal district court sits. That information is found under the heading "Courts" in the state law digests in the last volume of the Martindale-Hubbell directory of lawyers. Find the city where the federal court sits for the district which includes the county where your case is pending.

This preliminary selection of a city defines the list of law firms you will consider. Of course there are more and larger firms in larger cities. Few attorneys will turn down your business by suggesting, at the initial contact, that you need someone from a different city. However, the burden of traveling any distance to the courthouse has an impact on cost and sometimes on the outcome. You are on your own in making this first choice.

The term "home-towned" describes what happens to outsiders in some courthouses. The official line is that everybody receives equal treatment from the judges. A young attorney once had a motion pending in one of the northern suburbs of Chicago. The adversary was a prominent local lawyer. He failed to appear at the 9:15 a.m. calendar call. The judge said to come back at ten o'clock. The local lawyer did not show up, so the judge said to come back at three o'clock. The young attorney did, and waited around until after four o'clock, when the local lawyer arrived at last. The motion was disposed of in about five minutes. The Judge then asked the young attorney if he had missed the last train to Chicago. He should have been embarrassed when he was told that the young attorney's office was across the street. Hire a local attorney to minimize being "home-towned" by the judge and the clerk.

A *Chicago Tribune* story about a leading personal-injury attorney included a photo showing the attorney marching to court along with an associate carrying a portable podium. The attorney had found success with Chicago juries by presenting a formal, three-piece-suit image. He always spoke with great authority (self-assumed) from behind a podium. That worked in Chicago. The independent ranchers of western Oklahoma are responsible for their own businesses, facing the threats of drought, tornado, and the commodities markets. The authoritative approach would be taken as an insult. They are more likely to accept gentle guidance from a "good old boy."

The Adversary

The Martindale-Hubbell directory of lawyers purports to list every lawyer in the United States, by city and state. It does a good job. It is a multivolume set. In each volume, there are two parts. First is an alphabetical list of every attorney in each city. The second part, called the biographical listings, is organized by law firm, listing information about each attorney in the firm. In cities of more than about 10,000 population, the law firms with a business practice are very likely to have entries in the biographical listings. The special value of Martindale-Hubbell is that it lists all lawyers.

Look up the opposing attorney, your adversary, in Martindale-Hubbell. In the listings by city you will find the year of his birth, the year he was first admitted to the bar, where he went to school (not important) and when he graduated, and the address or name of his firm. Martindale-Hubbell also rates lawyers. Any lawyer may make application for a rating. The publisher then circulates questionnaires to other lawyers in the locality. Applicants who qualify are permitted to place a paid listing in the biographical section. The biographical listings include a brief sketch of each lawyer in the law firm, a description of the practice, and sometimes a list of representative clients or references. In selecting your own trial attorney, consider people who are a few years older, with a few more years experience, in a slightly larger firm, than your adversary.

Type of Case

State in two or three words the obvious nature of the case you are concerned with. Most cases fit recognizable types. For example, automobile negligence or medical malpractice cases are readily recognized as bodily-injury matters. Collecting a bad debt falls under commercial litigation, code words for bankruptcy and collections. More subtle matters such as an unfair trade practice, which may violate antitrust statutes or a general duty of good faith and fair dealing, cannot be adequately described in a few words. The purpose here is to look for a match in law firm entries in the directories which also inadequately describe the types of cases handled. Ordinarily, you would choose firms that describe their practice using business terms combined with litigation.

In-House Support Capability

What is your in-house ability to support the trial attorney? You may not have the time, inclination, or ability to give your attorney much help. In one instance, because of internal management chaos, a lender was not even able to calculate the interest which had accrued on a loan. A larger firm, with more resources, may be better equipped to satisfy such a weak client's needs. If you are unable to help with the case, you need to accept being dependent on the law firm's internal management and controls. Such dependence justifies a relatively greater investment in the selection process, and higher fees for handling the case. Contrast that with a situation where you have confronted similar cases in the past, know pretty much what is required, and just need a local attorney to handle the presentation in court.

Responsiveness Required

The ability to meet a court-imposed deadline is essential. Similarly, time is critical if you are hiring an attorney to file an involuntary bankruptcy to void preferential transfers. You may need to get a job done on a holiday eve. Larger firms are more likely to have someone available who is relatively indifferent to a pending holiday or celebration. If your case is going to take up 100 percent of one or more person's time for several days, a smaller firm may not have the available capacity.

Discovery Burden

The litigation process is basically one of preparing evidence for presentation to the court. The evidence may be mostly in your possession, or in the possession of adverse parties. In an automobile accident case, the plaintiff has most of the evidence—medical and employment records and witness statements. Obtaining the evidence is straightforward. A complex business case involving price fixing and conspiracy usually requires that evidence be extracted from the adversary. Large volumes of documents produced by the opponent will be combed through in the search for a "smoking gun." The document search and other discovery drudgery will require the labors of young associates, paralegals, and data-entry clerks, suggesting a larger firm.

Intricacy of the Law

The intricacy of the legal issues varies from case to case. Admiralty law, for example, has a long, complex history and is understood by only a few specialists. State and federal efforts to control various investment swindles have made securities law a hopeless tangle. Although any case can have a few tricky issues, those kinds of cases are more likely to require a scholarly approach. You are more likely to find the needed research capacity in larger firms, or among in-house lawyers.

Sharpness of Fact Disputes

In most criminal cases, the defendant says that he did not do it. The criminal defendant either is, or is not, the same person who, for example, pointed the gun at the clerk and demanded money. In most business cases, the facts are not really disputed. Somebody does not pay what they owe and then looks for an excuse. The parties all agree that Exhibit A is the contract, but claim that they don't agree on what the words mean or what was intended. Often there is much bluster about what is unfair and threats of punitive damages if a jury gets a chance to decide who wins. The best hope of avoiding the risk of a runaway jury, apart from settlement, is to persuade the judge of the merits of your position through meticulous discovery and research. When the factual disputes are vague, a larger firm may be better suited to blow away the smokescreen with a discovery paper storm and get a decision by summary judgment. Where there is a genuine fact issue, firm size is less important.

How Much You Can Spend

Attorneys who represent business interests expect to be paid in full each month. The contingent-fee lawyer is more typically a solo practitioner representing individuals in personal-injury claims. You may have a very good case that will take years to prove, but not have the funds to pay for all of the legal services as they are incurred. Smaller firms are more likely to be able to devise a mutually satisfactory payment plan. Larger firms, with more overhead to cover, may charge more in fees.

Identifying Candidates

Using the profile portion of Fig. 4-1 to assemble your analysis defines what kind of an attorney you are looking for, what city she is in, and what size law firm she is with. Now you are ready to start searching.

Seek Referrals

The conventional advice on how to find an attorney is to ask someone you know to make a recommendation. In reality, you are not likely to know anyone who can give you useful information about a trial attorney in some of the remote places where courts sit. How many people do you know in Wampsville, New York, or Boise City, Oklahoma? Gather all the information you can to make the procedure more effective, but rely on the procedure.

If you do have someone you can ask, that person will have little knowledge of what your needs are. You won't know the basis of their recommendation. Most referrals are to friends, fraternity brothers, old army buddies, or brothers-in-law.

Reliance on referrals can create problems. Getting an introduction from an acquaintance may help you get a positive response from the attorney when you first approach him, at the price of some dilution of loyalty. The attorney may make an extra effort in the hope of further referrals, or may seek to reward the source of the referral directly. Your gratitude to the person who gave you the referral may keep you from asking tough questions, demanding quality service, or firing the attorney. The source of the referral becomes an added source of complications.

You should quickly survey your sources for referrals. Make inquiries through your business connections in the place where the case is. Ask your dealer, trade association, collection agency, or claims adjuster. With a pending deadline, you don't have time to wait for your calls to be returned by someone who probably cannot help you. So make the calls, but move on. Do not spend any time asking at the courthouse; court clerks and judges should never make recommendations of attorneys. Check within your company and with your regular outside counsel. Expect to pay for time spent by outside counsel. In each instance, inquire gently into the basis of the recommendation.

List the names of any attorneys recommended on the checklist, Fig. 4-1, under candidates. Then go to the directories, including Martindale-Hubbell, and start the real search.

Use Directories

Look in the directories for the listings in the city where the court sits. There are many legal directories. Most states have a directory of lawyers in that state, by city. There are commercially published directories of negligence, automobile, corporate, and collection lawyers. The value of any directory is limited if you do not know how those listed are selected. The *Prentice Hall Law & Business Directory of Litigation Attorneys*, a two-volume set introduced in 1990, costs $300 and merely lists the membership of the litigation section of the American Bar Association, open to any lawyer willing to pay the dues. Also in 1990, WESTLAW, the legal research databases, introduced a legal directory which can be searched with a personal computer and a modem. If your business requires frequent collection efforts, there are organizations of commercial law specialists with published membership lists.

Some directories don't list enough lawyers to cover every county seat. They are of little value except for narrow, nonlitigation specialties such as municipal bonds or patents.

If the directories show only a few lawyers in the city of interest, expand your search to other cities in the same county. Only after you have exhausted these sources should you begin to look in major cities.

Using Martindale-Hubbell, a quick survey of the alphabetical listing of lawyers in the target city will tell you if you have a small enough number of lawyers to deal with. If there are too many—more than one page—use the biographical listings, by law firm. In either case, look at the range of law firms which are available. The fact that a lawyer is in a firm suggests that there is enough stability to be in business, enough compatibility to get along with one or more other persons, and some backup if the lawyer is ill or otherwise unavailable. Absent other considerations, these advantages rule out solo practitioners for most business matters. The largest firm in town tends to be somewhat self-satisfied and expensive. Placing your business with a smaller firm increases your impact and value as a client. The bias is therefore toward the smaller firms in the mid-range of sizes in the particular city. You adjust this bias with the considerations profiled on Fig. 4-1.

By focusing on the size of the firms, you have winnowed out a small enough number for close examination. Each entry describes the types of work in which the firm claims expertise. Look for those which match your needs. Read the list of representative clients. Firms that represent several insurance companies defend personal-injury claims. Firms that represent several banks do mortgage foreclosures. Look further at firms which list clients like your company. If you are familiar with the city, note the proximity of the firm offices to the courthouse.

Examine the list of individual lawyers and note their ages. What is the age distribution of the partners? Are all of the partners very old or very young, with none in between? That is the pattern where the talented junior partners quit. Are there enough associates to help the partners, which is important if your case will have a heavy discovery burden? Are there signs of hiring sons and grandsons, a great tradition that ignores merit? Lists of multiple bar memberships are meaningless unless they disclose a special interest. Firms in which most of the lawyers graduated from the same law school have a narrow outlook.

Within these firms, look for an attorney who is a little older and a little more experienced than the adversary attorney. Find at least three—partners only, do not consider associates—and add them to the referrals you want to follow up on, at the bottom of Fig. 4-1.

Criteria for Choosing Trial Attorneys

Every client would like to know the win–loss ratio of the trial attorneys under consideration. One crafty old attorney tried a big case before a bad judge. The judge ruled against him. The judge was reversed on appeal. Does that trial count as a win or a loss? The same old attorney handled the appeal of a case that had been tried to a verdict by another attorney. The old attorney won that case on appeal also. Should that initial trial count as a win or a loss? Maybe attorneys who take the tougher cases have more adverse verdicts, but smart attorneys are supposed to know enough to settle the losers. Just knowing which party prevailed is not enough to know how the attorney affected the outcome.

Few attorneys actually try a case all the way through to a jury verdict in any one year. For example, in one year, of the 12,000 lawyers in Chicago, only 1000 had a trial that went to a verdict. Only a few hundred had more than one complete trial. The attorneys with the most trials handled the defense of claims for the housing authority and the transit authority, cases which might be difficult but are not complex. A complex commercial case takes more than a year to prepare. Most are destined to be settled. The attorneys who handle such cases rarely try them. The test of ability is in analysis, preparation, cost control, and negotiation. There are no simple statistics to measure these functions.

You might be able to judge who is the best available trial attorney, based on past cases, reputation, and perhaps direct observation of courtroom performance. Unfortunately, the advocate who was excellent last year may have peaked, the intensity of trials being such that sustained high performance is unlikely. Or maybe he looked good because he had the right case at the right time. Good results are not the result of luck, but good fortune contributes to extraordinarily good results.

Winning attorneys often succumb to the temptation to trade on a reputation established by a few spectacular successes. They become "rainmakers" for the firm, selling the firm's services under the label of their talent. A great trial attorney may have little ability to inspire equal performance from younger and presumably lesser talents. If you must seek out the great man, have in mind how you will ensure that your case gets his attention.

The best choice is a team, with a blend of talents: a leader to get the best out of the others; an analytic technician to figure out what is important; a diligent grind to get everything done on time; a persuasive diplomat to draw the adversary into a settlement; and a brilliant presenter to sway the jury.

Making the Choice

At this point you have a list of about five candidates from which to choose. The best way to make the choice is to visit the law firms and interview the partners you have identified. Realistically, a credit manager trying to collect a $2500 debt cannot fly across the country to interview attorneys. Which lawsuits justify travel is a business judgment. When travel cost is not a factor, visit the firms.

The interview process is conducted in two stages. In the first stage a telephone inquiry is made, followed by a written request for information. In the second stage, the information received is used as a basis for either a second telephone interview or a visit to the firm. Figure 4-2 is a telephone contact record you can set up for each candidate. Using this form while talking will ensure that you cover all the points, and help you keep track of whom you are talking to.

Initial Phone Contact

In the initial call, be sure to identify yourself and your company fully. Spell out names for the receptionist. Then ask for the attorney you have identified. If that person is not immediately available, leave a number for him to call you back. If he will not be available within a few hours or the next day, ask to speak with the most senior partner who is available. Your choice may be engaged in a trial, or on vacation, and a senior partner may be able to fill in for him. If you are asked what the call is about, state that you are trying to arrange for local representation, and give the case name and number and the court.

When you have made contact, keep in mind that you have not yet established a confidential attorney–client relationship. Be sure the attorney has your name, and the case name. Tell the attorney briefly what the case is about. If it is a collection case, say so. Not all attorneys want to accept all cases. So make it clear what kind of a case it is and see if the response is enthusiastic. If the response is lukewarm, the service will probably be likewise. Tell the attorney what your deadline is, and ask directly if he has time to attend to the matter. The answer should be yes or no. If he says he can get someone else to handle it, beware. That is the wrong way to start. It means that the case is already being delegated. If the case is delegated to an associate at this stage, you will never get a partner's attention.

Ask for a conflict-of-interest check. In a small firm, the attorney may

> ### Candidate Attorney Phone Contact Record
>
> Case name:
>
> Attorney name:
> Firm name:
> Phone number:
>
> > Date called:
> > Time called:
>
> > Identify yourself and your company by name.
> > Ask for a specific attorney and leave a call-back number.
>
> When contact is made:
>
> > Identify the case name, court, and file number.
> > State the type of case.
> > Tell the attorney what the deadline is.
> > Ask if she will be able to handle that type of case.
> > Request a conflict-of-interest check.
> > Read or fax a list of the parties to the suit.
> > Request a call back after conflicts are checked and cleared.
> > Request a firm résumé and hourly rates by fax or overnight mail.
>
> Evaluate materials received in response:
>
> > Hourly rate schedule
> > Firm résumé
> > Cover letter
> > Promptness
>
> Second conversation after conflicts are cleared:
>
> > Evaluate the promptness of the call-back.
> > Describe your company.
> > Describe the case in detail.
> > Set up a visit at the offices of the law firm.
>
> Or, if there is to be no visit:
>
> > Test enthusiasm and interest in the case.
> > Share ideas about the case and see if the response is creative.
> > Ask for predictions of time and expense; are they reasonable?
> > Ask for a description of the attorney's relevant experience.
> > Ask for designation of the team.
> > Ask for designation of the lawyer to handle the case day-to-day.
> > Ask for first actions proposed for handling the case.
> > Ask for commitment to the budget and schedule.
> > Explore the billing system and cost-recovery charges.
> > Determine the billing policy for travel time.

Figure 4-2. The candidate attorney phone contact record is a checklist to ensure that the important points are covered in telephone conversations.

be able to tell you positively that there is no conflict of interest. In larger firms, it may take several hours to survey the records and ask the attorneys if there are any existing clients of the firm who might have interests in conflict with yours. Occasionally a conflict will slip by. A benefit-plan trustee hired a law firm to collect unpaid employer contributions under a union contract. There were no apparent conflicts. Several days later the law firm received an angry phone call from a long-standing client which owned the defaulting employer, using a different corporate name.

In smaller communities it may be worth your while to inquire if minor conflicts can be waived. Waiver requires express consent of both clients. Where a conflict arises from representation of other parties against a common adversary, there may be benefit in sharing the attorney. The surest and quickest way to tell the attorney who else is in a defense case is to send or fax a copy of the caption of the complaint. As a plaintiff, send a list of all anticipated parties.

Tell the attorney that you are considering him for the work. Do not promise it to him. Tell him that you will send him a letter, generally following the form of Fig. 4-3, by fax or overnight mail and ask him to reply the same way. That way you can test the firm's communications capability, responsiveness, and marketing acumen. Conclude by telling the attorney that you will call him back the next day and set a time for that call.

Also tell him that you are sending a form, Fig. 4-4, the litigation cost estimate, for use in estimating the cost of the litigation. Make sure that the attorney understands that the litigation cost estimate is not a bid, and that your decision will be based on other factors. The dates and assigned personnel are as important as the amounts estimated. What you will find out is if the law firm is willing to work with you in the management of the case.

Out of five initial calls made to candidates, some will not call back. Others will be unavailable, because of conflict of interest or the press of other business. You may reject some because of "bad vibrations" during the phone calls. It is sufficient to have two or three to work with.

As they come in, look at the firm résumés and hourly rate schedules. Are the hourly rates for any individual lawyer you have selected out of line? Is your choice the most expensive person in her own firm? Are any of the firms showing rates more than 20 percent higher or lower than the others, comparing attorneys of like age and experience? Hourly rates are meaningful only when considered together with the number of hours expended. Keep the hourly rates in mind when you discuss the litigation cost estimate and the number of hours that associates are expected to bill each month. A high billing requirement coupled with a high hourly rate will translate into low value.

Getting a Trial Attorney When and Where You Need One 63

XYZ COMPANY LETTERHEAD

Current Date

Prospective Lawyer
Law Firm Name
Street Address
P.O. Box Number
City, State, Zip Code

Via Fax (111) 555-1111

Re: Case Name
Court and File Number
Representation of XYZ Company

Dear Mr. Lawyer:

Thank you for taking the time to return my phone call of today. We are in the process of arranging for representation of XYZ Company in the above-referenced matter.

Please determine if you are free of conflict of interest and able to undertake such representation. We are sending you a list of parties or a copy of the caption of the petition.

Please send us, by overnight mail or by fax, your firm resume and a schedule of hourly rates charged for your services.

We are also sending you a form for estimating the cost of this litigation. Please provide rough figures for discussion.

We are working under a deadline, so please give this your prompt attention if you wish us to consider you and your firm to represent us. I am looking forward to discussing this further with you.

Very truly yours,

XYZ Company

_____

By: Charles Smith, Credit Manager

Figure 4-3. The initial inquiry letter to a candidate trial attorney invites the submission of information.

Litigation Cost Estimate

To: Your Company
    Your Town
                                                                Date:

From: Law Firm
      Other Town

Re: Case Name
    Court and Court File Number
    Litigation Cost Estimate

The following estimate of cost, including fees and disbursements, and time required to represent the interests of Your Company effectively, is made prior to the submitting firm having been retained, and without any reliance upon any independent investigation of the facts and circumstances of the case. It is a mere estimate, not intended to define either the maximum or the minimum expense for fees, costs, and disbursements. If retained, the actual fees charged will be based on the time actually expended at the hourly rates shown for the attorneys performing the services.

The scope of our assignment is: (type in a simple description, for example, foreclose mortgage of debtor, complete sale of collateral, obtain judgment for deficiency).

Task	Cost in dollars	Complete date
Investigation and research		
Pleadings		
Affirmative discovery		
Responsive discovery		
Dispositive motions		
Trial preparation		
Miscellaneous negotiations		
Trial		
Execution of judgment	———	
Total estimated cost	$_____	
Target completion date		, 199__

Partner in charge: Rate:
Associate: Rate:

Figure 4-4. A simple estimate of the time and cost of handling a lawsuit reveals the way the attorney is approaching the case.

Are the firm résumés useful? If they are merely duplicates of Martindale-Hubbell listings, not much advantage has been taken of the opportunity to persuade you. A good résumé will tell you of the special expertise of firm members. Can you identify a leader? Is the résumé intended to please everybody, or is there a strong identity and focus on strengths. Did the firm send you a cover letter giving helpful, factual information?

Work through the second stage, either a visit or a detailed phone conversation, with at least two firms. Working with more than one firm assures a conscious choice and a basis for comparison. Making a deliberate choice helps establish the appropriate relationship between you and the attorney. An attorney chosen in such a deliberate manner knows who the client is and how to communicate with you.

Visit the Firm

There is no better way to gain insight into a law firm, and to get your representation off to a good start, than to visit the firm before making a commitment. The visit is not a beauty contest or a design competition; rather it is an opportunity to observe and to establish a relationship. If an actual visit is not possible, asking the questions and listening carefully to the responses in a telephone call may accomplish some of your objectives.

At the law firm, you will want to see the entire facility. A 10-min walk around will tell you if the space is adequate, properly lighted, and ventilated. A cramped, crowded space indicates that inadequate reinvestment of profits is being made. Look in the file room, mail room, and copy room. Is it an efficient workplace? Files scattered about, lack of work surfaces, and dirt are cause for concern. You want to be sure that your files are complete and can be found, and that mailings of legal papers are properly assembled. In small firms, ask how high-volume copying is handled. Subcontracting is OK, especially if they promptly identify a nearby copy shop.

Look at the office of the partner you are seeking to retain and any associates working with him. Are these the offices of people who can command the firm's resources? Are the offices of the associates who are to work with the partner close to the partner's office? You are going to pay for the time spent walking back and forth.

Look at the attorney too. The attorney you hire will be a representative of your company. He owes it to you to look the part. Attorneys have a great burden of persuasion. Their dress and personal effects should not be an impediment. Although sometimes distinctive dress is part of an image used to affect juries, most lawyers do not operate at that level.

Look at the library. Does it contain federal materials? If not, ask where they go to do research on federal matters. Do they have WESTLAW or Lexis electronic databases?

Does the firm have an adequate reception area? Are there conference rooms or other space sufficient for depositions? If not, ask where they do depositions. In some locations the court reporters provide deposition rooms that are perfectly satisfactory. What provision is made for parking, for your witnesses? How close is the office to the courthouse, state or federal?

The purpose of looking at the office facilities is to create an opportunity to observe the people you are thinking of entrusting your matter to. If the offices are impressive, whether tasteful or gaudy, remember who is paying for it. Offices are intended to make a statement; you need to look behind that statement.

Does the partner you contacted greet you with some enthusiasm and interest in your case? Managing the case means working with this man. Is he receptive? You are there to listen to him, but is he listening to you? Does he hear what you are telling him?

Tell him about the case, what you know about it and your ideas of what an appropriate response might be. Does he understand what you are saying? Does he respond creatively with ideas of things to do? Does he consider your suggestions?

Mention the concept of a litigation budget and note his response. Does he immediately launch into a dissertation on how unpredictable costs are? Does he display familiarity with the concept? Is he willing to use a budget as a tool to develop strategies?

Ask how the firm keeps track of pending matters and due dates. Does the system they describe, often called a "diary," "tickler," or "docket," have cross-checks, or does it rely on a single individual? Ask how the quality of legal work is assured. Is each lawyer's work reviewed?

Ask for a description of the billing system used by the firm. Tell the attorney that you will expect a monthly billing with detailed statements of what work was done, the time expended, and by whom. If there is a problem with billing in that format, find another attorney. Ask how the bills are prepared and reviewed. Does someone look at the bills to ensure that associate time charged is consistent with value? Is the partner you hire going to do that, and does he have the power to write off excessive time? You only want to hire the person who is going to be responsible for your bill. It is important that the person who looks at the bill be intimately familiar with the work being done. Establish the identity of the attorney who will have the day-to-day responsibility for your case. That person must be a full partner, must have the authority to command the law firm's resources, and must review your bills.

Ask about recovery of costs and disbursements. You should know from your own business what copies cost. A law firm that charges more that the actual cost for copies may be focusing on the wrong profit centers. On the other hand, firms that do not pass variable costs such as long-distance telephone and copying charges through to the clients for whom they are incurred overcharge the clients who do not use those items. The cost for copies, envelopes, and postage for a simple motion for a receiver in a simple foreclosure can, if there are many junior lien claimants, exceed $150.

Ask to meet the others on the team that will handle your case. This will include associates. Does it include paralegal and secretaries? Do the attorneys you meet have secretaries? If you are paying over $100 per hour for their time, you want to be sure that the time is not spent filing and making copies.

Ask who they will go to for help if they find themselves in over their heads. Is there a "lawyers' lawyer" in the background who can back this team up?

What is the relationship between your attorney and the other members of the team? Do all of the good ideas have to come from the boss? Is there obvious respect and affection within the team? Do the young associates know enough to take notes?

Ask the partner how hard the associates work. If he starts to brag that the associates produce more than 150 hours per month, you may be in a sweatshop. Ask what the minimum billing for associates is. The absolute maximum practical for second-year associates is about 150 hours. Anything over that means time is being padded and the troops are not being rested properly.

Ask about trial experience. Ask what cases have been handled in the past few years, what stage they are in now, and how the ultimate resolutions are being brought about. Do this by asking if the partner really has time to handle your matter. Since few attorneys actually go to trial in any given year, see if this attorney ever handles minor cases just to get into the courtroom and maintain proficiency. Comments about how to get cases settled will indicate the philosophical approach of the individual. Does it match yours?

When you have touched on all of these points, it is time to leave, or end the conversation. Say good-bye and tell the attorney you will get back to him tomorrow. Any firm should look good by itself, but the strengths and weaknesses show up clearly when compared to another firm.

The final decision is an exercise in intuition. This procedure generates a basis for intuition. Assuming basic competence, the relationships between people is most important. Advocacy, a persuasive art, is about people. Of the attorneys who are actually willing to handle your case, pick the one you like best.

Having made that decision, you need to implement it. Telephone the attorney selected and tell her that you are sending a retainer letter and the documents on the case. Attorneys frequently request an advance on fees, commonly called a *retainer*. The practice of law necessarily involves dealing with deadbeats. Attorneys are always concerned about being paid. Litigation is rarely a happy experience for the client. When it is over, clients are not highly motivated to pay. It is normal to advance a "retainer" of about 2 months' estimated fees, to be kept in the firm's trust account and applied to the final bill. If cash flow is a problem, offer to pay bi-monthly bills to reduce the retainer.

The Retainer Letter

The retainer letter establishes the terms of the services contract with the attorney and her law firm. You should prepare this letter. Figure 4-5 is a form retainer letter intended to be adapted for your particular needs.

The retainer letter should state who the client is, and who has authority to speak for the client. The attorney then knows from whom she should take direction. This is particularly important when the contact with the attorney was made through an intermediary, such as your regular outside counsel.

Describe the scope of the work. In litigation matters this is ordinarily the name of a case. In nonlitigation matters the scope of the attorney's responsibility should be broad enough to require a response to unexpected developments.

Identify the particular attorneys who are committed to work on your case, and their hourly rates. The law firm needs some flexibility in staffing the case, but you want to avoid having the file passed around from associate to associate.

Be explicit about the billing procedure. The bills should be sent monthly or bi-monthly. The fees are based on hourly rates, for time shown on the invoice. The detailed time records should show the identity of the person doing the work, by name or initials. The work performed should be described in plain English and in enough detail so that you can tell what is being accomplished. This means that proper names of people talked to, specific issues researched, and the like, are written out. Time charged for a phone conversation should include who was talked to and what about.

Travel time should be expressly provided for. A day that starts at five o'clock in the morning and ends at eleven o'clock at night in a strange hotel room is truly 18 hours long. String a few together and the recovery time is real also. But if the day includes 10 hours riding in airplanes and taxis, billing for the full 18 hours may be excessive, especially since some time, e.g., meals, is clearly nonworking. It does not matter what the agreement is, so long as it is fair and mutually understood. Some-

XYZ COMPANY LETTERHEAD

Current Date

Individual Attorney Name
Law Firm Name
Street Address
P.O. Box Number
City, State, Zip Code

Via Fax or overnight mail

Re: Case Name
Court and Court File Number
Representation of XYZ Company

Dear (insert name):

XYZ Company has authorized me to retain you and your firm to represent it in the above-referenced matter and related matters.

As we discussed at your offices (or by telephone) on (date of visit or call), you have agreed to personally provide the necessary legal services. We understand that you will be assisted in this representation by your partner, Paula T. Ripper, and your associates, Edgar Y. Answorth, William G. Associate, and Warren D. Goode. Please let me know before involving any additional attorneys in this representation.

We will pay for your services at the hourly rates indicated in your letter of (insert date), and reimburse you for your actual expenses and disbursements. You have agreed to render monthly bills. The bills will include a detailed statement indicating for services: the date, identity of the person, the exact service provided in plain English, and the time expended. The description of the service will be sufficient to identify persons, issues, or events. Expenses and disbursement will also be identified in detail. In addition to the billing detail, you will provide an invoice summarizing by attorney the hours, hourly rate, and amount charged for services and the total due for disbursements.

We agree to reimburse you for expenses and disbursements at your actual cost. This may include such items as long-distance telephone, postage, and copying. It does not include secretarial services, word processing, local messenger, or other ordinary office operations.

We have agreed to advance the sum of $0000.00 as a retainer to be held in your trust account as security for payment of our bill. We will remit payment in full of your invoices, subject to a reservation of rights including the right to audit the bill and require adjustments, within 5 business days of receipt, taking a 2 percent discount against services only.

Figure 4-5. A form of retainer letter for trial attorneys.

Where practicable, we prefer to pay the expenses of this matter directly on vendor invoices. Therefore, although we will rely upon you to arrange for all necessary services, including experts and consultants, please have them bill us directly or forward their invoices.

Please forward copies of all papers received or filed in this matter, including correspondence, as well as memoranda of law, evidence summaries, and other materials that reflect the status of the case. Send routine copies to the attention of Mary Doe, Analyst, at this address. Separately report important developments to the undersigned by telephone or letter. Please send drafts of all pleadings, motions, briefs, and discovery materials you intend to file on our behalf to the undersigned, early enough so that our comments, if any, can be reflected in the finished document.

The files you create and maintain on this matter shall at all times be the sole and exclusive property of XYZ Company. You agree to waive any claim of a lien on said files and to deliver them upon demand. Any copies made for your own use shall be at your own expense.

Please report lack of cooperation by any employee immediately, so that our goals and objectives can be clarified by the undersigned.

(no budget option)
Please prepare a schedule of the work you presently expect will be necessary to handle this matter, including your estimate of the fees and disbursements. We would like to have this in hand before the first pleading is filed on our behalf.

(budget option)
As we discussed, we wish to have a detailed budget and schedule prepared for this matter. Please advise when you might be ready to meet for that purpose. If you can, please send the undersigned a copy of the local court rules, particularly any that relate to pre-trial conferences.

Enclosed for your information is a copy of the board of director's resolution delegating authority to handle legal matters to the undersigned. Also enclosed is a list of affiliated companies and trade styles of the company.

Enclosed, and covered by a separate letter, are the documents relating to this matter. Please telephone the undersigned if you have any questions.

Very truly yours,

Fred XYZ, President

Figure 4-5. (*Continued*)

times, paying for first-class travel recovers some of the lost time for working purposes. In that case, require that the work be done for you. No attorney should ever attempt to handle confidential client matters while riding in coach.

A lawyer from Oklahoma City went to Las Vegas in the summer of 1988 to meet his client and an adversary to discuss settlement of some lease disputes. He had never met the adversaries, who were from Dallas. Imagine his surprise when he heard his seatmates, who had boarded in Dallas, discussing in detail a case just like the one he was handling. He did not speak up at first, not realizing it was the same case. Then he was alternately embarrassed or engrossed. The adversaries were indeed unhappy to see him arrive at the meeting that afternoon. The lesson is simple: Good lawyers do not work on airplanes.

The provision for expense and cost reimbursement should be at the law firm's actual cost, with no markup. The copy machine as a profit center makes no contribution to your case.

Outside experts, court reporters, and other vendors who require large cash outlays should contract directly with you and be paid directly by you. This reduces the cash-flow burden to the law firm and avoids markups.

If there is a retainer or fee deposit to be made, state that it will be retained in the law firm's trust account to be applied to unpaid fees or returned at the end of the case.

Having been specific about the bills, be specific about the payment. Agree to pay in full in 5 business days, but reserve the right to review the bills later.

Tell the attorney how you want to be kept informed, using methods described in Chaps. 15 and 16. You may ask that copies of correspondence, court filings, memos of law, and evidence summaries be sent to a manager. Early drafts of documents prepared on your behalf should be submitted to you for review and comment. Do not rely on your copies alone, but require the attorney to report directly regarding significant developments and decisions you must make.

State who owns the file. There are two problems where ownership of the file comes up: replacing attorneys for unsatisfactory performance and storage of closed files. As client, you pay for everything in the file, including "work product." You would not tolerate one of your employees developing a system on your time and then denying you its use after he quit. So specify that you own the entire file. Of course, the law firm can make copies for its own purposes, but at its own expense. If you must fire the attorney, you can demand, and get, immediate delivery of your file to your new attorneys. When the file is closed, there is no reason to leave it with the attorney. Get it back and destroy what you do not need to retain.

In a big case, where you are going to use a budget, ask for a copy of the local court rules. Most court clerks can supply copies of the local rules, which may be only a few pages in state courts or over 100 pages in some federal courts. The requirements for getting the case set for trial and trial memorandum or pretrial order are often detailed there. Asking for the rules shows the attorney what you expect. If this is a big problem, everything will be a big problem. You might as well find that out early.

When you get the signed retainer letter back, advise the law firms that you rejected. Figure 4-6 is a form letter for that purpose. This is more than a mere courtesy. Once an attorney has talked to you, with a deadline pending, he runs the risk of a malpractice claim if you do not expressly relieve him of responsibility for the matter.

XYZ COMPANY LETTERHEAD

Current Date

Prospective Lawyer
Law Firm Name
Street Address
P.O. Box Number
City, State, Zip Code

Re: Case Name
Court and File Number

Dear Ms. Lawyer:

Thank you for your cooperation in our process of selecting local trial counsel in the above-referenced matter. We have chosen another firm to represent XYZ Company in this case. You and your firm will be considered should we have another need for representation in your area.

Very truly yours,

by_____
Mr. XYZ, President

Figure 4-6. A rejection letter relieves a prospective trial attorney of concern about the deadline in your case.

Getting a Trial Attorney When and Where You Need One 73

1. Analyze requirements of your situation using the trial attorney selection checklist, Fig. 4-1, to record:

   Location
   Adversary information from legal directories
   Type of case
   Profile of case

2. Identify candidates:

   Seek referrals but do not delay.
   Use legal directories.

3. Contact two or more candidates:

   Interview by telephone using candidate attorney phone contact record, Fig. 4-2.
   Clear potential conflicts of interest.
   Evaluate materials received in response to inquiry.

4. Visit best candidates and evaluate:

   Facilities efficient and orderly
   Lead attorney has apparent authority within law firm
   Appearance consistent with desired image
   Library and electronic research capability
   Proximity to courthouse
   Enthusiasm and interest
   Receptiveness and creativity
   Cost sensitivity and use of budget
   Fees and billing procedures
   Follow-up and quality assurance systems
   Back-up legal talent
   Role of associates
   Lead attorney commits to work on your matter
   Actual trial experience

5. Exercise your informed intuition and judgment.

6. Retain chosen candidate:

   Use retainer letter, Fig. 4-5.
   Describe scope of work.
   Identify specific attorneys chosen.
   State fee and billing arrangement.

7. Advise other candidates that they have not been selected.

Procedure: Retaining attorneys for trial or any ad-hoc matter.

5
Getting the Right Stuff from Your Outside Lawyers

Your lawsuit will have a satisfactory outcome if the court understands the true facts and applies the correct law. Law professors, political scientists, and legal philosophers assume that courts' decisions are based on actual truth and that the questions of law are about the actual dispute between the parties. In truth, the "facts" presented in court are only shadows of reality cast in the dim, flickering light of witnesses' testimony on the rough surfaces of the juror's minds. The legal issues that determine the outcome often have nothing to do with the underlying dispute between the parties.

The reason you hire an attorney for litigation is to make sure the court makes a decision that, from your point of view, is right. The adversary legal system depends on opposing attorneys presenting the best evidence and most convincing arguments. Looking back when the matter is finished, you may sense that the outcome was controlled by the wrong legal issues, or the real facts were ignored. It's too late, then. The value of any legal service, from forming a simple corporation to negotiating a merger, depends on getting the facts and the law right.

You rely on your attorney's expertise and experience, instead of doing it yourself. Second-guessing an attorney is like helping someone play poker. You don't know what the hole cards are, and you don't know how she bluffs. If you definitely knew what all the facts were, why they were relevant, how to prove them, what the legal procedures were, and what the law should be, you could direct and control your lawyer.

But that would still be a mistake. The practice of law is an art. Achieving your objectives requires creativity and imagination, which is stifled by tight control. At the beginning of a case, no attorney knows all the answers or how she will reach them. But you can know how well an attorney is performing. You can make a judgment about whether or not your attorney is doing the things that produce a satisfactory result while the matter is going on, while you can still do something about it.

A basic element of legal performance is getting the job done. Hollywood produces amusing fantasies depicting lawyers at work. Typically, the hero is romantically involved, able to prowl about through the night, often inebriated, and wins the jury's votes by a brilliant argument delivered in a hushed courtroom. The reality, alas, is different.

The trial attorney must marshal evidence and get it into the courtroom. The logistics of hauling overhead projectors and VCRs in and out of a downtown courthouse each day of a trial may by itself defeat the effort to present a case. Is the electrical cord long enough? Is there an electrical receptacle? Live witnesses present other challenges. Can the witness be found and served with a subpoena? Is the witness sober? The evidence must be presented within a legal framework that changes constantly, and that must be custom-crafted to fit the available facts.

Even a lawyer performing a seemingly routine task, such as drafting a contract, faces the problem of getting the law and the facts right. For example, an oil-well operator accepted a bid from a service company to clean up a drilling site for a price of $13,800. The clean-up included hauling away soil contaminated with drilling fluids. The service company did the job and then sued for an additional $32,007.95. A tariff filed with the state regulatory authority required payment of $62.54 per hour per vehicle plus a service charge for each barrel of oil-field waste material moved. On appeal, the court held that in spite of the agreement of the parties, the tariff amount must be paid. Had a lawyer been involved in drafting that contract, adequate performance would have required careful, tedious library research to find the tariff requirement.

This chapter is about the performance of outside lawyers, what it is, and how to motivate it. Just as an automobile designed to go fast requires more fuel or a tire sacrifices long wear for increased traction, cost is a consideration in shaping optimum performance. But you do not always get more by paying more. Good performance means that you get all you pay for.

Do Outside Lawyers Manage Themselves?

Judges repeatedly tell the same amusing story. At the crucial argument of the big case, the renowned senior partner rises to address the court.

Well into the presentation, the judge asks some questions, perhaps not about the point under immediate discussion. The senior partner stumbles, then asks if he may consult with his associate. The associate, having done all of the work on the case, knows the answer, and attempts to whisper it to the senior partner. The senior partner returns to the podium, not knowing the legal theories, not knowing the facts, and not knowing what is persuasive to the court. The senior partner knows only what he can pick up from the whispered prompting of his associate. That is weak advocacy. Considering how often judges tell the story, it must happen frequently.

Relying on Your "Rainmaker"

The process of selecting regular outside counsel and trial attorneys, described in Chaps. 3 and 4, emphasizes hiring an individual matched to your needs or your particular case's requirements. Much of the actual legal work to be done is the execution of technical procedures, the type of work done by lawyers. There are such technical procedures, either routine or highly specialized, in both the defense of a complex lawsuit and in handling the ordinary problems confronted by every business. The individual you have selected may have good reason to have someone else do such work.

If the individual you have selected is in a law firm and not a solo practitioner, she will be able to delegate technical procedural work to associates. This is often presented as a cost-saving measure, because the associates charge lower hourly rates. More experienced lawyers should be more efficient, however, accomplishing the same objectives in less time and thus neutralizing the rate differential. Also, any cost saving must overcome the burden of internal communication, the time taken to explain the problem to the associate, and the time needed for the associate to explain the answer.

Two valid reasons to have work done by associates are the work load of the individual attorney or counsel you have selected and the need for special skills. The operations of a law practice are driven by time limits. Deadlines have to be met continuously. Your individual counsel or attorney may not have time available at the instant you need it. Many routine tasks require great skill; for example, research in electronic databases is easily and efficiently performed by lawyers trained in their use. A routine mortgage foreclosure goes quickly for a lawyer who knows the court clerks, judges, and sheriff.

Trial attorneys have another reason to delegate much of the trial-preparation work to assistants. Only a small percentage of cases are actually presented in court. Courtroom technique—that is, jury savvy—is developed and maintained only by actually presenting cases. One person, working alone, cannot prepare enough complex business cases to obtain the necessary trial exposure. However, there is a difference between working closely with assistants and turning cases over to associates.

In the early 1980s, a prominent Salt Lake City attorney was retained, with his firm, to defend a claim that a plaintiff had been injured by exposure to boric acid. It is generally agreed that boric acid is not harmful to most people in the manner claimed by this plaintiff. The case was assigned to a junior partner and an associate. The plaintiff's claims were supported by two physicians, each located in a distant state. As trial approached, the young attorneys proposed deposing these so-called experts, the usual procedure. Under the rules, the defendant would have to pay the experts' fees for the depositions. Because the experts were out of state, the plaintiff could then use the depositions as evidence at trial. The plaintiff's case was not strong, and it was unlikely that the plaintiff's own attorney would spend the money to bring the experts to the trial. The effect of following the usual procedure would be for the defendant to finance the plaintiff's case. The prominent attorney relied upon by the client had failed to deliver his own wisdom.

In complex cases and ongoing business representation, no single individual will be able to provide the capacity to get the job done well. For solo practitioners, that means some work will be referred to other firms. In law firms, work will be assigned to associates. Adequate performance by the individual you have selected requires both sufficient continued involvement so that you receive the benefit of their skill and wisdom, and sufficient leadership and management so that resources are effectively brought to bear on your matter. You must decide if the attorney you have chosen is a good enough manager and leader to delegate your work.

Relying on the Law Firm Management

Ordinarily, your relationship to a law firm is with an individual lawyer who initially attracted you. That individual is your contact at the law firm, acting somewhat like an account executive and supervising all the work done on your behalf. With the passage of time, however, your company may become a "firm client." That implies that you are relying on the internal management of the law firm itself, and not an individual partner, to look after your matters.

Law firms are partnerships or corporations owned by professional employees. When marketing efforts are effective and business is plentiful, the firm may be tempted to distribute earnings to partners and fail to make adequate investments in space, staff, and equipment. As the business grows, more associates are hired to do the work, but they are squeezed into the same space. Conference and work rooms disappear. File space is filled, and boxes of papers pile up in offices. The associates are not supported by stenographers and file clerks, and clients pay lawyers' hourly rates for typing, filing, and running the copy machine.

The most effective lawyers will use current, though expensive, technology. As this is written, fax machines, multitasking personal computers, legal research in electronic databases, large screen videotaped depositions, and computer simulations of accidents are current. The impact of technology is greater on routine paper shuffling than on counseling clients. The cost to the client of inadequate investment shows up in more associate hours for such paper shuffling. As you work with the lawyers, you may notice that they are frustrated by difficulty in completing tasks, examples being getting documents typed, getting current materials into your file, getting copies of items received sent to you, obtaining copies of appellate opinions or statutes. Such problems are symptoms of inadequate investment. If the firm's response to shortcomings is to increase pressure on the associates, any improvement will be temporary.

The principal resource of any law firm is its personnel. Rapid turnover of associates in your regular outside law firm imposes a retraining cost on your company. What you will notice is that cases or projects are started by one associate who leaves before its completion. Associate turnover may be caused by inadequate compensation, poor working conditions, inordinate work loads, or negative group dynamics. You will see the effect in increased time charges and delay.

A sure sign of deficient management is the shifting of files from associate to associate. This means that when an associate becomes stuck on a problem, no help is available, so the work stops. Then, instead of teaching the associate how to do the job, the lack of progress is addressed by shifting the matter to another associate, with the cost of that associate becoming familiar with the matter. It also means that the work is not being matched to the capabilities of the people assigned to do it.

Good management in a law firm is indicated by the use of systems to keep track of the work and assure quality. Case management software that runs on personal computers is available. How well it is used is a matter of discipline. More important is a system by which each lawyer's work is reviewed by other lawyers. Your direct observations, and feedback you may get from the firm's associates, will guide you in deciding if you can rely on a law firm management to assure the performance of lawyers working on your matters.

Elements of Performance

You don't have to rely on the law firm or the rainmaker to judge the performance of lawyers working on your matters. You decide if your employees know what they are doing, work hard, and are honest. The same kinds of things — competence, diligence, and character — describe the performance of lawyers.

Competence

Undoubtedly there are some lawyers who know so little about the law that they cannot handle any matter adequately. You should be able to avoid them by asking questions during the selection process. Your real concern is whether the attorney knows what is needed to handle your particular case. It is more important to know how to find the current law than to have a vast knowledge of what the law was yesterday. Lawyers know more law on the last day before taking the bar exam than they ever will again. There are signs of incompetence. If a case does not progress, the attorney may not know local procedures. If predictions about how the court will rule on preliminary matters are consistently wrong, the attorney may not know how to find the applicable law. If the matter does not involve litigation, however, deficient legal skill is hard to detect. Ordinarily, you must rely on the system by which lawyers are licensed to ensure a fundamental level of legal knowledge. As a lay person, although gross incompetence may be obvious, you may have difficulty in discerning the difference between a tough legal question frustrating a good lawyer and a simple question stumping a poor lawyer.

It is not incompetence to ask for help. The most expert trial attorneys recognize the value of consulting with specialists on both legal issues and factual issues. Some legal issues are outside the experience of all but a few. So reassure your trial attorney that you will not pull the file if she seeks advice from a specialist in an unusual case or she comes to you for factual expertise.

A less esoteric aspect of know-how shows up in how the paper flow in the office is handled. As a business client, your file should contain copies of almost everything your lawyer has, including everything she gets from the adversary and everything she sends out. The copying to client files is just good office practice. The lawyer's files should be up to date, with everything filed. Nothing should ever get lost. If a lawyer tells you on the phone that she cannot locate a document, start worrying. If it happens a second time, you are in jeopardy. Losing papers is a sign that critical dates may be missed. You can lose a case for failure to respond to a motion for summary judgment within the time limit.

Creativity and Imagination. Intellectual involvement by the lawyer always helps the client. As an example, consider a matter involving the value of a particular parcel of real estate. The usual evidence of value is appraisals. Appraisal testimony is usually thought of as "expert" testimony, that is, opinion testimony. There is nothing wrong with opinions, but it is difficult to distinguish valid opinions from purchased testimony. The professional societies of appraisers have written procedures by which data are assembled and analyzed for the purpose of establishing a foundation for the appraiser's opinion. In litigation, experts on each side will have written reports that generally follow the procedures. To cross-examine effectively, an attorney must understand the economic and social theories on which the procedures are based. Then the attorney must find a way, artistically, to make the jury understand the real meaning of the expert testimony.

The same appraisal may come up in a situation where you wish to purchase the real estate. Effective representation may depend on understanding what is motivating the seller, and ignoring the appraisal. Intellectual involvement manifests itself as curiosity, inquisitiveness, and a somewhat theoretical approach to the law and your matter. Its value to you as a client is that it creates new and additional options.

People Skills. Legal problems are predominantly people problems. The first problem every lawyer faces is getting the facts. The shy or diffident attorney who accepts the first answer given, and is afraid of offending you or your managers, will never find out the truth. Reports from operating people that attorneys are demanding, impatient, and brusque may indicate that the right questions are being asked. A lawyer must listen to the client to find out what the real problem is. A lawyer must listen to witnesses to hear what is not being said. A lawyer must hear everything a witness wants to say, and assure the witness of his ability to tell the truth.

The ultimate objective of the trial attorney is to present the evidence persuasively. Most evidence is testimony, and even physical evidence must be explained. Once the story and the physical evidence are put together, the witnesses must be conditioned to testify. Everyone has some reaction to being interrogated in front of onlookers, judge, and jury. Some witnesses have obnoxious personalities. Other witnesses are performers and may only feel excited or keyed up. Some take the witness chair with a flat affect, a sign of depression. Whatever the particular personality type, the trial attorney must condition the witnesses so that they are comfortable and able to concentrate on telling the truth while testifying.

Real trial attorneys know that they are dependent on witnesses to carry the burden of persuasion to the jury, and, as a practical matter, to create a plausible threat in depositions. Conditioning witnesses to enable them to tell the truth is a psychological art. The witness is relieved of the burden of ego, fear of failure or embarrassment, so that his or her mental capability is available to listen to questions and form truthful and understandable answers.

Witnesses need to be taught how to listen to questions and to answer only the question asked. Properly conditioned witnesses have had an opportunity to talk about the case with an attorney long enough so they have said everything they want to. Only then will witnesses trust the attorney to ask the right questions.

Beyond conditioning, witnesses should be substantively prepared. That is, all of the documents of interest, and the facts, should be reviewed with the witness so that the witness can speak confidently. No witness should be surprised while under oath. All of this should happen more than "two sleeps" before the actual testimony. Otherwise, the last thing the lawyer puts in the witness's head will be the first thing out under oath.

Sometimes a witness is asked to come into town the night before he or she is to testify and meet with the attorney to "go over the testimony." Attempts to prepare a witness the evening before generally ruins that night's rest and really softens up the witness for the next day. A more extreme example is calling a witness into the attorney's office in the morning, asking all the embarrassing questions, ridiculing the answers, telling the witness his testimony is very important and then leaving him alone to drink his lunch before going on the stand. It happens.

When a sincere witness has a devastating experience, at trail or deposition, the attorney's people skills have failed. The importance of working with people, sharply defined in the litigation situation, is equally true in nonlitigation matters.

Straightforward Advice. Anyone who is a lawyer has proven, in law school and in the bar examination, a basic ability to write and speak the English language. In practice, lawyers sometimes wrap their advice in so many words that the client cannot find any meaning. Advice burdened with erudite prose is often worthless, either because you can't figure out what it means, or because it has no meaning. If a lawyer cannot state advice in plain English, the lawyer doesn't understand it either. Some clients, or employees, prefer vague advice so they can avoid responsibility for not following it.

Using words that really mean something is the easy part of effective communication. To be useful, the lawyer also has to deliver the advice when and where it is needed. Like the lubricant in an engine, advice has to be put on the load-bearing point.

The Jones Act is a variation on the Federal Employer's Liability Act (FELA), a federal statute enacted to provide compensation to employees in interstate commerce who are not covered by state workers' compensation statutes. The Jones Act covers the crews of offshore drilling rigs. The statute provides that if an injured employee can prove that any neglect of the employer contributed to his injury, the employee is entitled to a damage award to be set by a jury. During the oil boom of the early 1980s, offshore injuries increased. One law firm, the old attorneys, had been doing a good job of defending a drilling company for a long time. The work was handled by a lead partner and two associates. The drilling company management became dissatisfied with the large sums being recommended for settlement and the large awards in cases that went to verdict. Management wanted to know why.

At the time, that management needed to be fully informed about every case, and as major cases developed, to be told in advance what was coming. The old attorneys had two problems. First, after many years of dealing with a few claim agents and one in-house lawyer, the old attorneys had forgotten who the client was. Second, they felt that giving more information would not contribute to the success of the defense effort. The old attorneys were unhappy at what they saw as lack of confidence in their work. The company management was having difficulty in accepting the settlement recommendations and was further distressed when cases not settled generated big verdicts. Eventually, new attorneys were selected and the old attorneys ceased getting new assignments. It was a sad end to a long relationship. The new attorneys did not do any better in the defense of cases, but the management had more confidence in its own decision making.

The old attorneys had failed to deliver the advice where it was needed, to the management decision makers. Your lawyer should communicate to you what you need to know for the decisions you need to make. You need to decide what your settlement posture is—that is, how much money you will pay to make the case go away. You also need to decide what steps need be taken in the operations of the company to control risks. In the matter of the Jones Act cases, the sudden increase in damage awards was a direct result of deviations from company policy by line supervision regarding the hiring of crews and the repair and maintenance of equipment. Without input from the lawyers, management had no way to know that the company's policies were not being followed.

Your lawyer should get out of her comfortable office and deliver her advice to you. Your questions should be invited, to ensure complete understanding. The advice ought to be free of double talk and come down to a straightforward recommendation. When you understand the advice, you can make a decision to either follow it or not.

Diligence

Most legal cases start off with a flurry of activity. You find and hire an attorney. A pleading is quickly filed with the court. A strategy is sketched out. Diligence is about what is happening 6 months later.

As a practical matter, diligence means that the individual you have selected is working on your case. This does not mean just having an associate churn out a stream of paperwork. Diligence is shown by focused creativity on the dull tasks of learning the facts, finding the proof, studying the law, and assembling it all into a finished product for presentation, and doing it all on time. Diligence means continuing to work on the matter until it is done, completely.

Every lawsuit can be seen as having a "slow side" and a "fast side." Usually the defense is on the slow side, but not always. On the slow side, you do not want the case to get to trial soon, hoping that witnesses will die, forget, or move away. If the plaintiff is not pushing the case, the defendant may just stand by and wait for it to go away. The defendant runs a risk, in taking action, that the plaintiff will be stirred into action.

Diligence on the "slow side" of a case requires both prompt action and patience. For example, a long-time employee of a national jewelry chain had quit, or been fired. He was emotionally distraught at the time. Soon after, he sued his former employer for wrongful discharge. The defendant's attorney quickly asked exactly what the plaintiff's claims were. After responding, the plaintiff's attorney did nothing. The defense attorney continued to gather documents and sworn statements, but did nothing to stimulate the plaintiff's attorney. Eventually, the case was dismissed by the court for lack of prosecution.

A group of disgruntled graduates of a proprietary school sued. They were unable to find satisfactory employment in the field in which they had trained. The attorneys exchanged some documents. Then the plaintiffs' attorney stopped working on the case. When one of the plaintiffs moved out of town, his deposition was requested by the defense attorney. He did not want to incur the expense of coming back, so his claim was dropped. Gradually others dropped out of the plaintiffs' group. Eventually that case "died a natural death."

Insurance companies, and the lawyers they hire, learned long ago that many plaintiffs will not really get their cases ready. The Friday afternoon before the Monday trial date is a time of bluffing and guessing, most cases settling in a process that much resembles an auction. In the few cases where the trial does start, as soon as the judge figures out what it is about, the parties will be pressured to settle. In such circumstances, why bother to prepare?

Not preparing is risky. Plaintiffs' cases are most dangerous when not recognized. An all-terrain vehicle (ATV) tipped over while descending a steep slope. An occupant, whose ankle was broken, sued the ATV manufacturer in California. The ATV manufacturer did not think it could be liable to someone crazy enough to drive down the side of a mountain. The plaintiff's attorney quietly assembled a case on the new theory of failure to warn. The defense attorney and the defendant's employees did not get along well. The in-house engineers were not prepared for their depositions. The case was set for trial in mid-December, an inconvenient time for the company's employee witnesses to travel from the Midwest. The plaintiff's lawyer, who had seemed boorish in discovery, was ready at trial, rejecting all settlement offers. The verdict for the plaintiff, over $600,000 in compensatory damages and over $1 million in punitive damages, was a surprise to the defendant.

Diligence requires that your attorney have a theory of the case. Working on the theory, and finding the facts and law to support it, keeps your attorney involved in achieving your goals, rather than just reacting to the adversary. That way, you and your attorney have some control of the case, even when you are on the "slow side."

Extensions of Time as Warnings. A request for an extension of time filed just before something is due is a warning about diligence. Some time limits are short. For example, some federal courts may require that a motion for summary judgment be responded to within 15 days. Such responses may require more than 15 days to prepare. Any request for more time should be filed long before the standard time expires. If your attorney is running to the courthouse to seek an extension on the afternoon of the last day, there is an uncontrolled risk that the extension may not be granted. Postponements and continuances are signals that preparation is not proceeding in an ordered and deliberate manner. Of course, whenever your opponent asks for more time, you should always agree. Why spur him to action?

Character

Character is a basis for trust. Lawyers who are trustworthy and are trusted by other lawyers, including adversaries and judges, spend less time and money getting things done. Any short-term benefit from sharp practices and "cute" tricks are quickly wiped out by strict enforcement of every petty rule by the legal community.

Even when asked directly by a client to do something tricky, an attorney with integrity will refuse. If the attorney is an associate and the corporation is a major client of the law firm, some interesting questions are raised. Does an employee of the client corporation have the authority to ask the attorney to do something shady? Who takes the blame if the misdeed comes to light? Can the attorney jeopardize the client's good name on the say-so of an employee? Judges and other lawyers know which attorneys have honor. Often, when an attorney of established integrity drops a client with no explanation, they draw an inference of misconduct by the client.

What kind of client asks an attorney to break the law? In a lawsuit, the procedure requires disclosure of documents and other evidence. This is information, a form of company property. The client often wants to protect that property, either because it is a trade secret or because it hurts the client's position in the lawsuit. By sharply interpreting the information request, an attorney might evade disclosure. Do you want to risk punishment for this the kind of representation?

Prudence. Prudence requires that an adequate amount of work be done on each matter. The problem, for clients who can pay, is that an excessive amount of unnecessary work is done. Some large firms apply the motto: "Leave no stone unturned." Turning over all of the stones generates fees. Other lawyers are tempted to do nothing, hoping the matter will settle.

Prudence also requires the maintenance of cordial relationships with the adverse attorneys. You ought to expect, and may demand, that your attorney not let her adversary get her goat. Your justified anger at the other party is no reason to pay your attorney to be mad at the other party's attorney. When the attorneys get emotional, the costs go up.

Prudence also requires that positions not be pushed beyond their supporting facts. The analogy with the card game, bridge, is overbidding a hand. Aggressive attorneys often urge clients to "take them to the mat," forcing ordinary business disputes into litigation and doubtful cases to trial.

Loyalty. The lawyers' Code of Professional Conduct mandates loyalty to the client. The problem of loyalty is not that lawyers are tempted to sneak over to the adversary side to make a deal. The problem is a conflict between the lawyers' need to earn fees and the best interests of the client. It is a betrayal of trust for a lawyer to say: "Copy everything, the client will pay." Excessive depositions, unnecessary motions, and wrangling over petty disputes are really just forms of padding the bill, a breach of the duty of loyalty.

Candor. Candor is the unwelcome virtue, the burden of the true professional. An example illustrates the nature of candor. The company founder had built a business from nothing over a period of 15 years. In the early years his wife had worked with him, but as success came she withdrew from the business. An attractive younger woman took her place in the business and in the affections of the founder. The founder attempted to conceal the liaison with the younger woman. The senior management of the business was painfully aware of the relationship, because the younger woman had been promoted far beyond her abilities. The nature of the business was such that it presented opportunities to embezzle federal funds. An audit revealed that the younger woman had at times supplemented her income with an independent embezzlement scheme. Senior management was reluctant to tell the founder that his paramour had been stealing.

Eventually the problem was brought to the law firm dealing with the federal agencies conducting the investigation of the theft of federal funds. Here is the burden of candor. The founder needed to know that the younger woman was a thief, but he could be expected to deny his personal involvement with her. It fell to the trail attorney to bear the bad news.

That explicit example of candor illustrates two factors. First, the news is bad. Second, the client, you, are wrong. Clients usually think they are right about the law, right about the facts, and right in their judgments about other human beings. It is not easy to tell a client that he is wrong and then collect a fee for doing so. Candor is often a matter of courage.

Lawyers value impartiality highly, particularly in forming opinions about the merits of cases. Clients do not value impartiality, probably because they know, or think they know, the merits of their case. An attorney who colors his advice to make the client happy will collect more fees. Sophisticated clients will seek candid, impartial counsel to improve their own decision making.

Motivation, or Lawyers Are People Too

Considering the amount of fees charged, it hardly seems fair that you should have to motivate your lawyer in addition to paying her. But you as a client are interested in results, and a small effort to motivate will pay off in improved performance.

Intensity is the mark of a trial attorney. At trial, the attorney must focus on the task of persuading the judge and the jury, while fending off the attacks of the adversary, and complying with the technical requirements of getting evidence admitted. There is no time for holding your hand, except when the attorney finds such hand holding a way to relieve her own tensions. All that you can do to help is answer questions, run errands, and give moral support.

Most attorneys maintain their concentration by immersing themselves, and their egos, in the case. It takes a healthy ego to bear the responsibility of making on-the-spot tactical decisions that are binding on the client. At times things go badly. Objections are overruled. Witnesses change their stories. The adversary's objections are sustained. The judge is in a bad temper, perhaps abusive. Through it all the attorney must look like a winner, because the jury is watching.

How do you motivate such people? Trial attorneys, themselves masters of psychological manipulation, will not respond to the kinds of pressures that drive ordinary employees. You hope that when a particular trial attorney completes a case, there will be no more cases in that location. Any promise of future business is empty. A best effort by the attorney includes keeping the fees down, which is directly contrary to the attorney's business interest. You are left to providing psychological rewards: a sense of achievement for a job well done; the respect and gratitude of knowledgeable colleagues; and the power to influence events.

The selection process itself is the first step in motivating the attorney; the effort demonstrates the importance of the case to you. That is reason enough, by itself, to visit the law firm. Then, follow up by having an authorized person systematically and formally provide feedback.

Provide a Contact Person

All lawyers who serve clients, and particularly trial attorneys, are people oriented. Ideas and things may be important, but in the law, things happen because people make decisions. Lawyers talk mostly to witnesses, informants, or the persons who made the mess. In business situations, these persons are often employees, not the client.

Lawyers can interact with and be stimulated by a live human being, who "is" the client. This is particularly true of trial attorneys, who have absolute power to bind their clients in open court. The intensity of the work, the need to exercise authority with confidence, and time pressures all create need for a direct connection with the client. The middle of a trial, or a negotiation, is no time for petty corporate politics about who is in charge. At those moments, immediate action is required. Hesitation destroys opportunity.

Having a clearly designated person to deal with the lawyer provides a contact for interaction and feedback. Ideally, this person's authority should come from the board of directors. Also, this person should not have a personal interest, apart from the company's, in the outcome. That is, if your credit manager screwed up on a credit line, the lawyer trying to collect should have someone else to whom to talk.

Communicate Regularly

There is a fine distinction between positive feedback and nagging. Nobody, including lawyers, likes to be nagged. Nagging is avoided by regular, systematic communications. Budgets, billings, and draft review procedures create a framework for the exchange of ideas. These exchanges are the practitioner's opportunity to show you the results of her effort and creativity, and your opportunity to motivate with admiration and praise.

The telephone is an efficient method of communication, both friendly and flexible. It is also a nuisance. A busy practice may keep a lawyer away from the office much of the time. A trial attorney is out to court, in depositions, interviewing witnesses, or in the library most of the time. Returning phone calls, often in the evening, turns into telephone tag. It is more efficient to write letters to your lawyer. Use the fax if time is pressing. A letter can be handled at a time when the lawyer can give it her full attention. A letter both commands and permits a studied response. A letter is a physical piece of paper that hangs around until it is answered. A letter creates a record, important in a case that may go on for years. A letter can be proofread before it is sent, a chance to call back angry words without embarrassment. Finally, a letter is serious. The lawyer builds her case according to what you tell her. You would not change engineering specifications without writing it down, and you should not change a lawyer's instructions without doing so in writing.

Pay the Bill

The statement that "patients who do not pay do not get better" is attributed to Freud. Clients who do not pay their lawyers don't resolve their legal problems. An example from criminal law illustrates the point. An individual's sentence to 2 years in prison was suspended subject to probation. The probation conditions included periodic meetings with his probation officer and psychological counseling. He didn't show up for the meetings and didn't bother with the counseling. His attorney beat the first probation revocation on a technicality, but he failed to get the fee in advance. The individual never did pay and also failed to meet the probation conditions. The next revocation application did not have any technical defects. That individual had to go to prison to find out that probation was serious. Paying the attorney's fees could have driven that message home. When the fees are not paid, the client operates under a delusion about the real costs of legal problems. Lawyers all have a sense that clients who do not pay continue to have legal problems.

Delusions about cost lead some clients to refuse to consider settlement. Generally, when your case is a clear winner or a clear loser, the fees are relatively small. In close cases, where the proof is difficult to find and the law requires in-depth research, fees build rapidly. Tons of documents are copied and processed. The persons whose names appear on the documents are called for deposition. Travel expenses and court reporters' fees are added on top of hourly legal fees. As the months pass, the attorney tells you that more is needed to have a winning case. The bills give a more specific message about the cost of a victory. If you do not pay the bills, you will miss that message.

Ordinarily, in a business matter, the amount of the bill should be a calculation based on hourly rates or percentages, as agreed when the lawyer is hired. You may hear lawyers speak of "value billing" or "premium billing," the idea being that you pay more money if the lawyer does a good job. It is not clear, in light of the basic billing rates, why the lawyer should demand more because of a good result. The basic fee should get the best effort from the lawyer. Without an objective criterion, after-the-fact bonuses for outside attorneys do little to encourage extra effort. On the other hand, late or slow payment of billings is a powerful disincentive. Not paying the bill when due is a strong statement of your opinion of the worth of the services. The lawyer's ego is wrapped in the invoice.

Working on complicated cases generates significant overhead. A slow-paying client is a cash-flow problem. If a case is close to trial, the court is dictating the completion date of each task. The lawyer must maintain cash flow by working for other clients who pay promptly. For most law firms, the capital investment in library and equipment is less than 3 months' revenue. Accounts receivable are the major capital account. The combination of thin capital structure and court-imposed time pressure always affects the quality of work done for slow-paying clients.

Although a close review of the bills for legal services is an important way of keeping track of what your lawyers are doing, quibbling over details is counterproductive. Hectoring the lawyer for more detail, rejecting items after the fact, and arbitrarily cutting fees on the assumption that they are padded will drive good lawyers away. The lawyers who remain will have figured out how to beat your system.

You motivate performance from your outside lawyers with communication, and by performing your side of the retainer agreement. But there are situations where mere motivation cannot be expected to overcome problems.

The Dysfunctional

Lawyers, like house painters and cowboys, have reputations for hard drinking. The performance of lawyers is impaired by abuse of alcohol or other drugs, mental or physical illness, and business or marital difficulties, just like everybody else. You cannot expect an impaired lawyer to perform satisfactorily. Your response to a situation where you discover your lawyer is impaired should be determined entirely and solely by your needs.

You cannot rely on a dysfunctional lawyer. If she is in a law firm which recognizes the problem and takes prompt and effective steps to ensure that the your needs are served, you can leave the case with the firm. If the law firm does not move promptly and decisively, get another law firm.

1. Attend to performance while the case is in process.
2. Law firm management:
   Continuing involvement of "rainmaker":
     Delegates tasks, not strategy; or
     Delegates to specialists
   Adequate support staff and equipment
   Turnover of associates working on your matters
   Quality assurance system
3. Performance:
   Competence:
     Knowledge of law, shown by:
       Accurately predicting rulings; and
       Asking for help
     Error-free office operations
     Intellectual grasp of facts and theories
     Working with information sources and witnesses
     Delivery of usable, understandable advice
   Diligence:
     Continuing effort
     Full preparation for each proceeding
     On-time completion of every task
   Character:
     Integrity; always tells the truth
     Prudence; always realistic
     Loyalty; always fair to you
     Candor; always tells you what you need to know
4. Motivation:
   Show the attorney that the matter is important to you.
   Provide the attorney with a direct contact with the client, able to respond to requests for direction and assistance.
   Communicate regularly with the attorney.
   Pay legal bills as agreed.
5. Fire attorneys who are dysfunctional.

Procedure: Recognizing and motivating outside attorney performance.

6
Hiring In-House Lawyers

A half-century ago, very few lawyers were employed in-house. As government regulation and other legal considerations have increasingly intruded into the affairs of business, more businesses have chosen the in-house option.

Lawyers are sometimes hired in-house to solve a special problem. In the mid-1970s, heavy-equipment manufacturers were confronted with the then-new problem of product liability. Jury verdicts from all over the country found that products were "defective" in a way that engineers did not understand. The insurance companies did not seem to be able to control the losses. One major company's response was to hire an experienced personal-injury trial attorney from Chicago. His assignment was to aggressively manage the defense process to assure the best attainable outcomes. He had access to top management and to the best engineering resources of the company. That company survives today, competing effectively in the world market.

Another heavy-equipment manufacturer in the Chicago area, with a historically significant name, took a less aggressive approach. That company's top management was focused elsewhere. Its in-house lawyers, traditionally tied to the corporate secretary function, were limited in their ability to effect change within the company. Good, creative people, they formulated and lobbied for legislation to limit product liability. That legislation was passed, in one form or another, in several states. However, the company name has faded from the scene.

The surviving company chose a high-impact attorney to cause internal change. The fading company did not see its lawyers as a source of change. The lawyers in both companies performed as intended by the managements.

Some surprisingly small companies find it advantageous to have a salaried lawyer. One real estate developer, who has been through a couple of booms and busts and knows most of the hidden traps, provides a staffed office and a salary of $500 per week to a young lawyer who agrees to work about half-time on a flexible schedule. The turnover is fairly high, but the developer can depend on having documents prepared quickly and carefully, and the young lawyer gets practical experience.

The decision to hire an in-house lawyer implies that some change is occurring. The hiring process may start because of a need to replace a lawyer who has left the company, to add a lawyer in a program of planned growth, or to deal with a special problem.

Even when hiring a replacement for an existing position, change should be expected. Every professional should bring a unique creativity to the task. You cannot change lawyers, scientists, engineers, or artists like light bulbs. When you change professionals, the job is changed. The new lawyer should be expected to bring new insights and imagination to improve or replace existing procedures and systems.

Defining the Position

The decision to create a new in-house legal position is driven by frustration over high costs and unsatisfactory service from the existing arrangement. Your analysis of your total legal outlay, as described in Chap. 2, shows if you are spending enough to support an in-house lawyer. The real costs include more than just dollars. Legal problems distract managers, delay projects, and disrupt relationships. Your real objective in hiring in-house lawyers is to reduce these nondollar costs. An in-house lawyer should quickly become a "specialist" in the business, and know what needs to be done. That knowledge will speed things up. An established working relationship with operating people should smooth out the process. To accomplish this successful result, you have to put the right person in the right position.

Defining the Role

Identify what you want to change. Service in routine matters and cost concerns are met by a lawyer role. Understanding and presenting the company position to outsiders suggests an attorney role. Reducing the distraction of management by legal problems is consistent with an in-house counsel role. The legal access chart you prepare as described in Chap. 2 categorizes legal services you have been using. Implicit in these categories is consideration of the level of skill and experience, and hence the compensation required. Understanding that the roles of lawyer, attorney, and counsel may overlap, does the tentative decision to create an in-house position match up with the analysis of actual expenditures shown on your legal access chart? A business owner might sense a need for an in-house counsel, but that implies a major change if the legal access chart indicates a small expenditure for counsel at the executive management level.

Reporting Structure and Team

With whom is the new lawyer going to work, and to whom will she report? The in-house lawyer works for the client, that is, for the company. The lawyer–client relationship poses a particular management problem, discussed in Chap. 8. As a practical matter, your new lawyer will report to and receive assignments from one or more managers. In addition, the lawyer will work with other persons. For example, a person hired to supervise the defense of product liability cases may receive assignments from a claims manager, but often work with marketing people (to prevent statements of features and benefits in advertising material from causing liability), and be supported in litigation activity by engineers and the engineering records clerks. A lawyer hired to work on labor relations matters will get into the finance department to talk about ERISA, and into the production department to talk about OSHA, in addition to the personnel department for EEO matters. In preparing your legal access chart it is suggested that you show at least two but no more than five or six levels of management. Place the new lawyer's position on your legal access chart at the level of the company where she will actually "plug in."

Establishing a Budget

As suggested in Chap. 2, the base salary of new school teachers can be used to calculate the approximate amount that must be budgeted for each legal position. The budget figure should include about 60 percent for compensation and about 40 percent for overhead. Obvious overhead is office space, secretarial support, and law books. Less obvious are professional dues, license fees, and recurrent training. A company which had some in-house patent attorneys connected to the engineering department once hired an in-house lawyer without making any provision for overhead. He sat in the bookkeeping bullpen for a year, begging help with typing and keeping his files in a desk drawer. Needless to say, his productivity was disappointing. Two years later the same individual was keeping a secretary and a paralegal busy full time, and a serious product liability problem was coming under control.

At this point the personnel department will want to help. After all, they have the expertise and the responsibility for hiring employees. Although the personnel or human resources department can help, lawyers are different from other employees. Professional licensing and regulation affect the relationship with the employer, who is also a client.

Your personnel department may use a system that involves writing a detailed job description, assigning points to the various factors, and adding up the points to assign a "grade." Commercially published salary surveys can then be used to derive a salary range. If the salary survey does not match the calculation based on teachers' salaries, take another look at the job description. Employee-grading systems are not designed to attract and retain the type of individuals who have invested substantial time, treasure, and talent in becoming learned professionals. For such individuals, salary may be a secondary motivator. But low esteem expressed as low pay undermines other sources of motivation. An employee-grading system that cannot be reconciled with both the market and the company's need for legal services will cause mischief.

Qualifications

The basic qualifications for legal positions relate to licensing, academic background, general experience, and professional experience. Applicants should be admitted to practice law, or be eligible for admission, before the courts of the state of the company's principal place of business. Academic and experience qualifications that create arbitrary barriers should be minimized if you are seriously looking for the best candidates. Particularly with young lawyers, there is an emphasis on academic qualifications. Some law schools are surely better than others in that they have higher admissions criteria, larger libraries, and more illustrious faculty. Harvard comes to mind. No doubt the very best students at the best law schools are very bright indeed. There is also no doubt that the very best students of mediocre law schools are also very bright. In the real world, away from smart classmates, the big library, and the illustrious faculty, the differences in ability among the best students fades to insignificance. At the bottom of the class, the poorest students from the better law schools will tend to be adequate. Even the poorest students from the mediocre law schools may make up in "street smarts" for academic weakness. Nonetheless, academic records are available information, so you might as well evaluate it.

Prospective candidates always know their class rank. You want to know the class rank at the end of each semester. Someone in the bottom third at the end of the first year who has risen to the top third at the end of the third and final year has been learning something. Honors such as "Law Review," "Moot Court," and "Order of Coif" are all based on grades in the early years. You will hear excuses from those whose grades declined that such extracurricular activities are the reason. Listen respectfully. This is good-quality advocacy on behalf of an indefensible position. Do not ask if "Law Review" is more demanding than raising children. It does not matter. Grades are a poor predictor of success, but if you must focus on grades, note that grades on elective courses, in the later years, are slightly better predictors. Consider also whether students were attending law school full or part time. Full-time attendance indicates commitment, but it takes real dedication to finish a part-time program at night while working a regular job. Grades measure only skills in academic activities. A strong undergraduate education in English literature and political science will prepare a student to get good grades in law school. A scientific or technical undergraduate degree will prepare students to think creatively and work hard, but a weakness in communication skills may hurt grades.

Years of work experience as an engineer, salesperson, or accountant greatly enhance a lawyer's abilities. With a variety of work experience, a lawyer is better equipped to see different aspects of any problem, particularly the human aspects. A candidate who has had some false starts in her career has also tested her limits. This can be the subject of a meaningful discussion in an interview. An individual's explanation of a past failure may reveal much about her character.

The most useful information in evaluating a candidate relates to her professional experience. You want to consider the substance of the experience, the amount, and the variety.

Lawyers and the quality of their work are ultimately tested in the courtroom. Live courtroom experience is what teaches lawyers to do what you pay them to do. The drafter of a document seeks clear expression with an ear that has heard such documents read aloud to juries, and heard jury verdicts spoken in judgment.

The quickest way for a young lawyer to gain courtroom experience is as a prosecutor, for the offices of a United States Attorney, a state attorney general, district attorney, county prosecutor, military judge advocate, or in various municipalities. It does not matter how big the cases are; witnesses lie in all courts. Getting into court and confronting witnesses teaches the problem of proof. If a lawyer has not done it herself, alone, she does not understand. Once she understands, she is never the same again. Another place to find lawyers with courtroom experience early in their careers is in personal-injury defense offices. The Chicago

Housing Authority and Chicago Transit Authority staff lawyers try many cases to verdicts before juries each year. Some law firms that defend insured cases have young lawyers trying cases in the second year.

Government employment, other than being a prosecutor, is also excellent experience. Working in any kind of regulatory process teaches a useful understanding of all bureaucratic processes.

Lawyers working in corporations learn the skills necessary to operate within organizations and the specialties relevant to the particular corporation's operations. Management skills also can be acquired in this environment.

Most legal careers start in law firms. The size of the firm is important. If a young lawyer could not find a job, she may have hung out her shingle and gone looking for clients. After a few years of running her own business, she knows about overhead, personnel, taxes, marketing, and other practical things. Solos know how to collect fees, and how hard it is to get customers. If you really need a business lawyer to handle all of your needs, value the solo's experience highly.

A bright young lawyer who has spent years studying the documents in a single antitrust case, never having any real contact with clients or witnesses, will have learned little of value to your business. The fact that associates in large law firms are profit centers limits their development. If the young lawyer is not going to be made a partner, her training will not be expanded for the benefit of subsequent employers. The principal value of large-firm castoffs is their knowledge of how such firms operate, which is useful in supervising such firms.

A beginning lawyer with no experience is a poor choice for a company unless there is an existing in-house staff which will provide training and support her professional stature. The role of a lawyer requires that advice be given or procedures followed with certainty. The company's operating personnel will assume that the lawyer knows her "law" but will attack her every time she imposes a burden or restriction. Self-confidence, eroded in such circumstances, can be maintained or restored by handling real cases in courtrooms, or by associating with other lawyers. The sole lawyer in a company needs the confidence born of experience.

Personality and character are even less objective than academic record and experience. The fact that an individual has a license to practice law implies that her character has been examined, and fingerprints checked. Actually, the character examination is superficial at best. The fact of being a lawyer does mean that the individual persisted through law school. This will be a strong individual. Do you want a strong individual? A person who firmly identifies herself as a lawyer, who is a member of the appropriate bar associations, is likely to have an impact on your organization. You must make a judgment about how strong a person you want in your company.

Do you have room for an inquisitive person? A curious poker into dark corners, seeking the facts, may upset some of your old-timers. Would you prefer a mere functionary, a processor of paper? Is initiative a desirable quality in this position? Will persistence in problem solving cause unhappiness in the departments to which this person is to provide services? Is self-direction, the seeking of new problems to solve, desirable?

Appearance is easier to deal with. Advocates are presenters; just like actors, they must pay attention to how they look. Appearances affect the ability to influence. Some are flashy, others are modest. Either can be a persuasive style. Modest is better for corporations. Sometimes appearance is irrelevant. The lawyers in the land department of an oil company may not wear suits and ties to work. If your in-house lawyers ever deal with outsiders, however, they need to look like lawyers. Lawyers wear somber clothes.

Beyond work, you are hiring permanent employees. A well-balanced life includes recreation, physical activity, and a role in the social and political life of the community. These things lend stability. In the interview, a reluctance to discuss such outside activities may be a product of fearing to offend. Would you hire a sky diver? A SCUBA diver? Such people are usually deliberate risk managers, a good quality in a lawyer.

Age, sex, and handicaps are often a concern. Among lawyers, older tends to be better, but variety of experience is more important than merely passing time. The practice of law is gender neutral, even if some individual lawyers are not. Sex is a nonissue. Physical handicaps are little impediment to a lawyer's function for an individual who can get through the bar exam. There are no physical demands that cannot be handled by an assistant. Computer databases for research have even provided relief from the handling of heavy books.

Lawyers occasionally brag about the ability to "think like a lawyer," saying that it is the main thing to be learned in law schools. There is a problem-solving approach unique to the law, just as there is for engineering and science. "Thinking like a lawyer," mainly a concentration on facts proven by evidence and application of principles of law instead of common sense, is adequately demonstrated by completing law school and passing the bar examination. You are looking for lawyers who are able to relate legal concepts to business practicality, a form of intelligence.

In the corporate environment, the value of a lawyer comes from the application of creativity and imagination to business problems. As a practical matter, many bright lawyers are buried in a flood of minutiae. To be productive in a meaningful way, an in-house lawyer must have a systems approach to the practice of law. The systems enable clerical staff to control details, so the lawyer can control problems.

You are looking for someone to work with the people in your company. The handsome, witty, intelligent, hard-working, self-centered egotist may not make a net positive contribution. Indeed, sometimes persons of great talent overshadow others. The others move so that they can get some light as well, even if that means moving out of the company. Any employee who soaks up management time and attention is depriving coworkers of needed feedback and stimulus. Typical legal problems are complicated enough to call for a team response. In-house lawyers need to be able to communicate with operating employees, who may be the cause of the problem. This requires tact and diplomacy.

The ultimate capability of an in-house lawyer, the prerequisite for survival of the human species, is the ability to adapt. In the late 1960s the idea of "environmental law" was beginning to develop. A young patent lawyer with a major law firm in Houston was assigned some of those cases because of his "technical" background. By the late 1970s he gave up all pretense of being a patent lawyer, having evolved into an environmental specialist. In a large law firm such a specialty makes sense. For an in-house lawyer, narrow specialties become obsolete within 5 or 10 years. The thrust of in-house practice moved from shareholder derivative suits in the 1950s; to antitrust and trade regulation in the 1960s; to equal employment opportunity, occupational safety and health, and product liability in the 1970s; to mergers and acquisitions in the 1980s. The 1990s are likely to be an era of intellectual property and international trade. The more or less continuous ebb and flow of social and political issues requires in-house lawyers to be able to meet and adapt to unexpected problems.

Finding Candidates

With these kinds of considerations in mind, you must set about the task of finding an individual who satisfies the company's needs. Selecting the right person is the most important step in managing legal matters. In hiring lawyers, the lead should be taken by the manager responsible. Knowledgeable lawyers are aware that jobs filled by the personnel department are not considered important by the company's management. The best lawyers are not interested in unimportant jobs.

Prospective employees are apt to be found readily at hand in the professional circles of your present employees. The current buzzword is "networking." Let it be known that you are looking and see what résumés come to you. You may want to screen out the sons-in-law and neighbors. If you have retained the unsolicited résumés received in recent years, take them out and review them. Candidates who recruit themselves demonstrate both initiative and an interest in your business. With a defined set of qualifications, you may be able to identify some excellent candidates.

The outside law firms you are using are also a source of candidates. The partners will urge you to hire their rejects, associates who will never be asked to become partners. The law firm hopes that some residual loyalty of ex-associates will help them keep your company's business. Also, placing weak lawyers inside helps keep the client dependent. That is the source of the impression that in-house lawyers are second rate. Ask your own employees to identify the sharp associates they work with in outside firms. Approach those associates directly, without going through the partners.

Using Headhunters

Sometimes the network cannot be used, perhaps because you are looking for a high-impact lawyer to effect some major change, or you want to keep the fact that you are looking confidential. You may be tempted to use a legal headhunter. *The National Law Journal* listed 282 firms in the business of recruiting lawyers in 1990. Some are better than others, and none are inexpensive. Inexpensive alternatives are placement services operated by some state bar associations, usually a book of résumés, sometimes sorted by area of interest and location.

The common practice of headhunters is to run advertisements in the trade press and *The Wall Street Journal*. The résumés generated are screened by some arbitrary standards, usually by low-level clerks. The résumés of higher potential get a follow-up call, some more screening, and the net result is sent to you as a package. This level of service is not worth much. The biggest weakness is the arbitrary screening.

A better grade of headhunter will call around to similar companies looking for referrals. He is trying to find a candidate with experience in your line of business. That way it is easy to convince you that the candidate's experience is valuable, without dealing with either the candidate's abilities or your long-term needs. Raiding competitors to fill positions may be satisfactory for some functions, but it totally misses the pool of available, experienced lawyers who are seeking an opportunity to put legal skills to work. Headhunters, and executive recruiters, do not have a collection of qualified candidates on the shelf. They start each search from scratch, looking for someone they can sell to you.

The best headhunters are really management consultants. They help define the job with enough precision so that the search is orderly. Their fee is based on the service provided, not the contingency of finding someone you like well enough to hire. The procedure described in this chapter, painstakingly implemented, will generate the same results.

Advertising

Placing advertisements for prospective employees gives you access to a pool of candidates with new ideas and new solutions for old problems.

The traditional method of filling professional positions, the "old-boy" networks, has one advantage: Everybody thinks the same way. That is hardly a virtue in competitive international markets. Publishing advertisements is consistent with government policies of equal economic opportunity, a consideration if you are a government contractor.

The most effective place to advertise is in the journals of the state bar associations of the states where you wish to recruit. Membership in state bar associations, mandatory in some states, will attract about one-half of the lawyers in states where it is voluntary. Membership in a voluntary state bar association indicates a desirable attitude toward the law as a profession. A state bar journal ad is targeted precisely at your prospects at a very low cost.

Major metropolitan areas have daily legal newspapers. These newspapers are read by lawyers with a local courthouse practice. If you need a litigation-oriented lawyer in a particular city, those newspapers reach the most likely candidates effectively.

The major metropolitan newspapers occasionally carry advertisements for lawyers. Such advertisements are relatively expensive. It is a matter of chance whether or not any desirable candidates will read the help-wanted classifieds on the weekend your ad runs.

The licensing requirements of each state impose a heavy burden on lawyers wishing to move from one jurisdiction to another. The expense of applying for admission to the bar is often in excess of $1000 in fees alone. Taking a bar examination is a major ordeal, requiring intense preparation. Admission based on "reciprocity" between states is not available to lawyers going to, or from, some states (Florida, New Mexico, Arizona, and California are examples). The requirements of reciprocal admission can be difficult for older and more experienced lawyers to meet.

If you require some unique qualifications—for example, a patent lawyer specializing in electronic arts for a location in North Dakota—you may need to extend your search to other states. The state bar journals of the states from which the general population is migrating (the Rust Belt in the late 1970s, the Oil Patch in the late 1980s, and the Northeast in the early 1990s) and the destination states from which young adventurers may be ready to return (New York and California) are targeted on pools of likely candidates. If you need national coverage, *The National Law Journal* and *The American Lawyer* are widely read, especially by associates in larger firms. The broadest coverage is probably through *The Wall Street Journal*. Ads run in regional editions are republished nationally in the *Weekly Business Employment Journal*.

You may wish to conceal your company identity in advertising an opening. Prospects' reluctance to respond to blind ads can be handled by using a consultant as an intermediary and making an express commitment to keep replies confidential. Or, if it is true, you can state that your own employees know of the ad.

The job should be described in terms of areas of law most likely to be encountered. Terms such as "compliance" or "litigation" are so broad as to be meaningless. A job with a limited potential for advancement will have a precise description, such as: "Develop and implement compliance programs in connection with the marketing of pharmaceutical products and supervision of related litigation"; or "Supervise documentation of security interests in floor plan and field warehouse arrangements and manage collections and liquidation litigation." A small company needing adaptability and broad interest might describe an entry-level position as: "Conduct or supervise litigation in defense of claims against the company"; or "Draft documents and advise operating management regarding general business transactions."

An experience requirement will narrow the response. Requiring "3 to 5 years" will exclude potentially desirable responses from individuals with perhaps 10 years, of which the most recent few years may be applicable directly to your situation. Titles do not define experience requirements. "Senior counsel with 3 to 5 years" is nonsense in a profession where careers extend beyond 40 years. The use of minimum levels of experience seems to have the fewest disadvantages.

Describe the company's location with enough precision that the prospect can tell what license will be required and can evaluate the cost of living. A job offer in southern California or New York City has entirely different cost considerations than an offer of similar work in Topeka.

Finally, disclose the big secret, the compensation budget. A salary reveals how important the job is to the company. There is little reason to have experienced counsel applying for jobs budgeted at $40,000, or beginners responding to jobs valued at $125,000. Some compensation flexibility is retained by indicting the amount in the budget.

Ask interested individuals to send a brief résumé and salary history. The response may be directed to a box number, or to a consultant. Ads calling for a reply to the personnel or human resources department suggest arbitrary screening for a low-level job. You would not approach a prospective chief executive officer, or even a vice president, that way. Many of the most desirable lawyers will not respond to such an approach.

Sorting Out Applicants

Your recruitment efforts should yield a large stack of résumés and cover letters to sort through. All are worth a look; you may see something unexpected. Advertisements draw a wide range of responses, some of which are totally inappropriate. Licensing, compensation, and experience are a basis for a preliminary screening. Since all lawyers function to some extent as communicators, some will be rejected for failure to make an effective, attractive presentation with the cover letter and résumé. This negative process of screening and rejecting candidates might well be delegated to a headhunter or personnel department. You will want to handle the positive process of considering candidates.

Résumés are a poor device for decision making. The applicant tries to disclose as few negatives as possible. The employer is trying to screen out as many as possible. More information is needed for either to go further. Continued involvement of a consultant will enable you to keep your identity confidential. A letter to the applicant requesting more information and enclosing substantial information about the company will start the relationship on a professional tone. If you are ready to disclose your identity, enclose your 10-K, proxy statement, and shareholder report, or some product brochures, to introduce yourself. If confidentiality is still a concern, have the consultant prepare a description of the company and its business. You give some information, and you ask for a lot of information in return. Use a form letter—Fig. 6-1 provides an example—to request more information and to test creativity by asking for information the applicant thinks will be useful to you.

If you are hiring lawyers with less than 7 years experience, ask for an ordinary (not certified), copy of their law school transcript. Academic achievement is not relevant to most jobs, but transcripts are a useful topic for discussion in interviews.

Ask for an example of their written work. Junior lawyers may not get to sign briefs or memoranda they prepare. Published articles may have benefited from unacknowledged editorial efforts. More experienced counsel seldom write anything that is not confidential to some client. The best writing sample is a filed brief or pleading. The writing sample may give you an idea of the applicant's style of presentation. Is the document lengthy, or short and to the point? Is it easy to read? Does it make sense to you? You may not be able to judge the quality of the research, but you will know if you cannot understand it. Give extra consideration to a trial attorney imaginative enough to respond with a transcript of an examination of a witness.

Ask applicants to respond to a questionnaire of three to five items designed to reveal their personality and philosophy. You want them to tell you what they think is important about legal work and human relationships. A list of questions that might be used for this purpose appears as Fig. 6-2. When you read the answers, look for clearly expressed ideas. The fundamental quality you seek in any lawyer is the ability to have ideas, and to express them.

> I. M. Consultant
> P.O. Box 456
> Chicago, Illinois 60000
>
> Current Date
>
> U. R. Applicant
> Street Address
> Anytown, Illinois 60000
>
> Dear Ms. Applicant:
>
> Thank you for responding to our recent advertisement of an opening for a lawyer. We have many well-qualified candidates, like yourself, to consider.
>
> The enclosed materials relating to the prospective employer may be of interest to you.
>
> Please forward a copy of the transcript of your courses and grades in law school. It is not necessary that the copy be certified. Please indicate your class rank at the end of each semester.
>
> Please provide us with a written sample of your work. This should reflect your creativity and your analytical ability.
>
> Please answer the enclosed questions in the spaces provided. Finally, please provide us with any information that you think will help us in considering your qualifications for this position.
>
> Very truly yours,
>
> I. M. Consultant

Figure 6-1. A letter requesting further information from an applicant for an in-house position.

Your reading of the responses to the questionnaire and the writing samples will give you a basis for offering interviews. At this point, continued concealment of your identity is insulting. You should be building a professional relationship with each applicant still under consideration. Send the regular employment application form used by your company, to be filled out and brought to the interview. Also, advise the applicant that you will want names, addresses, and telephone numbers of references and licensing information brought to the interview. A form letter, like Fig. 6-3, invites the applicant to telephone you to set a date. Be sure to cover travel costs in the letter.

Select one or two from each group.

Personal Motivation

What courses did you enjoy most in law school and why?

Why did you choose to become a lawyer?

Describe and explain your life goals and ambitions.

Explain why you have left previous jobs.

What jobs have been most interesting to you in the past?

Given a choice of positions in New York City, Columbus, Ohio, Dallas, Texas, Telluride, Colorado, and San Diego, California, which would you choose and why?

Professional Focus

How do you stay up to date with current developments in the law?

How have you applied current technology—personal computers for example—to your practice of law?

What current developments in the law do you think will have substantial impact on business in the next 5 years?

How will you prepare to handle assignments involving areas of law with which you have no experience?

Legal Philosophy

Describe the proper role of a lawyer within a business organization.

Confronted with a client intending to act in violation of the law, what should a lawyer consider in choosing between being candid and being fired, or continuing the representation in the hope of changing the client's views?

How should a lawyer help a client in negotiating a contract?

Do you think the law is to be found in precedent and statutes, or is the law to be shaped in response to social, political, and economic pressures?

Figure 6-2. A list of questions you might use to find how an applicant for an in-house legal position thinks.

Hiring In-House Lawyers

XYZ CORPORATION
XYZ Street
Othertown, Your State
(335) 555-1212

Current Date

U. R. Applicant
Street Address
Anytown, Illinois 60000

Dear Ms. Applicant:

Thank you for the material you forwarded to our consultant, I. M. Consultant, regarding your qualifications for the legal position we are considering. We would like to discuss your qualifications further with you at our offices.

A copy of our regular employment application is enclosed. Please fill it out completely, for our records.

Please bring the names, addresses, and current telephone numbers of references who can attest to your ability and character.

We would like to proceed promptly, so please call my secretary, June December, collect at (335) 555-1212 to make an appointment. She will handle your travel arrangements and reservations.

Very truly yours,

Mr. XYZ

Figure 6-3. A letter inviting an applicant for an interview.

The Interview

Interviewing is a learned skill. It involves listening. An experienced lawyer should be good at it. Although interviews are not entirely satisfactory as a selection device, there are no better alternatives. The following suggestions are intended to give the conversation sufficient scope and depth so that you can make an intuitive judgment.

Ask the candidate what she would like to know about the company. Do the candidate's questions reflect a reading of the materials you sent? Has the candidate made any effort to study your company or your industry?

Put pressure on. Ask the candidate if the writing sample submitted is what she thought was the best instrument for its intended purpose or, alternatively, if she thought it was what would impress you the most. The glib response is that the sample is both—best for its purpose and most impressive. The relationship of attorney and client so often involves a clash of ideas that such challenges have a proper place in the interview.

Discuss the law school transcript. Ask which courses were electives and why she selected those particular areas of study. Ask what else went on in her life while in law school—marriage, children born, sickness, divorce, financial distress. Is the applicant defensive about grades? Can the applicant handle criticism without excessive involvement of her ego.

What is the story of the rest of her life? Undergraduate school, part-time jobs, military service, and nonlegal full-time work all contribute to an individual's point of view. Law students who seek out summer jobs with law firms have a narrow picture of the world. These people are going to spend the rest of their lives in law firms; why would they waste their youth in dusty libraries and file rooms?

Find out what the candidate reads, both books and periodicals. We all tend to overstate our reading, but see if you can detect an information gatherer. Individuals who clip and save articles from state bar journals and publications of the "sections" of the American Bar Association (ABA) are demonstrating an interest in the law. Find out if she routes or otherwise redistributes articles of interest, a very desirable trait for in-house professionals. Find out what professional associations she belongs to, and who pays her dues. Memberships in sections of the American Bar Association and state bar associations are an important indication of professional interests.

After some rapport is established, you need to ask the hard questions about legal experience. What was done in each job? What kinds of matters were worked on, and what did the candidate actually do herself? In a litigation practice, did the candidate actually present any cases to a jury? Was she the "lead" attorney or "second chair"? Was the outcome satisfactory? Other than jury trials, what is her experience in presenting cases to the court. Nonjury proceedings, divorce, custody, probation violations, various motions, and the like are a real test of persuasiveness and judgment. How much contact has she had with clients and employees of clients? Does she think clients were receptive to her advice?

How many paralegals, secretaries, and files clerks worked under her direct supervision? How many lawyers? Who supervised her? How did she motivate her subordinates? Who designed the systems she relied on, and what systems did she design herself? Did the systems work well enough to be useful? Did she have to fire anyone? Why? Ask her about disciplinary actions by the courts and bar associations. You need to know if she has ever been sanctioned, censured, suspended, or disbarred. Tell her that you will need certificates of good standing from the courts to which she is admitted. Ask her for references and permission to contact them.

Use of psychological tests of lawyers may be misleading. All lawyers are good at taking tests; the bar exam is a classic stress challenge. Lawyers as a group tend to be pretty smart, maybe smarter than psychologists. Personal-injury lawyers are likely to have worked closely with psychiatrists using such tests to prove damages from psychic injury.

Describe the job to each promising candidate, and ask if the job seems desirable, and what special quality she can bring to it. Offer to answer questions about the job and the company.

Show her the working environment. The actual office designated for the job, and its furnishings, reveals a great deal about the position within the organization. Show her the library and tell her what her materials budget will be. Let her observe how friendly and helpful the support staff is, and get a feel for the atmosphere of the workplace. Introduce her to, and let her interview, lawyers and other professionals on your staff.

Choosing

The entire purpose of the interview is to provide you with an opportunity to observe the candidate. The observations are a basis for intuition. Demeanor, presence, and personality contribute to the selection process. In the end, it is a matter of judgment.

Before acting on your judgment, check all references. Use the telephone; you can hear things in a phone call that would not be written. Confirm all bar admissions and current status. Contact past supervisors and coworkers to ask if the work described on the résumé matches their recollection.

You should be able to rank your choices. You must rely on your intuition to make a largely subjective choice. Remember, you are hiring someone whose wants to be valued for the advice she gives. To succeed, she must gain your trust and confidence. If she cannot do that, she fails. Ask yourself if you are willing to go through an emotionally draining experience with this candidate at your side. That is what a trial is.

Having made a choice, offer the best candidate the job. Although a telephone call is more friendly, a formal letter will help set the tone of the relationship. Figure 6-4 is a form that can be used for this purpose. When you have an acceptance, it is courteous to let other candidates know that they are no longer being considered. Figure 6-5 is a form for that purpose.

XYZ CORPORATION
XYZ Street
Othertown, This State
(335) 555-1212

Current Date

U. R. Applicant
Street Address
Anytown, Illinois 60000

Dear Ms. Applicant:

As we discussed by telephone, XYZ Corporation hereby offers to employ you as a staff lawyer on the following terms. You must complete a probation period of 9 months with satisfactory productivity. During the probationary period you must meet the requirements for admission to practice law before the courts of this state. The company will reimburse you for your costs incurred in gaining admission to the bar.

Your compensation in this position will be $47,500 per year plus the benefits provided under the various benefit plans, from time to time, to all salaried employees.

Your employment begins on the last day of March, and employee benefits, including medical insurance, will go into effect 30 days later.

This offer is contingent upon your ability to pass a physical examination. Please contact the office of Fred Smith, M.D., at (335) 555-1212 for an appointment.

Please telephone me if you have any questions. If employment on these terms is acceptable to you, please sign the enclosed copy where indicated and return it to me.

We are looking forward to having you join us at XYZ Corporation for a long, enjoyable, and productive career.

Very truly yours,

Mr. XYZ

Figure 6-4. A letter offering in-house employment to a lawyer.

> XYZ CORPORATION
> XYZ Street
> Othertown, This State
> (335) 555-1212
>
> Current Date
>
> N. D. Goode
> Street Address
> Wrongtown, Iowa 60000
>
> Dear Mr. Goode:
>
> Thank you for helping us in our search for an in-house lawyer. We have selected another candidate. We were impressed with your qualifications, and wish you well in your endeavors,
>
> Very truly yours,
>
> Mr. XYZ

Figure 6-5. A letter advising an applicant of the selection of another candidate.

1. Define the focus of the position:
   Efficient implementation of procedures; or
   Effective advocacy outside of company; or
   In-depth understanding and advice for decision making
2. Define the lawyer's position in the management structure:
   Identify who will receive most of the legal services.
   Identify to whom will the lawyer report.
3. State qualifications:
   License to practice law
   Law school, considering full or part time while working; and grades, class rank, and honors
   Nonlegal achievements, employment, and training
   Amount, scope, and variety of professional experience
4. Find candidates:
   Survey informal sources:
      Employee and business community referrals
      Attorneys in outside firms
      Unsolicited résumés
   Use employment services:
      Bar associations and law schools
      Employment agencies which advertise and screen
      "Headhunters" who recruit from similar employers
      Consultants who provide guidance
   Advertise qualifications, compensation, and location:
      State bar journals of target states
      National legal publications.
5. Seek more information from qualified candidates:
   Writing sample
   Response to written questions from Fig. 6-2
6. Interview candidates:
   Prior completion of standard employment application
   Discuss education and experience
   Discuss candidate's non-work-related interests and experience
   Evaluate candidate's listening skills
   Evaluate candidate's interest in helping coworkers
   Evaluate questions asked by candidate
7. Check references and confirm credentials.
8. Rely on informed intuition and judgment.
9. Make explicit offer of employment, in writing, to best candidate.

Procedure: Hiring in-house lawyers.

7
What to Expect from In-House Lawyers, and How to Get It

The hope of saving money often motivates the hiring of in-house lawyers. Any business with a significant amount of legal work can save money with in-house lawyers. However, the short-term effect of an in-house lawyer is likely to be an increase in legal expenditures. The new lawyer will recognize "needs" for additional legal work that you might otherwise do without. Some of the additional work will be sent to outside lawyers, either because of its location or because special skills are required. At the same time, the in-house lawyer who formerly billed 1800 hours per year in private practice will do well to generate half that amount of "productive" time as an employee. The in-house lawyer spends more time talking to other employees, has periods when there is no work to attend to, and is on the job fewer hours per week.

Comparing a $48,000 annual salary, with benefits and desk space, to an hourly rate of $100 suggests a 50 percent cost advantage to in-house lawyers. Actual cost savings from hour-for-hour substitution are elusive. Such savings are achieved only when in-house lawyers are more efficient and effective than their outside counterparts. The increase in efficiency follows from ease of access to accurate information. Much greater savings result from changes in the company's operations. The in-house lawyer, a specialist in your business, can find and fix small things to avoid big problems. This creative change is what saves you money, not simply substituting for work by an independent outside attorney. A comparison of the total legal outlay from year to year will show the effect of in-house lawyers if you can adjust for all other variables. An elaborate cost accounting system may give you such information, after the fact. Or you can evaluate in-house lawyers by the impression they make on you. Of course, you will be most impressed by the people handling the biggest problems, not by the people avoiding little problems. Unfortunately, the beneficial effects of in-house lawyers are subtle and often unnoticed. How can you tell if they are doing a good job when they seem to be fussing over petty details? Failed efforts of in-house lawyers give some insight.

A manufacturing company sold its product directly to retail dealers. To induce dealers to stock their show rooms with this seasonal product, 30–60–90 terms were offered. Dealerships were much sought after, and were often family businesses. There were some credit losses. When suits were filed to collect unpaid accounts, it was frequently discovered that the dealer name (debtor) represented nothing. The annual contract renewal had been signed "Jones Store," but "Jones" had been dead for years. An in-house lawyer recommended that the marketing department check the dealer names during the annual contract renewal cycle, basically by looking at the sales tax collection certificate in states where there was a sales tax. Marketing refused, wishing to avoid offending its customers. The credit losses continued.

Another company packaged and marketed lubricants that met SAE and industry specifications. Over the years, the company had acquired several distinctive and well-established trademarks for such products in the course of mergers and acquisitions. The trademarks were not essential to current marketing programs. An in-house lawyer recommended that the trademarks be affixed to packages of product shipped in interstate commerce, because at that time continuous use was required to preserve the right to enforce the registration. The operating management refused to expend the effort to preserve the trademarks. Those trademarks, carried as nondepreciable goodwill, were lost to the company.

A company delivered a commodity product through common-carrier terminals. To meet price competition, customers were given 30-day terms against a credit limit. The terminals reported deliveries periodically, with a lag time of up to a month. An in-house lawyer recommended that the terminal contracts require daily reporting of deliveries. The marketing department refused to accept the cost. During the lag time, a San Antonio dealer picked up $500,000 worth of product, under a $25,000 credit line, sold it, and took the cash to the Bahamas. That same year, a Chicago area dealer, with a $100,000 credit limit, picked up $1,100,000 worth of product during the lag time, sold it, and went bankrupt. Those two losses wiped out the year's profits for that division of the company.

The first example is about gathering facts, the dealer identities. The second example is about making facts, interstate shipments of trademarked goods. The third is about avoiding facts, deliveries in excess of credit limits. In each, the in-house lawyer found the right facts and applied the correct law. But the effort failed to benefit the company. The lawyer did not get the job done.

For an in-house lawyer, good performance is conduct that results in success, that results in changes that avoid future legal expenses. How do you know you are getting good performance when good performance means that nothing bad is happening? How do you know when an in-house lawyer, who is doing a great job at "winning" cases that never should have happened in the first place, is doing you more harm than good? How can you judge the performance of lawyers when they have no control over the "law" or the "facts"?

The performance of in-house lawyers can be judged accurately by their conduct while the work is being done. Competence, diligence, and character, as with outside attorneys, indicate the value of the contribution of in-house lawyers.

Competence

Listening carefully to everything your employees have to say is the only way the lawyer can discover the right questions or have a chance of finding the right answer to any problem. Especially in routine matters, the lawyer not only needs to hear the words, but also to pick up poorly expressed intentions and attitudes. This requires patient attention. After a few years with the company, a staff lawyer may feel that she ought to have quick answers. Such answers may be to the wrong questions. Some employees will blindly follow bad advice. Others, frustrated with legal advice that does not meet the problem or cannot be implemented, ignore the advice and rely on their own common sense. Either way, the lawyer's work is worthless or worse. Wrong advice indicates that the lawyer is not listening.

Just as a trial attorney must work with the intense emotions felt by witnesses, the in-house lawyer must cope with middle managers guarding their turf. The lawyer is seen as an intruder, a source of problems and a rebuke. An insecure manager will try to obstruct the lawyer, or shift responsibility for an impending disaster. Persuading middle-management employees to cooperate is an art. Young in-house lawyers soon learn of the need to charm secretaries. Charm often fails with crusty old managers who have real mistakes to hide. The ability to deal with employees' anxieties is essential to digging out the truth.

The legal problems of a business are complicated. All of the facts and applicable law must be considered. The in-house lawyer's job is to explain the legal aspects of the situation so that you, and any operating manager, can understand it. The explanation has to make sense both orally and in writing. Since you are familiar with the business and can ask questions, it is a lot easier to make things clear to you than to a jury. The same thing goes for contracts and other formal documents drafted by your lawyer; they should be easy to read and understand. You never want a judge to have to guess what a document means.

Beyond listening carefully, gently pulling out the truth, and stating the solution clearly, the in-house lawyer needs one more people skill: the art of persuasion. In each of the three examples of failure, the operating management was not convinced of the need to follow the legal recommendation. People skills are the most essential element of competence for in-house lawyers.

Just as a pilot navigates a ship past obstacles to a safe anchorage, an in-house lawyer guides business operations past legal entanglements to accomplish legitimate objectives. The lawyer needs to know two kinds of law. The first is the formal, written law, basically the statutes, appellate opinions, and regulations generated by legislatures, courts, and government agencies. However, a lawyer's useful knowledge grows by a process of specialization and continued study. The constant activity of the courts and legislatures requires lawyers to update their knowledge when responding to questions. Law is a scholarly art. Your lawyers should be reading periodicals and attending seminars to keep up with the jargon of their particular practice, and spending hours in the library with unfamiliar problems.

There is a second body of legal knowledge about how cases really get decided in courthouses. In-house lawyers become isolated from what is going on at the courthouse. Taking disputes to juries is the foundation of a kind of judgment about what is convincing, what will be believed, and what matters. When decisions are being made in board rooms, lawyers sometimes makes statements that begin "No jury would ever find...." That is wrong! Juries and judges do all kinds of strange things. A courthouse attorney who tells you that she does not believe she can convince a jury of some fact may be giving you a sound judgment. A lawyer who tells you what a jury will, or will not, do is giving you wishful thinking.

No lawyer knows everything. The competent lawyer knows when help is needed. The most routine matters are the most specialized. For example, a real estate foreclosure is not itself unusual, but most lawyers have never done one. Any small misstep in the lengthy and intricate procedure requires that the entire process be done over from the beginning. An in-house lawyer who never seeks outside expertise is dangerous. The need for help might occur because of the press of other matters or the novelty or difficulty of the problem. The ultimate test of competence is knowing who does know how to get the job done right.

In addition to changes in the substantive law, changes in technology and the way law is practiced have an impact on the effectiveness and efficiency of lawyers. Up-to-date lawyers use personal computers to access legal databases, Lexis or WESTLAW. The use of such databases can have a big impact on negotiations. For example, a national retailer was late with the rent on a shopping center location. A database search revealed SEC filings reporting serious financial difficulty. The shopping center operator accepted a quick settlement and avoided the effect of the subsequent bankruptcy. In the late 1980s, the use of fax, computer simulations, videotape, and word processing became common. The 1990s will bring other developments to be adopted as needed.

Beyond "people skills" and "legal skills," competence requires the ability to get the job done. In private practice, the market is ruthless in punishing lawyers who cannot get things done. They cannot collect fees. In-house lawyers, who don't face monthly overhead expenses, can become nonproductive. Some pioneers in the application of personal computers did not do a lick of useful work for months at a time. Lawyers with proven ability get bogged down in a single case. Young lawyers cannot get started. You don't pay a lawyer for what she knows, but for what she can get done. The best lawyers often start projects not knowing how to reach the objective. They find ways to get the job done by hard work, creativity, and imagination. You pay the lawyer to figure out solutions.

Diligence

Diligence is more than just working as hard as the company culture requires. For lawyers, diligence is working on the difficult matters. The two most common ways in which in-house lawyers look busy while avoiding productive work are hiding in the bureaucratic maze and having high-visibility meetings. Lawyers, like any employees, can while away their time, lost in a morass of meetings and memos about how something will be done if anyone ever does it. Among favored topics are: "document retention," "the file system," and "proofreading marks for use with word processing." This is much less demanding than legal work, and no one will ever know if the job was done right, because the job is never done.

Worse, because of a double cost whammy, is the high-visibility crisis meeting. This is where the lawyer, frequently conspiring with weak upper-level managers, eats up time in half-day units meeting with you in hand-wringing "ain't it awful" sessions. Nothing gets done, nothing is decided. But the lawyer is there, with yellow pad in hand. The reality of corporate life is that the high-visibility assignments involving top management, press conferences, and big meetings are the way to get ahead.

Such meetings, and the crisis, result from the failure of in-house lawyers to find and defuse problems. Good lawyers come to meetings to listen, or to explain and report, then go out and accomplish the objective.

Any legal matter is founded in a factual situation and has a history. A workers' compensation claim, for example, is founded in an injury, claimed to be work related, and loss of income. An outside attorney retained to defend the claim merely looks to the proof. The manager will urge that the claimant is malingering, or that the injury is not work related. The in-house lawyer must look deeper, into the conditions in which the claim arose.

Similarly, in collecting a past-due account the outside attorney files suit, but the in-house lawyer needs to figure out why the credit limit was too high and why the collateral was inadequate. For the in-house lawyer, diligence means going beyond the solution sought by the manager to the underlying problem. Solutions chosen to cover up an underlying problem cause mischief. It is the in-house lawyer's responsibility to dig out the actual problem and create a genuine solution. The easy way out is just to do what the manager wants, not what the client needs.

A member of a state commission told me that lawyers were "deal killers." He went on to say that the commission's in-house counsel always rendered opinions that projects could not be done and ideas could not be implemented. The law is complicated, and some problems require serious study. Perhaps a conservative or cautious lawyer will say "no" when another lawyer might say "yes." A lazy lawyer always says "no," because she has not studied the law and investigated the facts to find a way to accomplish the client's objectives. The state commissioner then said that he had found the right kind of lawyer in the office of the state's attorney general. The assistant attorney general always said "yes." Beware of the lawyer who always says "yes," especially when the lawyer does not have any direct responsibility for the problem. Just because a lawyer says something is OK, that does not make it safe or right. The diligent lawyer nails down the facts and the law that is the basis for recommendations.

Lawyers are notorious for delay. Probably, difficulty in collecting fees from clients is why lawyers have an ingrained tolerance for delay. There is no point in finishing a job until the fee is in hand. Getting paid is not a problem for in-house lawyers. In-house lawyers should attend to matters promptly. At busy times, priorities may have to be set in the law departments, but no project should languish without an expected completion date.

The contrast between a lawyer's view of timeliness and the view of a businessman was amply illustrated in a seminar on alternate dispute resolution. A business dispute was described. A lawsuit on that type of problem could be expected to take 1 or 2 years. A minitrial procedure, described in Chap. 13, could bring about a much quicker settlement. One lawyer proposed a schedule of 90 days. His adversary suggested that perhaps it could be done in 60 days. The businesspeople on both sides interjected a demand that the job be finished in no more than 30 days. The excuse of "demands of other clients" is not available to in-house lawyers. The in-house response should be prompt by business, not lawyer, standards.

Proofreading is dull. In private practice, where clients pay the full hourly rate while lawyers read boilerplate documents line by line, the cash provides the motivation. In-house lawyers, and all employees, should strive for excellence in the details. Documents should be well written, and carefully proofread. Spelling and grammatical errors are unacceptable. Files should be organized so that any authorized person can locate any item within a reasonable time. To the limits of the resources, the product of the in-house lawyer should project an image of quality.

Curiosity and intellectual engagement are essential if the in-house lawyer is to gain the special knowledge of your business needed to contribute value beyond what is available from outside attorneys. An in-house lawyer should be a student of the company, its business, and its people. If you make tires, the in-house lawyer should be interested in the coatings on bead wire. If you provide central station alarm services, the lawyer should care about burglary techniques. If you run a string of hamburger stands, the lawyer should not be a vegetarian. In-house lawyers doing credit work should care about the Uniform Commercial Code and the Bankruptcy Code. The interest leads to the identification of needs and potential problems of the business, and the development of solutions. An in-house lawyer who does not care about your business will do exactly what you ask, and nothing more.

Diligence is linked to productivity. Every management with a law department eventually attempts to measure lawyer productivity. The usual way is to require that the lawyers fill out some kind of a time report. A really clever outside consultant will recommend that a standard billing and timekeeping software package be purchased and used for that purpose. The purpose of timekeeping systems is to identify costs, not productivity. Law firms use costs to set fees in a free market. In-house lawyers have a captive market. Lawyers are smart enough to figure out that the required "productivity" numbers can be made by repeatedly solving the same problem. Those with experience in mid-size or larger law firms will have no trouble billing 200 hours each month. When they get to really churning the files, they can also drive up the billings from outside attorneys.

Character

The last step in the process of getting a license to practice law is approval by a committee on "character and fitness." The committee is made up of established lawyers appointed by the courts. The process, an exercise in taking tests, submitting fingerprints, and filling out questionnaires, concludes with a perfunctory interview. This all happens after one completes law school and passes the bar examination. Few committee members wish to deny the applicant a license that has been earned through long, hard work. As a practical matter, only outrageous conduct will stop an applicant from getting a license. Possession of a license to practice law is evidence of intelligence and perseverance, but not of character.

Occasionally, some clients have the thought that they might prefer a lawyer who is a bit of a crook. Such a thought might be expressed as: "Someone who can get things done." Most lawyers are intelligent, and clever. They are also smart enough to steal from you, if they are so inclined. The character of the lawyer is all that protects you. The character, or virtue, of a lawyer is significant beyond mere honesty.

Prudence is the quality of correctly assessing realities and possibilities. In drafting a contract, a prudent lawyer considers the possibility that the other party is a crook, and that the whole deal is fraudulent. In litigation, a prudent lawyer provides for the possibility that the star witness may disappear, die, or be proven a liar. This is more than competently applying the right law to the right facts. It is the withholding of judgment until all the available information has been considered.

A variation of prudence is that an in-house lawyer should not stir up legal controversy. Disputes often develop from emotional reactions to unexpected developments and bad information. A customer who does not pay what is owed may anger you. The emotion may drive a decision-making process that would be better based on a dispassionate analysis of rights and remedies. Your in-house lawyer owes you that cool, calm calculation of the likelihood of success of any proposed cause of action.

Among lawyers, fairness and integrity are essential to success. Much of the problem in the legal system is caused by the lack of trust between adversaries. Attorneys have to trust each other in order to work together. Serving the same client, outside attorneys who cannot rely on the fairness and integrity of in-house lawyers have to find other ways to be sure that they are being told the truth and that their advice is reaching you.

Far more important is the absolute integrity of the in-house lawyer in dealing with you. The privilege of confidential communications between lawyer and client, discussed at length in Chap. 8, permits the in-house lawyer to speak and write the truth without fear of harm to the client. Only the lawyer's integrity assures that the truth will be fully and fairly told. Only the lawyer can speak freely of business matters, saying what needs to be said under a legal cloak of secrecy. An in-house lawyer who colors her advice to advance or protect any interest other than yours, including her own career, abuses the relationship, the privilege, and you.

Loyalty to the client, an element of integrity and fairness, requires an in-house lawyer to place your interests before her own. Overt disloyalty, purposely acting against your interests, is easy to deal with by termination and professional disciplinary action. More subtle is the effect of loyalty eroded by the in-house lawyer's perception of how she is being treated as an employee. Diminished loyalty may be indicated by a failure to present a dignified image, a cavalier or casual attitude toward the company's legal affairs, or openly looking for another job.

Loyalty to the client also limits the relationships between the in-house lawyer and every other employee. Employees are potential witnesses or informants. Every manager faces the problem of getting too close to workers he may have to fire. The lawyer is similarly isolated by a potential conflict of interest with every employee.

An in-house lawyer should also give you the ordinary loyalty desirable in any employee. In-house lawyers should help the company enforce its rules by setting an example of voluntary compliance. That means showing up for work at opening time.

Finally, an in-house lawyer's duty of loyalty is to the company and not to management. A lawyer should also be loyal to her profession. These loyalties will sometimes require a lawyer to do and say things which jeopardize her job and even her career.

Temperance, not as abstinence from the use of alcohol but as the avoidance of overindulgence, has particular application to lawyers with respect to competitiveness. The legal system is based on competition. Two attorneys representing opposite sides of a case argue their respective positions before a judge or jury, and a winner is chosen. From the beginning of law school, every lawyer is trained for mental combat. The objective is to win, by advancing your own cause and damaging the enemy. This kind of ruthless competitiveness, necessary for survival in the courtroom, is destructive if it is exercised within a company. An ambitious lawyer advancing her own cause within a company can hardly expect potential witnesses and informants to be forthcoming. An ambitious lawyer's recommendations will not be embraced joyfully by fellow employees.

Unchecked ambition leads to cannibalism among in-house lawyers. You can foster a collegial atmosphere by making it clear that no lawyer can advance his or her own interests at the expense of another. If there is no "best" legal job, there will be no fight for it. Each lawyer's goal should be professional development, not corporate advancement. At the junior level, the clear message should be that internal competition will be ruthlessly crushed.

Personal courage is essential to in-house counsel's performance. Three common situations requiring courage are carrying the bad news, refusing to break the law, and sticking to recommendations. The typical bad news situation comes up when you want a deal that will not work.

Documents may not say what the proponents of the deal claim they say. For example, a customer seeking credit may claim that he has contracts for the sale of completed goods, which, upon examination may turn out to be blanket purchase orders that are not effective without shipping instructions. That can usually be handled by persuading the operating management that the lawyer's interpretation is correct.

More difficult is the not-uncommon instance when an employee tells the in-house lawyer to lie. A lawyer who is fired for refusing to lie has no claim for wrongful discharge because the client has an absolute right to end the attorney–client relationship. You should establish a policy with your managers against asking in-house lawyers to compromise their integrity. Unfortunately, as a practical matter, for most in-house lawyers the only way to preserve their integrity is to resign if they are asked to lie.

Courage is required in closer questions. Once, the president of a subsidiary company had been convinced by an outside attorney that he needed to file a lawsuit against a customer. The lower-ranking employees who actually dealt with the customer knew that the dispute could be worked out without a lawsuit. It appeared that the outside attorney was stirring up some fee-generating litigation. Approval of the parent-company CEO was required to start a lawsuit. In a meeting with the CEO, the proposed suit was recommended. A junior in-house lawyer, familiar with the facts, was present. When asked by the CEO for his view, the junior lawyer demonstrated clearly why the suit was a bad idea. The CEO killed the proposal. The junior lawyer was removed from assignments to that subsidiary and soon left the company. The underlying problem with the customer worked itself out in due course, with no lawsuit, and satisfactory profits.

Motivation

You expect competence, diligence, and character from every employee, not just lawyers. What makes an in-house lawyer different from other employees is the role of the court in the relationship. The lawyer's license comes with a code of ethics that the courts will enforce. For example, the ethics require loyalty to the client, even after the lawyer is fired. And while you may pay the salary, the lawyer's practice of the profession is regulated by the courts. Still, performance improvements can be motivated.

Widely studied motivation theories should be applied to lawyers with caution. With the education and relatively high pay of lawyers, you might expect that self-actualization would be a need felt by most lawyers. However, in-house lawyers exchange pure self-actualization for a steady paycheck. Another theory is that a need for achievement, power, or affiliation is dominate in each individual. Getting a license to practice law is a major achievement for anyone. A license to practice law is certainly a source of power, as can be observed in any courtroom. Yet a decision to accept in-house employment must reflect some desire for affiliation. Other theories weigh interest in the task against interest in people, coercion against self-interest, or rewards against punishment. Regardless of the general validity of all or any of these theories, there is little reason to try to fit all lawyers into any such categories. However, working with outside attorneys is clearly more "task oriented," and leadership of in-house lawyers is more "people oriented."

Lawyers as a group are self-motivated. Legal training is largely training for the clash of ideas from which only one winner may emerge. Those who do not like to fight, do not finish. Those who do finish, like to win. The motivation challenge is not to create energy and drive, but to focus and direct the existing drive.

Establishing a Performance Environment

Lawyers, like all other workers, need tools. Unfortunately, in many corporate cultures, tools become symbols of authority, status, and prestige. Questions of who gets to use the airplane, who has a corner office, and who has her country club dues paid are merely distractions at the top level of management.

In many companies, secretaries are disappearing, victims of new office technology. This is fine if you can afford to pay your lawyers to do their own filing, and to have their functions stop when they are traveling. Most companies limit the size of offices by grade. Lawyers need space to handle witness interviews, and to spread out the voluminous documents that are often required in litigation. If the offices are not big enough for a library table, then conference and work rooms are needed.

A lawyer without a secretary, paralegal, speaker phone, fax machine, personal computer, and office and conference space is necessarily limited in performing services of the type substituted for outside attorneys. The usual way in which in-house lawyers find the small changes that yield big benefits is by doing such ordinary legal work. The nature of the lawyer's work causes many of her tools to be seen as "perks." When given the tools to get the work done, other employees at the same compensation level may view such things as mere symbols.

In one well-managed company, the grade level of lawyers required that they work in an open office environment. The furniture was nice, but there were no walls. There was also no confidentiality, destroying the privilege of attorney–client communications.

Parking space assignments, wood furniture, access to the executive dining room, and other symbols of privilege and status are clear signals to all employees. Your middle managers decide whether or not to follow the recommendations of in-house lawyers based on their perception of the power of the lawyer. The real value of in-house lawyers may be lost if the lawyer has low status.

The cheap way to give status is with titles. Calling a lawyer with 2 years experience "Senior Counsel," or "Deputy Assistant General Counsel" will not fool anyone in your operating management. The simple title "Lawyer" is enough, if the authority is really there.

For lawyers, like all other employees, compensation is necessary to induce them to work. Also, the paycheck proves that you appreciate the value of their efforts. You should pay lawyers well enough so that they are not embarrassed. They expect to live in good neighborhoods, dress well, drive late-model cars, take vacations, and educate their children. If the pay of in-house lawyers is too low, the best will quit.

In addition to adequate tools (overhead) and fair compensation, a performance environment for lawyers requires a direct connection with the client. In larger companies, with many in-house lawyers, this connection is made by having the head of the legal department report to someone on the board of directors. Lower-ranking lawyers can report to the head lawyer, confident that their advice will reach the board of directors, i.e., the client. The same solution works in smaller companies. The board of directors, or the owner, delegates authority to receive communications and advice from the in-house lawyers to some individual. The key is to keep the management of the lawyers separate from the operations management. That will limit the ability of managers to punish lawyers who do a good job, in effect giving substantial power to the lawyers.

If it is necessary to give the lawyers the status symbols, and salary, and at least a connection to power, what is left to provide incentives? Three come to mind: challenges, personal and professional development, and positive feedback.

Specific Motivations

A newly hired lawyer who is assigned humdrum, tedious, time-killing tasks learns that she was hired, at that pay, to do those things. Later assignment of more interesting and more difficult jobs will be seen as a basis for asking for more money. If the increased compensation is not forthcoming, the lawyer will feel put upon and taken advantage of. Interesting work will be seen, not as a reward, but as a disruption of a nonchallenging routine. Once such a pattern is established, it takes heroic leadership to overcome it. You end up with a bunch of bureaucratic drones.

A new lawyer should be started with assignments that push her to the limits of her abilities and endurance. If the supervision is adequate, the new lawyer should be put next to the edge of disaster, in the midst of crisis. Lawyers who start out with tough, interesting cases or projects define themselves in terms of accomplishments. They rise to challenge. The salary level becomes incidental.

The first assignments should be used to establish the principle that challenges, where the action is, and important to the company, are rewards. Being asked to do the difficult is the true badge of status and prestige. The reward for being the best lawyer is getting the best, toughest cases.

What then, do you do with the boring tasks? If you have more than one lawyer, periodic reviews should include having each lawyer rank her assignments in order of preference. One person's poison may well prove to be another person's meat. Reassignment based on preference will relieve some of the tedium.

Usually the junior lawyer gets the dullest, most boring, and safest tasks. That is a formula for frustration. To make lawyers handling routine tasks available for more important matters, relieve them of the burden, but not the responsibility. Hire legal assistants or paralegals to do the paper shuffling. There is an important transition from doer to manager that must take place for this technique to be successful. The best managers will end up with staffs doing the dullest work. They will be the leaders. There is no reason to think that the best lawyers will be the best managers. If you find yourself with a brilliant lawyer who cannot delegate, make the decision to relieve her of the tedious matters.

Starting a new lawyer with a challenge is only the beginning of a long-term human development project. Young lawyers, offered an assignment that will lead to development of a specialty, may ask if it is a dead end. For lawyers, career development is a process that will stretch over 40 years or more. As an in-house lawyer, there are few opportunities for advancement that do not require sacrifice of professional status. The development of a long-term career track may be helpful if you wish to retain talented lawyers into their most productive years.

An incentive with a great deal of flexibility is further professional training. The licensing authorities in the various states are beginning to require a minimum level of continuing legal education (CLE) for all lawyers. Going beyond the required level of CLE is rewarding to the lawyer and beneficial to the client. The periodic meetings of various organizations of lawyers such as the American Bar Association, American Association of Corporate Counsel, Defense Research Institute, American Trial Lawyers Association, as well as state and local bar associations, usually have excellent seminars and presentations. Sending your in-house lawyers to such meetings is a prized reward.

Another incentive, especially for the in-house lawyer who is intently focused on the law, is general development seminars. Training in such things as time management, motivation and confidence building, psychology, and communications may have little to do with the practice of law, but the insights gained and the change of pace may be a genuine reward.

A cash incentive related to development is to allow individual lawyers a discretionary budget for use in purchasing books, periodicals, and other materials of a professional nature. You might allow use of the discretionary budget for professional dues and fees. As the 1990s begin, the annual registration fee with the licensing authority of each state is about $150. Annual dues of voluntary bar associations and the American Bar Association will be several hundred dollars more.

In a botched effort to intimidate an existing in-house legal staff, a newly hired chief lawyer ordered each lawyer to write her own job description. The stated purpose was to decide which jobs to cut. There was the germ of a good idea in the project. Lawyers, like all employees, like to know where they stand. They also like to have feedback on whether they are doing what you want. A written quarterly report in which each lawyer details accomplishments and goals, naming the operating managers involved and describing the small changes that can save big money, will give the lawyers a chance to brag. After a year or two, the effort becomes routine and should be dropped, but it can give you a short-term boost.

Special Problems

Abuse of alcohol and other drugs, mental illness, business or marital difficulties, and physical illness all affect lawyers as people. With in-house lawyers, it is a human resources problem to be handled in accordance with the company's policy. If you value human resources, compassion and loyalty dictate that efforts be made to see the person through the difficulty. As to the actual work to be done, someone else will have to attend to the duties of the impaired person. Addicted lawyers are sometimes spectacular performers for a while. Eventually, however, the harm done by the addiction impairs performance. With recovery, past performance is often exceeded. It is worth a try.

Your in-house lawyers were lawyers long before they ever heard of your company, and they will still be lawyers even if the company goes broke or is absorbed into a giant conglomerate. Their status and prestige comes from the court, not their employer. They will answer to the court for malfeasance, even if you excuse it. Such self-created people are unlikely to be moved by the exhortations of after-dinner speakers, or threats from bookkeepers.

If you know what performance is, you can recognize it, appreciate it, and motivate it. Reward competence, diligence, and character, and you will get performance. Performance earns respect. Respected advice is followed. Small changes are made. Value is achieved.

1. Performance
    Competence:
        Helps employees accomplish business goals by:
            Listening and understanding
            Sensitivity to emotions
            Stating advice clearly
            Persuading employees to follow advice
        Demonstrates legal skills:
            Knows the general law
            Aware of how legal system works in practice
            Recognizes the need for special expertise or research
            Aware of current legal techniques
        Completes tasks without bogging down
    Diligence:
        Works on difficult, meaningful tasks
        Avoids bureaucratic make-work
        Seeks genuine solutions
        Completes projects on schedule
        Attends to details
        Shows imagination and creativity
    Character:
        Honesty and integrity
        Prudence:
            Accurately assesses realities and possibilities
            Avoids instigating controversy
        Loyalty:
            Places your interests first
            Avoids potential conflicts of interest
            Conforms to company policy
        Temperance in personal ambition
        Courage:
            Gives impartial advice
            Insists on ethical conduct
2. Motivation
    Establish performance environment:
        Offices, staff, and equipment
        Adequate compensation
        Status within company
        Connection to top management
    Challenge individual's capabilities
    Provide continuing professional development
    Review and comment on work

Procedure: Evaluating and motivating in-house lawyers.

8
Why Lawyers Act the Way They Do

Lawyers offend businesspeople by what seems like arrogance. The legal profession claims a superior ethical stature, hides behind a privilege, and sometimes ignores responsible managers. You can work around, or with, such attitudes if you understand where they come from and how they are changing. The key to understanding lawyers is in the relationship to the client.

Legal Ethics, Demographics, and Economics

A "profession" is a public promise to abide by a standard of conduct. Traditionally there were three "learned" professions: the law, medicine, and the clergy. You entrust your soul to the clergy, your body to the physician, and your property and rights to the lawyer. The idea of law as a profession is deeply ingrained in those who practice it. The idea of any profession is that an ethical standard places the interest of the client, patient, or penitent above the interest of the practitioner. A true professional will act against his or her personal interest to protect the profession and the client.

The Code of Ethics

The first "Canons of Professional Ethics" were adopted by the American Bar Association (ABA) in 1908. The original canons urged reasonableness, and said of a lawyer: "He must obey his own conscience and not that of his client." Although the canons were not specific, there was nothing vague in the references to moral law, honor, fidelity, and duty.

The original canons were superseded by the Code of Professional Responsibility, adopted by the ABA in 1969. This consisted of nine short canons, elaborated by lengthy "Ethical Considerations" and "Disciplinary Rules." Subsequently, many state bar associations adopted the ABA code for the guidance of their members. More ominously, many state courts incorporated the 1969 ABA Code of Professional Responsibility, or some variation of it, into the procedures for punishing lawyers. When the Illinois courts adopted the 1969 code, the "Ethical Considerations" were excluded as "not necessary to a judicially sanctioned body of rules intended to provide a basis for discipline." The code of ethics had degenerated from a statement of principles to a basis for punishment.

Since then, the ABA has developed yet another set of ethics rules, called the "Model Rules of Professional Conduct." These latest revisions prompted one commentator to write: "The confidentiality provisions of the Model Rules go so far toward the 'hired gun' model that they are a public embarrassment."

Honorable people do not need codes of conduct to tell them what to do. Attempts to be ethical by following a code result in moral tunnel vision. Respected bar journals publish articles with titles like "The Practice of Law and Conflicts of Interest: Living Close to the Line." Under the pressure of demographics and economics, the ethics code, once intended to define a minimum standard, now also sets the upper limit of ethical conduct.

Demographics

The number of lawyers is quadrupling in the second half of the twentieth century, against an increase of 60 percent in the general population. In 1985 there were 655,191 lawyers in the United States, of whom an estimated 460,206 were in private practice. About 37,000 law degrees are granted each year. There will be about 1 million lawyers in the year 2000.

After World War II, education benefits were seen as a way to deal with the large number of discharged veterans. The program was a success. That generation of educated and productive people drove an extended period of economic expansion. The lawyers of that group, born in the mid-1920s and admitted to practice in the early 1950s, are now retiring. From the 1950s and into the 1960s, a steadily growing economy, and a smaller cohort of candidates reflecting the reduced birth rate of the Depression years, resulted in good prospects for young lawyers admitted to practice in those years.

The "Soaring Sixties," proclaimed such by the cover of *Time* magazine, were a time of changes. The baby-boom generation began to enter law school in 1967. At the same time the Vietnam war, the civil rights movement, feminism, and raised expectations in a booming economy motivated vast numbers of bright young people to seek the power and prestige of the practice of law. A much publicized recession in the aerospace industry made engineering seem economically unstable. Vietnam veterans returned with education benefits, adding to the flood of qualified applicants to law schools. The Watergate scandal and the toppling of a President suggested that power was in the hands of journalists and lawyers. Journalism jobs were scarce, but law was a growing segment of the economy. The net effect has been an influx, beginning in 1971 and growing into the 1990s, of large numbers of bright, well-qualified lawyers, male and female, drawn from all segments of society.

At first this flood of lawyers was welcomed. Legal services became available to people who had never before been able to afford a lawyer. The burning of the cities that began in the 1960s became the suing of the cities, and everybody else, in the 1970s. Smart young lawyers dreamed up new theories and exploited old principles on behalf of their clients. The establishment hired its own lawyers to defend every issue. The law business boomed. The relatively peaceful resolution of social, economic, and political unrest of the 1960s, was the flood of lawsuits in the following decades. Though it was slow, costly, and unwieldy, the legal system had become accessible to the masses.

Economics

The introduction of so many additional lawyers into society resulted in intense competition for the available work. The only effective product differentiations were factors such as price, location, and responsiveness, not unlike any business.

In the plaintiff's personal-injury practice, totally dependent on contingent fees, more difficult cases were taken on, and pressed with more vigor. These novel and borderline cases had higher risks on both sides, sending costs up and profit margins down. Most deep-pocket business defendants responded with aggressive defense tactics, further increasing costs.

Before the sudden increase in the number of lawyers, many legal fees were based on the value of transactions. Lawyers perceived themselves as underpaid and short of prestige.

The solution to the problem of being underpaid was time billing. The idea was that if lawyers focused on the amount of time required to do a job, billings to clients would be more fair. It avoids the unfairness of charging a large fee for a large but simple matter and a smaller fee for a small, complicated matter. This approach to setting fees shifts the emphasis away from benefit to the client and onto the costs of the lawyers.

The advent of time billing was a real boon to the profession and those who supplied it with timekeeping and billing systems. The annoyance of writing everything down was soon overcome by the joy of sending out ever-increasing bills. A study of clients by the Missouri bar showed that clients were willing to pay fees based on effort—that is, the time, put forth by the lawyer. The bills showed every detail of work performed and time expended. Clients were persuaded by the detailed bills to remit payment.

Soon time billing overwhelmed everything else in the valuation of legal services. The product of the lawyer came to be seen as billable hours. The legal services market is never efficient. Clients lack cost and quality information when making decisions and bear extraordinary costs in changing lawyers. Law firms discovered that if they had a "rainmaker," a partner who could bring work into the firm, making money was only a matter of making billable hours.

The courts get into the problem of setting fees when the losing party has to pay the winner's lawyer. The usual method involves selecting an hourly rate based on a community standard, then adjusting for the factors listed in the Code of Ethics. Those factors are: (1) the time and labor required, the novelty and difficulty of the questions involved, and the skill requisite to perform the legal service properly; (2) the likelihood, if apparent to the client, that the acceptance of the particular employment will preclude other employment by the lawyer; (3) the fee customarily charged in the locality for similar legal services; (4) the amount involved and the results obtained; (5) the time limitation imposed by the client or by the circumstances; (6) the nature and the length of the professional relationship with the client; (7) the experience, reputation, and ability of the lawyer or lawyers performing the services; and (8) whether the fee is fixed or contingent.

None of these factors is directed toward value to the client! The "results obtained" is measured against the difficulty of the legal problem, not the benefit to the client.

In reality, most lawyers bring high ideals to the profession. The ideas of honor, integrity, and the pursuit of justice are sincerely embraced. In the marketplace, some shed their ideals to gain a competitive edge. Under economic pressure from an excessive supply of lawyers, high ethical standards result in loss of income. The organized bar, recognizing this, has tried to shore up general principles with increasingly explicit ethical codes. The best lawyers are sensitive to and troubled by the matter of ethics, and will perform to their own very high standards.

The Canons of Ethics, now called the Model Rules of Professional Responsibility, cover numerous aspects of the relationship with the client, including client confidences. That is also the subject of the law of privilege.

Privileged Communications

Knowledge is power. Every prudent businessperson strives to keep knowledge about his or her company's activities away from the competition. Casual information in the hands of a competitor may be damaging. Consider your reception area. A salesperson from whom you never buy may overhear your receptionist tell your secretary to find you to take a message from Mr. X, a major prospect for your company's products. After the salesperson is turned down once again, he has no reason not to tell your competitor, his next call, that Mr. X is shopping the market. Suddenly, you are not alone. Even landing a big contract, something you might publicize, is information that a competitor can use to approach your established customers. The prudent course is to treat everything as confidential. Your employee handbook probably reflects such a policy.

The legal system depends on getting at the truth for use in resolving problems. The device used is the subpoena. This is an order from the court that a witness appear and answer questions under oath. A subpoena may require an appearance in open court, before the judge. Subpoenas are also issued for pretrial discovery, explained in Chap. 11. If you fail to obey a subpoena, the court can issue a bench warrant for your arrest. Then you will be dealing with the sheriff, perhaps taken into custody and required to post bail. The fact that the information called for is confidential does not, by itself, relieve you of the obligation to answer the questions. However, information which is "privileged" may be protected.

The purpose of the attorney–client privilege is to permit you to tell the whole truth to your lawyer without fear that it will be used against you. Much of what clients say is wrong, cannot be proven, or is not relevant. The lawyer cannot sort out the important information without knowing the whole story. So everything you say to your lawyer is protected, if certain conditions are met. Those conditions include: the person asserting the privilege must be, or be seeking to become, a client; the communication must be only to a lawyer, or lawyer's representative, acting in that capacity; the communication must be intended to be confidential; the communication must be of facts or advice based on confidential information; the communication must not be for the purpose of committing a crime or perpetrating a fraud; and the privilege must be claimed by the client and not waived.

Legal scholars, and some courts, view trade secrets and reports required by government agencies as "privileged" and subject to protection. To protect such material, you have to go to the court. The judge will usually require the disclosure of the material, subject to a "protective order" which limits who can look at it. To obtain such treatment, you will have to persuade the judge that the material is in fact confidential and valuable.

The key to any claim of "privilege" is the client's intent that the communication be confidential. The intent has to be proven by showing how the material was handled. It is essential to have evidence of procedures to limit access to the material and to protect against inadvertent disclosure.

Some lawyers recommend stamping confidential materials, in distinctively colored ink, with "Privileged – Do Not Copy – Return to Secure File," or words to that effect. Any copy not bearing the stamp in the distinctive color would indicate a violation of your company's rules. Work copies needed would also be stamped. The problem is that much confidential material may never be stamped. Perhaps the person preparing the material does not have a stamp. If you stamp everything, it is meaningless.

As an expression of intent to maintain confidentiality, confidential materials should be kept in secure files. For legal files, a lockable file drawer, cabinet, or room should be designated and used only for legal files. The key should be held by an individual in a position of confidence within the company. All attorney–client privileged materials should be returned to that locked file at the end of each workday. If some personnel need to work continuously with such materials, they should be provided with authorized copies and a secure place to keep them apart from their other files. Attorney–client privileged material should never be placed in operating files.

Most businesses maintain files by subject or project. The subject may be a store, factory, piece of equipment, or customer contract. Most of the contents of the file will not be privileged. If you consulted a lawyer for advice, perhaps regarding the purchase contract, lease, or accidents at the site, the legal matter must be kept separate or the privilege may be lost. Mingling confidential and nonconfidential material suggests that there is no specific intent of confidentiality.

The attorney–client privilege is limited to what happens between attorney and client. You know who the attorney is because of the bills you pay and the license hanging on her wall. It is more difficult for the attorney to know who the client is. In the corporate environment, determining which individual employees are covered by the privilege is a problem. That question was addressed by the U.S. Supreme Court in 1981. In essence, the Court held that communication to lawyers by employees in response to the lawyers' inquiry for the purpose of gathering facts on which to formulate advice is privileged. That rule is binding only in federal cases decided under federal law.

In cases governed by state law, the law of each state determines which corporate employees are within the privilege. To be safe, the initial communications of facts of any case should come from in-house lawyers or employees in a position to control or take a substantial part in a decision about any action which the corporation may take on the advice of the attorney or an authorized member of the group that has that authority. Generally, members of the board of directors, the CEO, and persons who report to the board will be deemed members of the control group.

Much of what attorneys do while working on a case is protected by the "work product rule." The U.S. Supreme Court established the concept in 1947, holding that, in the absence of prejudice, hardship, or injustice, an attorney could assemble information, sift what he considers to be the relevant from the irrelevant facts, prepare his legal theories, and plan his strategy with a certain degree of privacy, free from unnecessary intrusion by opposing parties and their counsel. In federal cases, the rule covers documents and tangible things prepared in anticipation of litigation by another party or his attorney, consultant, surety, indemnitor, insurer, or agent, except where it would cause undue hardship. The mental impressions, conclusions, opinions, or legal theories of an attorney or other representative are always supposed to be protected. Most states have some form of the work product rule.

The work product rule imposes some practical considerations on businesspeople who become involved with incidents, such as accidents or fires, where there is a pressing urge to investigate. For example, you may want to take photographs or tape-record statements at the scene. The emotion of the moment produces insights and candor unique to the situation. A court may hold that the interests of justice require that any such photos or statements be disclosed, because the adverse party has no way to obtain the substantial equivalent. You should have the expert advice of an attorney before you create evidence which may be incomplete or misleading. Your lawyer's involvement may protect the investigation under the "work product rule."

Even when all the conditions are met, the attorney–client privilege can disappear if materials are handled carelessly. The rule is that disclosure of privileged material, even accidentally or inadvertently, is a waiver as to all such material. The danger of waiver is illustrated by cases where privileged material has been thrown in the trash without being shredded or obliterated. The adversary's private detective snoops through your trash, and suddenly everything you have said to your lawyer is part of the public record. More frequent is the situation where the adversary, looking at unprivileged files, finds privileged material that has been left there by mistake.

Concerns about the ethical duties owed to the client, and the need to protect the confidentiality of communications with the client, force lawyers to give particular thought to the question: "Who is the client?"

The Lawyer's Dilemma: Who Is the Client?

Sometimes, customers do not pay. It is routine for your credit manager to retain an attorney to collect a past-due account. The ordinary arrangement is to advance costs and pay a contingent fee of one-third of the net amount collected. The debtor may dispute the amount due, or point to a lack of assets, placing collection of the entire amount in question. If the debt is $1000, the attorneys may be inclined to accept a prompt offer of $500, generating a fee of $166.67 and a net recovery to the client of $333.33. The loss to the company is fully two-thirds of the debt. The attorney seeks authority to accept or reject from your credit manager. Does the attorney know if the credit manager actually has authority to settle on these terms? What difference would it make if the debt was $100,000? How about a debt of $10 million? The collection attorney's client is the creditor company, not the credit manager. Any settlement offer requires a decision to accept or reject. The attorney has no way to know if the credit manager has the authority to make that decision. Asking the credit manager for documentation of authority implies a lack of trust, hardly a good way to get more business. The attorney has to make a judgment about the authority of the person with whom she is communicating.

Who Gets the Advice?

The difficulty of knowing whether the client's employee has the authority to ignore or reject the attorney's advice and recommendations was demonstrated in a freight tariff case. Deregulation of the trucking industry brought price competition, with freight rates being negotiated between truckers and shippers. The Elkins Act, which established the Interstate Commerce Commission, continued to require that common-carrier freight rates be calculated in accord with published tariffs. The trucker could establish a negotiated rate by publishing it as a point-to-point rate for a specific class of goods. Some truckers simply neglected to publish the negotiated tariffs, and then went broke. A business developed of buying the tariff undercharge claims of defunct trucking companies and suing the naive shippers.

There is no fair answer to a tariff undercharge case. The shipper has paid the rate agreed to in an arms'-length negotiation with the trucker. It is only the failure of the trucker to publish the tariff that creates the claim. The old statute had relied on published tariffs to put all shippers on an equal footing. Presumably, a shipper should know of the requirement to pay at published rates.

The "manager–administration" of a reputable company retained an attorney to defend a tariff undercharge claim of about $15,000. After investigation and research, the attorney recommended that the claim be paid on the best terms that could be negotiated. The recommendation was based not on what was "fair" but on the result of applying the law to the facts. The "manager–administration" rejected the advice. The rules of the federal court where the case was pending could require the loser in such a case to pay the winner's legal fees. (Such rules have since been rejected by some appellate courts.)

Since the attorney's monthly bills were paid, the "manager-administration" had apparent authority to hire the attorney. However, the "manager–administration" was responsible for his employer's shipping arrangements. He might be blamed for the liability because he did not confirm publication of the negotiated tariff. Did the "manager–administration" have authority to reject a settlement offer of 50 percent? Does it make any difference that he had a part-time business on the side, selling household items on commission? Does the fact that he was looking for another job make a difference in his apparent authority? Does it matter that the attorney never visited the "manager–administration" at the employer's place of business and never met any of his coworkers?

The "manager–administration" may have been a dedicated employee who was fully informing the boss and following instructions. Or the "manager–administration" may have blundered on the freight contracts and hoped to keep the mess under cover until he found another job. Perhaps he was afraid to tell the boss any bad news. What is your response to an attorney who asks you for confirmation of a subordinate's authority? Will the subordinate ever hire that attorney again?

Actual and Apparent Authority

Your banker deals with the problem of authority of employees directly. The bank requires signature cards and, for corporate accounts, a "banking resolution" by the board of directors. Sophisticated parties to complex transactions, especially those that advance money, require a formal opinion of counsel to the effect that a party is validly in existence, has the power to enter into the transaction, and that the persons signing on behalf of the party are duly authorized to do so. For a corporation such an opinion is based on examination of the certificate of incorporation, bylaws, franchise tax returns, certificate of good standing of the secretary of state, and minutes of meetings of the shareholders and board of directors, in light of the applicable corporate law. This is an expensive process.

The authority of every employee or agent is looked at from two aspects, "actual" and "apparent." The "actual" authority is exactly, and only, the amount of authority that the employer or principal intended to give. The secret intent of the employer is not binding on the rest of the world. Outsiders can rely on what they observe, the "apparent" authority of the employee. Generally, a salesperson or machine operator would not have authority to sign a lease for a corporate headquarters. Even the president of a corporation would not necessarily have authority to sell all of the corporate assets.

An attorney appearing in court on behalf of a client has absolute "apparent" authority to bind the client. The courts will not look behind the words of one of its officers, the attorney, to determine what the client has authorized. If the client permits an attorney to address the court on its behalf, it is bound by whatever the attorney says. Between the client and the attorney, the client sets the limit of what the attorney can do. An attorney who acts beyond the authority granted by the client can be punished through disciplinary proceedings and malpractice suits, but the client remains bound by whatever was said in the courtroom. This extraordinary power of attorneys imposes a duty on the attorney to make sure that whatever she does is in fact authorized by the client. The attorney needs to know how much "actual" authority any particular employee can give.

Settlement Posture

The issue of authority comes up in several different ways, even in a simple case. Consider, for example, a business that operates several retail outlets. If a customer slips and falls, a claim may be made. There are two basic issues. Is the company liable? And what is the amount of money damages that will fairly compensate the injured customer? Even if no claim is made, the company might consider what measures should be taken to prevent future accidents.

The issue of liability has many aspects. One is the question of whether or not the injured customer should have observed a hazard and could have avoided injury by taking reasonable care for her own safety. Does it matter that the injured person is a well-known community figure? Popular and well regarded? Usually slightly drunk? Engaged in an act of vandalism or shoplifting when the accident occurred? Elderly and frail, especially if the business caters to such customers?

The damages question also has many sides. Lost wages and medical bills can be calculated. Fair recompense for "pain and suffering" may be sharply disputed. What is the proper response to a claim of alcoholism caused by excessive drinking brought on by back pain with no observed objective symptoms? Should the store pay the entire bill for a hip fracture in an elderly woman suffering from osteoporosis?

A decision must be made as to what settlement terms should be offered, if any. Such a decision requires consideration of more than photos of the accident scene and copies of the medical bills. Is the business for sale? Will a lawsuit upset a pending deal? Will payment of damages attract more claims of the same type? Will a refusal to pay a fair claim hurt relations with other customers? This evaluation of all aspects of the case becomes the "settlement posture." Most courts require attorneys to state a settlement posture before trial. The lawyer can say that nothing will be paid, or offer a generous sum. The choice is the client's, subject to the insurer's rights under the policy. The lawyer will advise, but someone must decide on behalf of the client.

In the case of the store, should the line supervisor, the store manager, be the one to decide? Will the loss be charged against his budget? Will the loss affect his bonus? What if he is soft-hearted, or thinks only of pleasing customers?

Other types of issues may arise. If the slip-and-fall claim came up because of a crack in the pavement, who decides whether of not to fix the crack? The conservative attorney will tell you that at one time evidence of repairs was excluded from evidence of defectiveness, but admitted as proof of control. Fixing the defect may convince a jury that you are liable. Is fixing the crack a decision to be left to the store manager?

In cases handled by attorneys hired by insurance companies, much of the information about the case comes from the insurer's investigator or adjuster. The balance of the factual information comes from fact witnesses, perhaps including the store manager. The insurance defense attorney has little contact with the client and little opportunity to consider business aspects of the case.

Attorneys hired by insurance companies know who is paying the fees and who can send them more business in the future. Balanced against that is the client's right to the absolute and undivided loyalty of the attorney of record. However, the insured has a legal duty to cooperate in the defense of the case. The lawyer paid by an insurance company, hired only to defend that particular case, sees the outcome of that case as the highest interest of the client with which he is concerned. Therefore, the insurance defense attorney has little interest in the position taken by his client's employees regarding a settlement posture.

Sole Proprietors

You might not anticipate that there would be any difficulty in identifying the client in a business operated as a sole proprietorship. The name on the tax return is the name of the boss. The boss owns the business, has all of the responsibility, and all of the authority. This is true of a one-person operation. Some sole proprietorships grow into large companies, however, without ever going through the process of incorporating. Some are "family" businesses. Merely sharing the family name does not give an individual authority to hire and direct attorneys. A general manager or superintendent may have such authority, if it has been expressly given by the sole proprietor. As a sole proprietor, you would want any attorney first to confirm that your employee actually has authority before making binding commitments on that employee's instructions.

As an example, a hardy and vigorous 75-year-old man had built a nationwide business manufacturing and installing a specialty product. The business operations were now run by his 45-year-old son. The founder's only other child was a daughter who did not participate in the business. From time to time, the son retained attorneys to handle things that came up in the ordinary course of business. As the father aged, he became less aware of passing events. Without a formal competence proceeding, an insult which the old man would have resisted, the son lacked the authority to hire the lawyers to defend, or settle, lawsuits. Many sole proprietors leave the operation of a business in the hands of a general manager. Such managers have no implied authority to hire lawyers, but they can be given express authority.

Partnerships

In a partnership, each of the general partners has the power to bind the others. A lawyer may act on behalf of the partnership upon the direction of only one partner, although the entire partnership is the client. It is embarrassing when two partners, acting in good faith but without consulting each other, hire separate attorneys and give conflicting instructions on the same matter. As a practical matter, there is always a question as to which partner speaks for the partnership when talking to the lawyer.

Partners have differences among themselves. A lawyer who represents a partnership may have a conflict of interest in a dispute among partners. Some partnerships, especially limited partnerships set up as investment vehicles, have so many members that the attorney has no practical way of knowing if a dispute exists. Thus, if one partner hires a lawyer to interpret the partnership agreement, an opinion favorable to that one partner may hurt the other partners. Payment of the lawyer's fee with partnership funds implies an equal duty to all partners.

Corporations

It is the corporation that presents the sharpest problem of client identification for the lawyer. A corporation exists only in the sense that a statute says it exists. Shareholders are not liable for corporate debt, because the invested capital is subject to creditors' claims and under the control of the board of directors. Authority to act for the corporation rests entirely with the board of directors, which can delegate limited authority to officers.

Some states have specific statutory provisions for "close" corporations, where there are few shareholders. Typically, such statutes permit a board of directors which consists of only one person, the holding of corporate offices by only one person, and waiver of other formalities. Under any statute, the essence of a corporation is that there is some capital invested, to be owned and used by the legal "person" and controlled by a board of directors.

As the chairman of the board, chief executive officer, and largest single shareholder, you may feel that the corporation's lawyer works for you. In most circumstances, the interests of the company and of yourself are identical. After all, you created the company with hard work and good ideas. However, the interests of the corporate entity must be considered separately from those of the shareholders, officers, and employees. Many corporations are wholly owned by one parent corporation. But the subsidiary has separate creditors who may have a claim on the invested capital. Some wholly owned subsidiaries have issued publicly traded bonds, giving rise to lawsuits when the owner loots the corporate treasury, causing a default on the bonds.

A more common problem occurs when an attorney is working with corporate employees who may not have authority to make decisions required by a lawsuit. Typically, the attorney's only contact within the corporation insists on an action that violates some law or legal obligation of the corporation. Even if that contact is the CEO, the ultimate authority is the board of directors. If the decision threatens the continued existence of the company, the attorney has a duty to the corporate entity to refer the matter to the highest authority that can act in behalf of the organization as determined by applicable law.

Differences in opinions, or judgments, arise at all levels of a company's management. Consider a hypothetical example. The CEO's pet product is a perfume that, it is generally agreed, smells terrible, causes some people to break out in a purple, putrefying rash, and violates Food and Drug Administration Regulations. The lawyer and other responsible people have made every effort to persuade the CEO that the product should be dropped, with no success. The rules of professional conduct do not permit the lawyer to quit until after the issue has been presented to the board of directors.

The lawyer's duty is clear enough. One of two things will happen. The lawyer may ensure continued receipt of a paycheck by acquiescing to the CEO or whatever other management is acting against the best interest of the client. Or the lawyer can fulfill a duty to the client that is defined and measured against standards set by the courts of which she is an officer. The lawyers who meet this standard do not last long at the larger law firms. Law firms do not become big by biting the management hand that feeds them.

Whether your company is a sole proprietorship, a partnership, or a corporation, it is important for you to understand who is not the client. Staff lawyers, claims managers, credit personnel, inventors, personnel managers, operations managers, real estate managers, purchasing agents, and a myriad of others may choose the company's lawyers and attend to the payment of legal bills. But these employees of the company are not the client. The lawyer needs assurance that the persons giving instructions and directions are authorized to do so by the client.

Why Lawyers Act the Way They Do

The relationship between attorney and client differs from other relationships. To the business client, it is merely a business relationship. To the lawyer, it can be a matter of life and death for the client. In criminal matters, long years of incarceration may hang on a single comment, a single question in cross-examination. A misunderstanding in a divorce case may cause a child to lose contact with a loving parent. A poorly chosen word in a will may cause family conflict to linger through generations. It is the effect on clients that gives the law meaning.

The modern lawyer's relationship with his client is formed in part by an ancient and honorable ethical tradition. That tradition is now under great economic pressure. From that relationship arises a privilege, little understood by laypersons, which the lawyer must protect. In business situations, these duties may be owed to an entity which is acting through persons with differing interests. Lawyers, trying to relate to clients, may not always relate to people.

1. Protect the confidentiality of communications:

   Store confidential material in a secure, locked place.
   Limit access to confidential materials.
   Do not circulate confidential materials.
   Do not distribute copies of confidential material.
   Do not mix confidential material with ordinary files.
   Destroy confidential material before throwing it out.
   Use secure communication channels.

2. Establish the attorney–client relationship:

   For the purpose of obtaining legal advice or representation
   Not in furtherance of a crime or conspiracy
   Limit advice to "legal" matters

3. Communicate only to the attorney:

   The attorney must be licensed to practice law.
   The attorney's agent, acting in that capacity, may receive communications within the privilege.
   No one other than the attorney, the attorney's agents, and the client may be present, or able to overhear, communications intended to be confidential.

4. Privilege covers only facts communicated to the attorney and advice received from the attorney.

5. Internal investigations may be privileged or exempt from disclosure if conducted by attorneys.

6. Do not disclose any confidential communications from the attorney to any third party.

7. Have a confidentiality policy for all business information and for all employees:

   Your employee manual should state that all business information is confidential and to be released only upon specific authorization.
   Use a standardized stationary format for materials that may be released outside the company.

Procedure: Preserving attorney–client privilege.

9

When Employees and Attorneys Bump Heads

Lawyers are not involved in most business activities. The middle management of a successful business operates at something approaching zero defects almost all the time. They don't need lawyers' help to do their jobs. It is only when the transaction is unusual or out of control that the lawyers are called in.

A situation is a legal matter because a lawsuit, regulatory requirement, or tricky transaction creates a threat that the power of the state will be exercised on the company. The threat is that when all the court processes are complete, the sheriff will come and hold an auction on the front steps of the loser. The loser will be out of business. The paychecks will stop. The lawyer's job is to manage that threat. Precise drafting of documents and careful execution of procedures ensure favorable outcomes. Advocacy ensures that the true facts are properly considered before the ultimate remedies and sanctions are applied. Counsel seeks to avoid unnecessary encounters with the system. The lawyer's goal is to avoid or win the lawsuit, an event that occurs outside the company. When the case is over, the lawyer moves on. The employee's goals are broader, and closely linked to the company's long-term future.

Part of the problem is that lawyers are called in on the big, tough, exciting problems. Like a small-town police officer's murder investigation, these situations are an opportunity for the employee to shine. People who have worked diligently and efficiently on ordinary matters feel slighted when they are supplanted in the big deals by lawyers, especially if the employee's hard-won expertise is disregarded or denigrated. Excluded or embarrassed, the employee sees the lawyer as the problem and not the solution. You cannot fault employees for shunning lawyers who arrive on the scene, do a war dance, and then depart, leaving the employees with a mess to clean up.

A Hypothetical Case

You may be able to identify in your own company someone like the hypothetical Mr. von Slugger. Mr. von Slugger is the chief engineer of a small division that is located a half-day's travel from the main office. He joined the company shortly after graduating from the engineering program at the local state university. After working well into middle age under old Joe, the unschooled but brilliant designer of the division's principal product, von Slugger finally became the chief engineer when old Joe retired. In the years since then, von Slugger has kept the product alive, filling a unique market niche, although costs have crept upward and unit sales have gradually eroded. The rest of the engineering staff consists of four graduate engineers, four designers, a department secretary, and an engineering records clerk. The department has not succeeded in developing new, marketable products. Mr. von Slugger, a hard and loyal worker, expects his people to work hard and be loyal also.

In recent years, a new problem has had von Slugger's attention. People injured while using the division's products have been filing lawsuits. The claimants assert that the products are defective. This really upsets Mr. von Slugger. He knows the products are good.

In any organization, knowledge is power. Mr. von Slugger's job is to know everything about the product from an engineering standpoint. At any time, he may be summoned to the general manager's office and called upon to explain any detail. He has worked hard to keep all the necessary information either in his head or at his fingertips. He knows, better than anyone else, exactly what is going on with that product, how it is made, how it works, and what is wrong with it. Perhaps because von Slugger has it all in his head, the documentation has become a little thin.

All of a sudden, because of these lawsuits, in addition to the boss, attorneys are calling up von Slugger, asking a lot of questions. All company information being confidential, he is reluctant to answer. He is not sure just who these attorneys are. The explanation that the insurer hired the attorneys eventually satisfies him, but he worries about talking to a plaintiff's attorney by mistake.

Then von Slugger is distressed by the attorney's ignorance of engineering principles. Mr. von Slugger does not understand the questions. He doesn't think the attorneys understand the answers. He is impatient and frustrated. He knows all the answers. He is, after all, an expert by virtue of his long years of working with the product. His word alone should be sufficient for a complete explanation of any point.

The work load imposed by the inquiries from lawyers has become burdensome. Hundreds of written questions and voluminous requests for copies of documents tie up the records clerk, the copy machine, and von Slugger himself. The questions are nonsense, and the answers require long explanations. When Mr. von Slugger learns that objections can be made to interrogatories, he begins to refuse to provide answers, insisting instead on the filing of objections.

Occasionally he will delegate the task of working up answers to one of his subordinates, but he has to check each answer personally to be sure that it is correct. He reports to the boss that the burden is so great that he may have to add staff, and the reason why the new model year revisions are late is that he has to spend so much time on litigation. Also, sometimes he really has to pressure his people to make them understand exactly how to answer some of the questions.

Mr. von Slugger does not mention to the boss that he is concerned with the nitpicking and faultfinding that is going on in these lawsuits. Nonetheless, he resents the constant carping and criticism of this fine product by people who really do not understand what goes into it. He also resents the excessive demands and unreasonable time frames of the insurance company attorneys. He is afraid the boss will blame him if a jury returns a big verdict against the company.

On the other hand, von Slugger enjoys going to court to be an expert witness. The travel is a nice break. The lawyers entertain him well. He is the center of attention. He likes matching wits with the plaintiff's attorneys in court. Somebody has to tell those people what it is really all about. Being on the stand is no fun; you have to watch yourself every minute. Sometimes the other lawyers really are irritating, the way they pretend not to understand. But since there is nobody else who knows it all, the way he does, von Slugger will have to keep marching along and doing the job.

Since he is doing the job, one thing that annoys him is when the lawyers want to talk to someone else in his department. It is his department and his responsibility, so all communications should be directed to him and come from him. That is just good management practice, maintaining the chain of command. He will make the decisions, all of them.

Look at what Mr. von Slugger, dedicated employee, is doing to his employer.

Mr. von Slugger is controlling the attorney's access to information about the case. To be persuasive, the attorney needs all the information she can absorb. Mr. von Slugger knows a great deal more than the attorney can ever use. Controlling what the attorney learns limits what the attorney can teach to the judges and jurors. Here, von Slugger's knowledge is a disadvantage, because what is obvious to von Slugger is a total mystery to some stranger hearing it for the first time in a jury box. Jurors, unable to ask questions, reject what they don't understand. Attorneys, also ignorant, develop a basic presentation to use with juries by teaching themselves. Mr. von Slugger's concern with details prevents the attorneys from developing a clear, coherent presentation of the big picture.

Mr. von Slugger's explanation that he merely wishes to ensure the correctness of the information shows a lack of faith in the attorney. If trial attorneys are good for anything, they should be good at digging out the truth. It is the investigation that shows the trial attorney what the adversary will use as evidence at the trial.

No responsible manager has enough spare time to educate attorneys properly. If the burden of working with attorneys interferes with getting regular tasks done, Mr. von Slugger's unhappiness will infect the attorneys.

Mr. von Slugger is also ensuring his power over his subordinates by controlling the selection of witnesses. Even sincere managers choose witnesses poorly—typically someone waiting to retire. The person with the most detailed technical knowledge may not be able to simplify concepts enough for a jury. The least competent person in the office won't be any better on the witness stand, even if he is easily spared for that duty. Sending someone who can be sacrificed for losing may preordain a bad outcome.

Attorneys select witnesses, when they have a choice, on their personal interaction. On the stand, the witness must have confidence in the attorney in order to project confidence to the jury. Often the most knowledgeable witnesses are also arrogant, defensive, and unconvincing. Obviously, the manager's opinion of a subordinate's capabilities as a witness should be shared with the attorney. Compulsive drinking, or a history of stress-induced heart attacks, might be a concern. But attorneys choose witnesses to present facts, or to persuade, or to teach as experts. To be effective, a witness must be liked by the jury. An attorney choosing a witness is using her own expertise about juries.

Occasionally, Mr. von Slugger will want to keep the attorney away from the bad news. It is far better for your attorney to find the problems than to have your adversary show what looks like a problem to the jury, or worse yet, show the jury your employees' attempt to cover up. Most attempts to conceal serious problems will fail. Experienced plaintiffs' attorneys know intuitively that the flaw is there and will search backward to its proof. Plaintiffs' attorneys are not stupid, although they sometimes look that way.

Consider an example. Mechanical goods are manufactured according to a design. The design of each assembly, subassembly, and part is set out in engineering records that consist of a bill of materials, a drawing, a procedure, and a specification. All changes are documented. The changes are dated, the reasons explained, and responsible people sign off. The plaintiff's attorney proves defects with a series of questions. Describing the condition or situation involved in the claim, he asks what parts of the machine could malfunction to cause that condition. As to those parts, he asks how many units of each were sold each month or year since the product was introduced. Knowing that sales of a defective part are exceptionally high, then decline when the defect is remedied, he demands the documentation of parts with the suspect pattern. In that documentation will be admissions of the defect. The persons who signed off will be called as witnesses.

No case is perfect. You know the flaws in your own case. Much that you might want to hide is irrelevant and inadmissible. Your attorney cannot tell if certain unhappy facts are going to be evidence against you if she does not know about them. A flaw you have attempted to conceal becomes the center of attention, the "smoking gun" needed to sway a jury. That is the lesson of the Watergate scandal. Under no circumstances should a manager be permitted to deny a company's in-house lawyer or outside trial attorney access to any record or to any employee, free of review or censorship by the manager.

Mr. von Slugger's proper role is teacher and informant to the attorney. When an employee controls the attorney's access to information, he may begin to force tactical adjustments that are not consistent with a chosen strategy. For example, insisting that certain discovery be objected to may bring attention to sensitive areas or may jeopardize the attorney's credibility with the court. When operating managers dictate legal tactics, costs go up.

Employees like Mr. von Slugger will not let the attorney do the attorney's job. The artistic energy that should go toward crafting the best presentation of your case is spent overcoming the interference of uncooperative employees. When the case doesn't go well, the blame falls on "inept" attorneys and "stupid" jurors.

More subtle than Mr. von Slugger is an employee who likes lawyers, Mr. E. Z. Heels. Unlike von Slugger, who wants to do everything himself, E. Z. Heels is happy to send everything to the lawyer for approval. A dedicated drone, he wants to avoid responsibility for any decision.

As with all employees, E. Z. Heels knows a lot more about his business than the lawyers ever will. Of course, he flatters the lawyers by telling them he respects their judgment. What he doesn't tell them is the whole story when he submits a plan or program for approval. E. Z. Heels has figured out that he can manipulate the lawyers into approving decisions by telling them only what they need to hear. For example, an advertising claim of reduced price may be approved by showing that the regular price has been maintained for a period of time. There is no need to tell the lawyer that no units were sold during that time. The chances of being caught are slim. Or E. Z. Heels may ask the lawyer if it is permissible to flush organic wastes into the storm sewer. That technical question is beyond the competence of a lawyer who thinks "organic" means "natural."

What makes E. Z. Heels most happy is when he has a number of lawyers to shop his questions around to. He will eventually settle on a few favorites who ask fewer questions and are more anxious to please. Those will be the speakers invited to the sales meetings to play golf with the marketing staff.

Enhancing the Value of Legal Services

Employees like Mr. von Slugger and E. Z. Heels degrade the factual basis of legal advice. You enhance the value of legal services by fairly allocating the burden, informing employees, insisting that attorneys perform, and providing leadership.

Track the Legal Burden

All legal services have costs beyond the fees paid to lawyers. As a matter of management information, an account should be established for legal matters. All time, materials, and expenses of employees working on legal matters should be charged to that account. The operating budget of a department should not be burdened with extraordinary work done on legal matters. In the overall accounting scheme, the legal budget is probably overhead that will be allocated to the department. Such bookkeeping legerdemain has no effect on profits, but it may affect perceptions of departmental performance. If the legal problems impose enough additional work to justify more personnel, filling that need should not be seen as an expansion.

Document searches required for discovery are burdensome. Sometimes dozens of file drawers and thousands of files have to be looked at, analyzed, inventoried, and selected items copied. Outside law firms often recommend using their own paralegals to do such searches. Better results are obtained by your regular employees. They are familiar with the files, the job will be done correctly the first time, and the files will be put back together properly. However, the regular work must go on. The cost of temporary help to keep it current should be charged to the legal budget.

The attorneys may need a particular individual's expertise in order to prepare a case. Some cases go on for years. A risk to your company is that the individual's projects may fall behind schedule or go astray. The employee may fear that promotion opportunities will be missed if he is tied up in a lawsuit. Providing additional support and assistance will minimize these problems.

Recognition by the employer that working with attorneys is part of the job relieves some employee concern. One way to do this is to add working with lawyers to the job description, and cover it in periodic reviews or evaluations. In companies where such systems are used, they become important to the people subjected to them. Outside contacts are a routine part of job-grading systems, but few outside contacts are as demanding as being a witness at deposition or trial. Employees who become caught up in litigation need reassurance that they will not be penalized for the time lost or for the result of the case.

Provide Legal Liaison

Attorneys, perhaps selected and paid by an insurance company, come into a company seeking the most confidential and guarded information and imposing tedious and boring burdens. The employees with whom the attorneys work may not be close to the top management of the company or aware of the importance of any particular legal matter. Employees asked to help outside attorneys need to hear that request from a recognized authority within the company. An effective request both introduces the attorney and explains the employee's role in the matter.

Establishing a formal liaison helps improve relations with a difficult employee before serious harm is done. Some employees are not forthcoming with lawyers when asked for help. The attorney may not know she is having such a problem. A liaison may detect a lack of cooperation and take corrective action without putting the attorney into the role of tattletale. For that reason, the liaison is more effective if he is not in the direct line of command of the employee. Similarly, the liaison can handle complaints of overreaching by the attorneys. In either event, prompt and fair attention to personality conflicts will ensure that the energy being expended is directed at the adversary, where it advances the company's objectives.

The cost of the liaison function will easily be recovered in decreased legal fees. It is typical for a law firm to bring paralegals to a document search, at $40 to $60 per hour, to make copies. When this happens on your own premises, your clerks may be standing by idle while your attorney's paralegal runs your copy machine. Hours may be spent searching for files on a particular topic, while your file clerk looks on. Liaison can avoid such failures to use in-house resources to meet legal needs.

The loss from ignoring expertise residing in-house is more subtle. In almost any fact dispute there are employees, not witnesses, who can explain why things happen the way they do. The outside attorneys do not know which employees to talk to, and may not even know what to talk about. Attorneys can miss the point of a business case because they never talk to knowledgeable people within the company. A liaison can connect the attorneys with the right employees.

Any such liaison function requires systematic approaches to reporting and control as described in Chaps. 15 and 16. The fact that the attorneys are being supervised by a responsible management simplifies the employee's setting of priorities. Part of the liaison function is to define the scope of the attorney's authority. Questions of what needs to be done first can be worked out internally, without involving outsiders. To reach clear decisions, the liaison must have a clear source of authority. Employees may be more comfortable if the liaison is not himself a lawyer. The liaison's authority must be real, backed up with whatever it takes in your company's culture so that a manager will believe when told that he must, in fact, make all those copies, or go to the deposition, or whatever it is that is needed to satisfy a court's schedule.

This role should be performed by a person who likes lawyers and wants to make them effective. Marketing and production people are not likely to be suited for this task by temperament, since it involves sitting back and watching as other people do things. The better choice is someone who handles administrative matters, and who is willing to work with talents greater than his own.

Demand Attorney Performance

Most employees will rise to the level of performance demonstrated by attorneys. In litigation there are some tight deadlines, but most work can be accomplished in an orderly manner if it is attended to promptly. Unreasonable demands by an attorney may have to be met to save the case, but they should not be tolerated. The requirements of the case should be communicated accurately and promptly.

Insist that both in-house lawyers and outside attorneys present an image of authority to your employees. At a minimum, this means that they have to dress well, behave with dignity, and be unswervingly loyal to the client. To command the respect of witnesses and informants, a young lawyer might have to be a stuffed shirt; experienced practitioners should be charming.

It is essential to avoid competition between your attorneys, whether in-house or outside, and employees. Lawyers are trained in a highly competitive environment. If they are permitted to compete with your employees, your legal matters will be weakened. An employee will not trust an attorney with whom he is competing to protect him in the courtroom, where both his character and his competence are under direct attack. An outside attorney who forms an alliance with an executive will not be trusted by individuals who are competing with that executive.

The relationship between the attorney and your employees should be based on mutual respect. The employee should respect the attorney for the quality of her performance. The attorney should respect the employee for doing almost everything right. They should respect each other as human beings.

Lead toward Clear Goals

Managers strive to motivate employees to pursue concrete objectives. When an oil driller "makes hole," an accounts payable clerk processes invoices, or a purchasing manager orders materials, the enterprise is well served, as is the public interest when the police officer catches a criminal. But these commendable activities are not the ultimate goals. The goal of public safety also requires that the criminal be convicted after a fair trial. The ultimate goal of business enterprises is to return profits to the owner, a concept that is somewhat remote for most employees and often nebulous even to the owner.

Much popular management literature is about defining goals in real terms. A typical technique is writing "mission statements." Such goal statements are used by employees to define concrete objectives. Such techniques can effectively resolve the ordinary conflicts between employees and attorneys, if they are used by managers with sufficient authority. The technique works because the employer and the client are identical.

State the expected contribution of every lawsuit, or other legal activity, toward achieving your company's goals. A lawsuit filed to collect a bad debt might contribute to controlling credit losses so that maximum credit can be extended. The defense of a product-liability suit, while protecting company assets, might also contribute to improving products. The defense of workers' compensation claims may contribute to worker safety. The concrete objectives of individual employees should contribute to identical goals. The credit analyst's effort helps credit sales. The engineer wants to improve the product. A line supervisor wants to prevent injuries. A deliberate managerial effort is required to identify and describe such goals.

A shared understanding of the company's goals will generally keep attorneys and employees working together. Mere personality clashes should be overcome by the attorney's people skills. Genuine differences of opinion call for a direct choice by the client.

The turncoat employee poses a problem that cannot be overcome by leadership. The typical turncoat employee is a line supervisor who, having failed to correct an unsafe condition, conceals the truth when a resulting injury is investigated. The attorney may realize that she is not getting straight answers. The attorney–client privilege is critical in such situations. You must back up the attorney until the facts are brought out. Once the turncoat has been found out, you have a dilemma. If he is fired, the turncoat may seek revenge by testifying against you. If you do nothing, you risk punitive damages in this or a later case. In such situations, quick settlement is desirable.

Your employees and attorneys align their goals in support of a common cause. Tracking the legal burden, providing liaison, and demanding performance from attorneys only removes obstacles to cooperation. When the employee looks beyond a job description and the attorney looks beyond the outcome of a single case, their joint effort will serve your cause. Only you can make that cause clear.

1. Identify employee concerns:

    Threat, unusual, or loss-of-control situation
    Transient attorney-versus-permanent employee conflict
    Attorney overshadowing diligent employee
    Litigation claims that suggest employee fault
    Attorneys' questioning of employee integrity
    Attorneys imposing "nonproductive" work
    Attorneys disrupting managers' control
    Employee's fear of adverse outcome
    Attorneys asserting control of scope of testimony
    Attorneys ignorant of the "real" truth
    Employee's desire to conceal (unimportant) flaws
    Employee's desire to manipulate attorney's advice

2. Provide for imputed legal costs:

    Establish a legal budget for operating departments.
    Retain or supplement staff to meet legal burdens.
    Consider legal effort in employee evaluation and review.
    Include working with attorneys in job descriptions and classifications.

3. Provide legal liaison:

    Identify attorneys as company advocates.
    Introduce involved employees to attorneys.
    Provide a contact point for employees
    Provide a contact point for attorneys.
    Delegate authority to set priorities.
    Provide attorneys with access to top management.

4. Demand attorney performance:

    Make accurate and timely requests for assistance
    Project dignity and stature worthy of respect
    Abhor competition between attorneys and employees

5. Set clear goals:
    State objectives of legal endeavors.
    Define expected contributions.

6. Beware of turncoat employees.

Procedure: Creating shared goals for employees and attorneys.

10
What to Do 'til the Lawyer Gets There: First Steps When You Are Sued

It doesn't matter whether the sheriff delivered the court papers or they came by certified mail, or in some other way; being sued will always make you angry. The strong emotional reaction is caused by arbitrary exercise of power over you and your business. The power of the state is being applied to you. You are compelled to answer claims that, as far as you are concerned, may be entirely wrong. If you're mad, be as mad as you want to for the next 30 seconds; then get over it, because you have work to do.

Time is always critical in legal matters. Deadlines are part of the inherently coercive nature of the law. The law is power, and rigid deadlines are intended to make you feel the force of that power. If you have legal papers in your hands, you must act within the time limits they impose or your rights, including the right to defend yourself, evaporate. If you are late, you are wrong. Missing a deadline will always cost you money. In the most extreme cases, you may have only a few hours to respond. Therefore, when you are served with papers, read them immediately; do not put them aside until "later." Papers served in the morning may require a response after lunch.

Examine the Papers

Look at the papers you have received and find your deadline. If the time is short, the papers usually state a date and place where you are to respond. A *temporary restraining order* or an *order to show cause* may already be in effect, and the hearing may be set to begin within just a few hours. A *garnishment, attachment,* or *replevin* will also have a short fuse, perhaps less than 5 days. A *summons,* served with a *complaint* or *petition,* will have a longer response time, perhaps 20 days, or in Texas until the third succeeding Monday. So dig in and use Fig. 10-1, "Service of Process Control Record," to organize what you know about the papers.

A summons from a U.S. District Court, Fig. 10-2, illustrates how some of the information looks. The numbered arrows correspond to numbered blanks on Figs. 10-1 and 10-4. Figure 10-2 is a standard form for federal court summonses.

Figure 10-3 is a summons from a state court. The items are similarly indicated by numbered arrows corresponding to numbered blanks on Figs. 10-1 and 10-4. Although the forms used by the different state courts are not the same, the information generally follows this pattern.

Item 1 is the name of the case, which is basically who is suing whom. A complicated case may have many parties and many claims. Find your name in the caption's lists of plaintiffs and defendants. Occasionally the case name is shortened on the summons, indicated by "et al." The names of all parties will be shown on the caption of the complaint or petition. In a simple case you are probably the defendant. In a more complicated case, you may be served as a "cross-defendant" or a "third-party defendant." Shorten the name of the case by using the name of the first party on each side, indicating your own name in parentheses on the appropriate side.

The name of the court, item 2, is centered at the top of the summons. Federal courts are broken down by districts and divisions. State courts are commonly identified by county or parish. The full name is needed to determine where the court is located.

The clerk stamps the court file number, item 3, on the right-hand side of the summons and complaint when the case is filed. It will be typed on later documents. Judges and court clerks cannot do anything without the file number. You will need it to obtain any information about the status of the case by telephone.

Always keep track of cases by the name of the case, the court, and the court file number. A plaintiff's attorney may file separate lawsuits, in different courts, in regard to a single claim for a single plaintiff. Two different lawsuits with identical names are easily confused. Also, a single case may be moved from one court to another, keeping the same name but changing file numbers.

Service of Process Control Record

1. Name of case:

2. Name of court:

3. Court file number:

4. Date and time of day that the papers first came into the possession of a purported company representative:

5. Name and location of first purported company representative to have received the papers:

6. How delivered:
    Ordinary first-class mail?
    Certified mail?
    Sheriff?
    Private process server?
    Other?

7. All documents received are attached and consist of:
    Envelope
    Summons
    Complaint/petition
    Garnishment
    Attachment/replevin
    Order of court
    Subpoena
    Other

8. Apparent response time:

9. This record and the attachments were transmitted for further handling by hand delivery/courier/overnight mail/fax on the _____ day of _____, 199__ at _____ o'clock to:

10. These documents were reported by telephone to:

11. This record prepared the _____ day of _____, 199__, by:

Figure 10-1. The *service of process control record* is used to assemble information relating to legal papers and how they were received.

What to Do 'til the Lawyer Gets There: First Steps When You Are Sued   **155**

AO 440 (Rev. 5/85) Summons in a Civil Action

United States District Court

WESTERN _____ DISTRICT OF _____ OKLAHOMA

CONSOLIDATED MANUFACTURING CO.,
        Plaintiff,
V.
UR ENTERPRISES, INC., an Oklahoma
Corporation, T.H. BOSS, SR., an
individual; and I.M. CONSULTANT,
an individual,
        Defendants.

SUMMONS IN A CIVIL ACTION

CASE NUMBER:

CIV 90   3553R

TO: (Name and Address of Defendant)

T.H. BOSS, SR.
303 N.W. 63rd Street, Suite 700
Oklahoma City, OK   73116

YOU ARE HEREBY SUMMONED and required to file with the Clerk of this Court and serve upon

PLAINTIFF'S ATTORNEY (name and address)

JAMES A. SLAYTON
3711 North Classen Boulevard
Oklahoma City, OK   73118
(405) 528-4823

an answer to the complaint which is herewith served upon you, within ___twenty (20)___ days after service of this summons upon you, exclusive of the day of service. If you fail to do so, judgment by default will be taken against you for the relief demanded in the complaint.

ROBERT D. DENNIS, CLERK   OCT 07 1991
CLERK   DATE

BY DEPUTY CLERK

Figure 10-2. A typical summons from a federal district court.

AO 440 (Rev. 5/85) Summons in a Civil Action

RETURN OF SERVICE	
Service of the Summons and Complaint was made by me[1]	DATE
NAME OF SERVER	TITLE

Check one box below to indicate appropriate method of service

☐ Served personally upon the defendant. Place where served: _____

☐ Left copies thereof at the defendant's dwelling house or usual place of abode with a person of suitable age and discretion then residing therein.
Name of person with whom the summons and complaint were left: _____

☐ Returned unexecuted: _____

☐ Other (specify): _____

STATEMENT OF SERVICE FEES		
TRAVEL	SERVICES	TOTAL

DECLARATION OF SERVER
I declare under penalty of perjury under the laws of the United States of America that the foregoing information contained in the Return of Service and Statement of Service Fees is true and correct.

Executed on _____   _____
              Date   *Signature of Server*

_____
Address of Server

1) As to who may serve a summons see Rule 4 of the Federal Rules of Civil Procedure.

Figure 10-2. Reverse side of federal summons form for proof of services.

What to Do 'til the Lawyer Gets There: First Steps When You Are Sued 157

```
              IN THE DISTRICT COURT OF OKLAHOMA COUNTY
                         STATE OF OKLAHOMA


CONSOLIDATED MANUFACTURING CO.,    )
                                   )
          Plaintiff,               )
                                   )
v.                                 )   Case No. CJ-90-13333
                                   )
U. R. ENTERPRISES, INC., an ,      )
Oklahoma Corporation,              )
T. H. Boss, Sr., an individual,    )
and I. M. Consultant, an           )
individual,                        )
                                   )
          Defendants.              )


                            SUMMONS

To the Defendant:    T. H. Boss, Sr
                     303 N.W. 63rd Suite 700
                     Oklahoma City, OK 73116

        You have been sued by the above-named Plaintiff, and you are directed to file a written
answer to the attached Petition in the Oklahoma County District Court within twenty (20) days after service
of this Summons upon you, exclusive of the day of service. Within the same time, a copy of your answer
must be delivered or mailed to the attorney for the Plaintiff.

        Unless you answer the Petition within the time stated, judgment will be rendered against you with
costs of the action.

        ISSUED THIS  _10_  DAY OF  _March_____, 1991.

                                          TOM PETUSKEY, COURT CLERK
(SEAL)

                                          By: _____
                                                    Deputy Court Clerk

Attorney for Plaintiff:
Name:        James A. Slayton, OBA #12168
             JAMES A. SLAYTON, P.C.
Address:     3711 N. Classen Blvd.
             Oklahoma City, Oklahoma  73118
             Telephone: (405) 528-4823

        YOU MAY SEEK THE ADVICE OF AN ATTORNEY ON ANY MATTER CONNECTED WITH THIS
SUIT OR YOUR ANSWER. SUCH ATTORNEY SHOULD BE CONSULTED IMMEDIATELY SO THAT AN
ANSWER MAY BE FILED WITHIN THE TIME LIMIT STATED IN THE SUMMONS.

        A copy of this Summons, with Petition attached, was mailed at Oklahoma City, Oklahoma, by
certified mail, return receipt requested, and if to an individual, delivery restricted to the addressee.
DATE MAILED:_____, DATE RECEIVED:_____

                              _____
                                Attorney for Plaintiff
```

Figure 10-3. A typical summons from a state trial court.

Determine the Deadline

The papers will either state the exact date on which a response is required or will specify how to calculate the response date. If the response date is stated explicitly, enter it on Fig. 10-1 as item 8. More common is for the summons to require response within a stated time after service. Enter that time, 20 days in the two illustrations, as item 8. The determination of when service is made, and when the response time starts to run, is a technical legal question for your attorney.

The exact date and time the papers were first received usually determines when your time limit starts to run. Enter that date as item 4. This is the time the material was received, not when the envelope was opened. Proof of service usually involves a record of receipt, which is why certified mail is used. If your receptionist or mail clerk signs for certified mail, he must be instructed to bring such mail to a responsible person immediately and see that it is opened and attended to. Just throwing the certified envelope in your "in" box is inadequate. The time began to run when the return receipt was signed. If the papers came by mail, keep the envelope. The postmark or postage meter date may be persuasive to the court if there is a question of timeliness.

There is a federal procedure for service of papers by first-class mail, enclosing a form to be signed and returned that acknowledges receipt. Signing and returning the form needlessly shortens the time your attorney has in which to answer.

The papers you receive may bear several dates. The two illustrative summonses have dates on which they were issued, item A. On some documents, a date stamp is affixed when the document is tendered for filing. A summons is not filed until after it is served. The "filed" stamp on the complaint or petition tells you when the case was started. The state court summons, Fig. 10-3, also may indicate the date on which it was served, item C. After delivering the papers, the process server fills in this blank on the copy of the summons that is returned to the court.

Dropping the papers on the ground at the front gate, or leaving them with the security guard at an office building, may not be good service. Careful plaintiffs' attorneys, to be sure they get good service, may serve you twice, perhaps by personal delivery to a corporate officer and also by delivery to a designated agent. Corporations have to be careful about multiple service. When papers are served on the secretary of state, the response time begins to run immediately, even if the papers are not forwarded promptly. You may think the time started at a later time when a different set of papers were delivered directly to you. When you receive more than one set of papers on the same lawsuit, the earliest delivery date is controlling.

Enter the name of the person who physically received the papers, and where, as item 5. Depending on whether the defendant is a human being, a partnership, or a corporation, there are various ways in which legal papers can be served. For a human being, leaving the papers with any adult at the usual place of abode, or nailing the papers to the front door along with mailing them, might be sufficient. In some states, delivery by ordinary first-class mail is sufficient. Corporations can be served through officers, designated agents, or the secretary of state. The location needed is the state and county, not a street address. Your attorney needs to know exactly who received the papers, where, and what that person's capacity is.

The means of delivery, item 6, may affect the amount of time you have to respond. For example, notices sometimes are deemed served when mailed, and 3 days are automatically added for transit time. Each state has rules, which must be interpreted by your attorney.

All of the documents received should be kept together for transmission to the attorney. Item 7 is an inventory of what has been received. Legal papers have titles; the two examples are summonses, item D. Do not discard anything, even if it appears to be a duplicate.

Papers delivered to someone unable or unauthorized to act on behalf of the company must be sent to the proper person without delay. When the papers are forwarded, the person to whom they are sent should be advised by telephone that they are coming. Keeping a continuous record of who has the papers will help avoid a missed deadline. Items 9, 10, and 11 record that information.

Authorize Action

After you get control of the papers, someone with authority must take the next steps. You may not have the time to attend to these details. Perhaps you have a plane to catch on the day the papers arrive. A manager, in-house counsel, or regular outside counsel may be given sufficient authority to take the necessary immediate steps in responding to legal papers. If you don't have someone to turn the papers over to, you had better commit a couple of hours to this, even if it means you have to lose a "supersaver" airfare.

The person responsible for your response can proceed by completing the "Report to Trial Attorney," Fig. 10-4. This form must be treated as confidential and kept in a secure file. If it is handled properly, it should be exempt from discovery and privileged as an attorney–client communication, even if you have not yet chosen an attorney.

Read the papers that have been served. Read each document from the upper left-hand corner of the first page to the lower right-hand corner of the last page. Check the back of each page. Review the initial con-

Report to Trial Attorney

1. Name of case:
12. Apparent due date of response:
13. Notified of immediate compliance required:
14. Role in case (plaintiff/defendant/witness/other):
15. Type of case:
16. What is the claim against the company?
    Who makes the claim?
    When did the claim arise?
17. Name of person in company with information about this matter:
18. Who has paperwork (accident reports, contracts, personnel files, or other material relevant to the claims in this matter):
19. Sent to insurer? Name and date:
20. Name, address, and phone number of adversary attorney:
21. Contact adversary? Exact time, phone number:
22. Court:
    Which state?
    State, federal, or other?
    District?
    Division?
    County?
    Other?
23. City where court located?
24. Attorney retained:
    Name:
    Backup:
    Firm:
    Street address:
    P.O. box:
    City:
    State:
    Zip:
    Telephone number:
    Fax number:

Figure 10-4. The *report to trial attorney* assembles information about the case for sending to the attorney retained.

clusion about the response time. Look for three things: first, does the document require you immediately to act, or stop acting, in some particular way; second, does the document specify a date and place at which you are to respond; and, third, are there directions for calculating a due date? Make any calculation required and enter the apparent due date as item 12.

Some legal papers require immediate compliance, without any court hearing. "Garnishments," sometimes called "income executions" or "attachments," require you immediately to withhold payment to creditors or employees and report to the court. A mere notice that the bankruptcy court adjudicated someone who owes you money requires you to stop collection efforts. An injunction, or temporary restraining order, has already been signed by the judge, perhaps without notice to you. When immediate action is required, notify the appropriate person, perhaps in the payroll or accounts payable department, and indicate his or her name as item 13.

Any court order telling you that you have to do something becomes effective when the judge signs it. Such orders are binding on you when you are served. The order will set a date for a hearing to determine if it should remain in effect. Often the language is "to appear and show cause why" the order should not remain in effect. Disobeying an order after you have been served is treated as contempt of court and may be punishable by fines or imprisonment. More important, it really makes judges angry and will surely prejudice them against you.

Determine Your Role

Receiving a summons means that you are involved in the lawsuit as a defendant. It does not matter if you are a defendant, cross-defendant, co-defendant, counter-defendant, or third-party defendant; a defendant always needs an attorney to protect his interests. A class action may determine your rights as a plaintiff or defendant even without a summons. You can also be subjected to the courts' power when you are merely a bystander with information or assets that the court wishes to control. As a nonparty, you may not need an attorney.

If it is not clear who is suing you, it is most likely the party whose attorney prepared the summons you received. Court clerks do not type the documents they issue. The documents are prepared by the parties, or their attorneys, and taken to the court clerks to be signed, sealed, issued, or filed. The name and role of the person who prepared the document is on the papers. Each of the sample summonses were prepared by the attorney for the plaintiff (item 20). However, after you have been brought into a case, additional claims can be made against you without the formality of a summons. Therefore, you must always read every paper you receive to see if you, or anything about you, is mentioned.

If you are merely a witness, or a source of information, the court asserts power with a *subpoena*. A subpoena may require you to appear at a deposition or at a trial, and it may require you to bring the originals of specified documents or other things with you. You might want the comfort of discussing your testimony with your counsel and making sure you understand what you need to do to comply. Beyond that, there is little need for an attorney. If you have employees, you can routinely expect to receive subpoenas for employment records for use in personal injury and divorce cases. With the advice of counsel, you can train a regular employee to take care of such procedures.

A *garnishment* is a claim against somebody else which is being enforced against property in your possession or under your control. You are merely a stakeholder. Usually the claim is against an employee and the judgment creditor is trying to seize wages. The claim may be against rent owed to your landlord or an account due to a supplier. Investigate immediately and determine if you do owe that person money. Hold any pending payments, and report to the court as required. With the advice of counsel you can set up a routine procedure to handle garnishments, with care taken to comply with the partial exemption of wages from execution. Garnishments present a risk of penalties that may be greater than the amount you owed your employee or creditor. Make note of your role in the case as item 14.

Investigate Internally

The petition, complaint, or other pleading that comes with the summons tells you about the claim. You may be brought into a case by the plaintiff, and may have additional claims asserted against you by a codefendant. Therefore, you must read every pleading you receive, including those that come by ordinary mail, to see what claims may relate to you. You may receive papers about a single case at different times. It is important to connect any new papers to existing files, if any.

As you read the pleadings, you may find that you know nothing about the claim. Most cases fall into three groups: breach of contract, tort or negligence, and regulatory enforcement. If it is a contract problem, somebody in the company probably knows something about the claimed contract. If it is an injury claim, there may be an accident report. If an employee is making a workers' compensation claim, the claimant has a supervisor.

If the case is about a bodily injury, the date or a range of dates is usually stated. Contract cases usually state the date of the contract, and the alleged breach occurred after that.

With the name of the claimant, a date of loss, and the type of claim, which you can enter on Fig. 10-4 as item 16, you should have enough information to conduct a quick internal investigation. Someone else within the company might already be working on the matter. Any such knowledgeable person should be listed in item 17. All material on the subject matter should be consolidated into a confidential file as soon as possible. That includes any accident report, workers' compensation file, credit file, or contract file. Work on those files will need to be coordinated with the requirements for effective handling of the lawsuit. However, do not let this investigation delay getting these papers to your insurer or attorney. Indicate the name of the person in your company who can help the insurer or attorney in item 18.

It was once considered good form for lawyers to send a demand letter before filing suit. A draft of a complaint might be attached, for emphasis. The advantage of a demand letter is that it is an offer to negotiate. Some cases can be settled as soon as the parties each understand that the other is serious. Early analysis and communications may help you avoid unnecessary involvement of the courts. Treat demand letters exactly as if they were lawsuits. Open the same type of file and organize your response. If there is a lawyer on the other side, you will need a lawyer's assistance in preparing documents for a settlement.

Advise Your Insurer

Determine if there is any applicable insurance coverage. Questions about the scope of coverage of insurance policies are tricky. Insurance can be purchased to cover almost any risk. If you have business-interruption coverage, it may cover a breach-of-contract claim. Title insurance may respond to a mechanic's lien foreclosure. Even outlandish claims may be covered by general liability policies, at least to the cost of providing a defense. Unless you know that there can be no insurance coverage, all claims and lawsuits should be reported to your insurance agent or broker. Note the report to the insurer as item 19.

An insured always has a duty of cooperation in the defense of claims and a duty to promptly notify of claims. Failure to do so may jeopardize valuable coverage. Also, your insurance broker's commissions are justified, in part, by the advice he gives you. He should make you aware of your risks and the coverage available. Telling him of every claim against you shifts the burden of determining what insurance you need.

The insurer will get back to you quickly regarding their position on whether or not they think the policy covers the claim. If they agree that coverage is provided, they will tell you what law firm has been retained for your defense. Attorneys retained by insurance companies to represent your company have an attorney–client relationship to you. However, such attorneys also have obligations to the insurer, who pays the bills. The attorneys hired by the insurer cannot advise you of questions of coverage. You will need advice on coverage from your regular counsel if there is any doubt or dispute. Except for coverage issues, the attorneys selected and paid by the insurer are your attorneys. They owe you an undivided duty of loyalty.

You may know the person on the other side of the lawsuit. If the lawsuit arises from a contract or other business relationship, there was once mutual trust and an expectation of profits. There may be enough trust remaining in your relationship that you can avoid committing it to the legal system. If no insurance coverage is possible, consider calling your adversary on the phone immediately.

Every competent legal counsel will tell you not to contact the other party by telephone. If you do, you should expect to be taped, misquoted, and lied to. You will probably waive objections to service. Any insurer will claim that the contact violated the cooperation obligation. But you should also consider that once the lawyers gain control of the case, it will be difficult to reestablish direct communications. Settlement negotiations as such may be privileged, but concessions of fact are not. So expect anything you say in the call to be used against you. Where the dispute is about a business matter, sometimes a direct call to the person in charge on the other side will lead to settlement. Consider it in uninsured cases and either do it or reject the idea, quickly. If you do so, record the date, time, and phone number where you reached your adversary as item 21.

Even if you call your adversary, or especially if you do, you will need to consult with your counsel. Under most court rules, you are in default if you fail to answer or otherwise plead within the time permitted. An agreement by the opposite party to an extension of time is meaningless. The court controls the calendar, and a court order is required to obtain an extension of the time limit. Especially in the federal courts, the rules require that certain things happen within specified times regardless of the wishes of the parties.

Select an Attorney

Before you can select an attorney, using the procedure in Chap. 4, you have to determine where the courthouse is. Look at the top of the caption. What state or territory is it from? Is it from a state court, a U.S. District Court, or some other governmental agency? U.S. District Courts cover districts which may be all or only a part of a state. Some federal districts are split into divisions—for example, the northern district of Texas has divisions in Dallas and Amarillo. If it is a state court case, the courthouse is in the county seat. In Texas, unless it has been changed by a local election, the courthouse is located in the geographic center of the county. You may need an atlas to locate it. In large metropolitan areas, the state courts may have branches at several locations. Enter everything you can find about the court as item 22.

Particularly if you are sued in another state, you may not know what city the case is pending in. The last volume of Martindale-Hubbell has a digest of the laws of each state. Under the heading "Courts" you will find a list of the counties in each federal court district and the county seats of each county. There is probably a law library containing Martindale-Hubbell open to the public at your own county courthouse. Using it and the information on the papers, complete as much of item 22 as you can, and be sure to complete item 23, the city where the court is located. As noted in Chap. 4, you can also use Martindale-Hubbell to look up your adversary's attorney.

You can easily find out where the court sits by telephoning your adversary's attorney. That name, address, and phone number are on the pleadings, item 20. Calling the adverse attorney will probably be treated as acknowledging receipt of the papers and a waive of any objections to service. Since you may need to look at Martindale-Hubbell anyway, the better idea is to commit the time to go to the library. If you cannot do it, send someone, either a manager, an in-house lawyer, or your regular outside counsel.

Trial attorneys should always be selected to meet the needs of the particular case. A primary consideration is location. If your regular outside counsel is located in the vicinity where the case is pending, you may wish to refer the case to her for defense. Otherwise, you, or someone acting on your behalf, should go through the process of selecting a trial attorney described in detail in Chap. 4. The trial attorney selected should be identified as item 24.

Finally, the attorney should be sent the entire package, along with a retainer letter. Enclose copies of both the service of process control record, Fig. 10-1, and the report to trial attorney, Fig. 10-4, with the originals of the papers served on you. Retain copies of everything in your confidential legal file. You are now into litigation, a mysterious, arbitrary process. However, with a small understanding of how it works, you can exercise substantial control over your destiny.

1. Instruct all employees that all "legal papers" are to be delivered to a specified person.
2. Delegate authority to attend to "legal papers" to a specific person (with a backup).
3. Use the service of process control record, Fig. 10-1, to organize information about the "legal papers" and their receipt.
4. Don't throw anything away: Keep envelopes and duplicates.
5. Read the "legal papers" to find:

    Express deadlines:
    Date, time, and place to respond; or
    Order already in effect

    Express action required or forbidden:
    Notify persons affected

    What is your role:
    Party
    Class member
    Witness
    Stakeholder

    Type of claim:
    Contract
    Tort
    Enforcement

    Who makes claim

    When claim arose

6. Investigate internally:
    Do you already have a file on the matter?
    Who knows about the matter?
7. Assemble information on "Report to Trial Attorney," Fig. 10-4.
8. Notify your insurer.
9. If you are not insured, contact your adversary.
10. Hire an attorney in the appropriate location, using the procedure described in Chap. 4, and forward:
    All papers received
    Service of Process Control Record, Fig. 10-1
    Report to Trial Attorney, Fig. 10-4

Procedure: Responding to legal papers.

11
How Litigation Really Works

Threatening to sue is more effective in getting an adversary to do what you want than actually filing a lawsuit. The legal system is a morass. Litigation is costly and uncertain. No one wants to be involved in a lawsuit. Motivated by a desire to avoid litigation, you and your adversary can probably work out a better deal for each of you than either will get at the courthouse.

Starting a Suit

But not always. Sometimes, the power is all on one side and the fairness is on the other. A debtor who has the money may simply refuse to pay. A customer may refuse to accept your custom-made goods, having found a cheaper substitute. Or a competitor may pass off his goods as yours, stealing your customers and your reputation. In exasperation or in anger you may be forced to resort to the dreaded litigation as a plaintiff. Or perhaps you have no choice, being sued as a defendant.

Once the lawsuit is filed, the threat disappears. Your attorney talks to the opponent, papers are filed, fees are paid, and a year or two later your attorney is suddenly telling you to settle on terms that are less advantageous than you expected. The settlement is suggested under the threat of going to trial, which is what you thought you were going to do in the first place. Understanding how this comes about will guide you in working with your attorney to obtain a better result.

When you are the plaintiff, you begin by telling your story to your attorney. Your attorney listens to your story to find out the facts that support a legal theory that will support the granting of relief by a court.

Sorting the facts out of the story calls for the exercise of the attorney's judgment as to what is likely to be important. Promising parts of the story are explored in detail and the specifics noted. The reason for the claim is matched to broad categories of law, such as breach of contract, negligence, or fraud. By the end of the interview, the attorney will have decided, based on the story, what facts will form the basis of the lawsuit.

Finding the Law

When you leave, the attorney can begin studying the law. Considering the hourly rates charged, you might expect a lawyer to know what the law is. The problem is not knowing the law, but citing specific authority for each proposition of law. A lawyer's basic skill is finding the points of law that are pertinent to a particular matter. Every legal matter has unique facts. The lawyer's job is to identify the fact pattern, match it to the law, and determine which of the unique facts affect the result. To do this, lawyers use indexes, digests, treatises, annotations, and computer databases.

Law is found by studying reports of prior cases and legislative enactments. It is so difficult to get a straight answer to questions about the law because the law is constantly developing and changing. The best you can get is an opinion about what the law was, and a prediction of what the law will be in your case.

The reports of prior cases relied on as law are the formal opinions of appellate courts. Traditionally, only real cases involving real disputes are brought to the trial courts. Advisory proceedings are a recent development. The risk of losing a real dispute presumably spurs the parties to make the best possible presentation of the evidence and the law. A jury verdict or a judge's findings are the basis of a judgment. A dissatisfied party may appeal. There is no appeal from the jury's fact findings, but arguments about the rules of evidence sometimes result in a new trial. If the appeal raises a genuine question of what the law is, or should be, the appellate court's ruling takes the form of an *opinion*. Opinions state what has been decided and why. The opinions are called *precedent*.

Court opinions are retrospective, always looking backward at events that have already happened. The cases decided always have unique facts. Precedent provides only guidance as to how the next case should be decided. Precedent is never truly binding, because the facts of each new case are different. Attorneys argue about whether the differences in the facts should make a difference in the outcome.

Lawyers also study the enactments of the U.S. Congress and the state legislatures, along with various constitutions and treaties. In some matters, the ordinances of municipal governments authorized by statutes must be considered. Municipal ordinances have a direct and dramatic impact on businesses, affecting zoning, licensing of tradespeople and mechanics, and taxation. The state and federal governments also implement legislation through administrative agencies which promulgate regulations.

In theory, legislation cannot change the effect of events which occurred before the statute became law. Statutes are applied prospectively: They are rules which are to govern future events. Of course, the courts look back at the circumstances to determine if the statutes are applicable.

In addition to prior court decisions, constitutions, treaties, statutes, ordinances, and regulations, there are books about law. These include the textbooks used in the business and tax law courses taught in business schools. Such books, some of which are excellent, are useful for broad statements of principles, sources of ideas, and questions. But lawyers must update what is in such books with current cases and statutes.

Your attorney first studies the law to define the claim in very broad terms. Attorneys know what the law is. However, diligent attorneys check recent cases and statutes to be sure that all of the required facts have been identified, and to find the specific cases and statutes that determine what facts must be proven in cases like yours. In routine cases, this may be as simple as running down a checklist in a form book. In more complex cases, it may be necessary to research statutes and past opinions.

The lawyers, on both sides, will be studying the law all through the lawsuit. New issues are constantly turning up. Usually, the lawyer has an idea of what the law is, or should be, on any particular issue. However, with so much law to choose from, the opposing lawyer may have a different opinion of what the law is. The judge's decision on any issue must be based on the prior cases and the statutes, not on what the lawyers say. The lawyer seeks those statutes or prior cases that make the most persuasive arguments in support of her view of the law. Those cases and statutes will be presented, if necessary, in a brief submitted to the judge.

First Choices

The claim must be against somebody in particular. You usually have an idea of whom you want to sue, but your attorney needs to identify everyone who might be liable on the claim. There may be several potential defendants. In a product-liability case, the claim may be against the retailer, wholesaler, manufacturer, and designer of the product. An antitrust case may be against all of the conspirators. Each individual defendant must be accurately and fully identified. A claim might be against a partnership, a corporation, or an individual. Many business operations are conducted by corporations using trade names. A lawsuit must be directed to the underlying corporation. You can save some fees, and some time by giving to your attorney exact identification of the parties involved in the matter as possible defendants. The attorney will choose the defendants based on the legal theory developed.

Your attorney next has to figure out what court to sue the defendant in. State trial courts sit in each county and serve "venues" which may include more than one county and are often called circuits or districts. A "venue" is a geographic concept, a certain territory within which the court has power, usually a county or a state. "Jurisdiction" is the court's power to decide questions of a particular subject matter and the power to bind individual persons by the decision. In the past, a court's power could be imposed only on persons found within the boundaries of the venue, thus the common understanding of jurisdiction as territorial. Your attorney must select a court with both the power to decide the type of case and the ability to subject the defendant to its jurisdiction.

There is an additional and separate federal court system. It consists of district courts, sitting on one or more districts for each state, circuit courts of appeals for circuits which take in several states, and the U.S. Supreme Court. It also includes the bankruptcy courts, which are subordinate to the district courts. Federal courts have jurisdiction only to the extent provided by the Constitution and acts of Congress. Generally, the federal district courts have subject matter jurisdiction only over federal questions and actions between citizens of different states.

The Rules of Civil Procedure

The conduct of civil litigation in the federal courts is governed by the *Federal Rules of Civil Procedure*. Criminal law has a different set of rules. The Federal Rules of Civil Procedure completely changed litigation when they were adopted in 1937. These federal rules were intended to prevent the outcome of cases from being determined by the cleverness of trial attorneys. Before 1937, written pleadings were used to narrow the factual issues to be submitted to the court. When the fact issues were joined, a trial was held on just those points which, if proven, would decide the outcome of case. The difficulty was that the focus on "issues" was not a focus on facts. Attorneys went to trial with little information about what evidence would be presented. This "sporting theory of justice," or "trial by ambush," remains the popular conception of how lawsuits are tried.

The 1937 federal rules simplified the pleading process and provided for discovery. Trickery—particularly, concealing evidence—was to be prevented by requiring full disclosure of each party's case. This process of discovery was expected to eliminate courtroom surprise and bring the parties to the same view of the facts. With over a half-century of experience to look back on, the 1937 rules have succeeded in reducing the element of surprise. However, the cost of the discovery has itself become a problem.

Each of the 50 states has its own rules of procedure. Some states take great historical pride in their procedure. Many states still have a requirement that litigants plead "facts constituting a cause of action" or "a cause of action." However, all states have adopted rules favoring pretrial discovery. Many states have adapted the Federal Rules of Civil Procedure with only a few changes. The following description of how a lawsuit proceeds follows the federal rules. Each state's rules include minor variations. For example, in some states the complaint is called a "petition," or a deposition is called an "examination before trial." However, the general outline of the federal rules is a fair guide to the practice in any state.

Pleading

A lawsuit is commenced by filing a complaint with the court. A *complaint* is supposed to be a short, plain, simple, concise, and direct statement of what the plaintiff claims and what the plaintiff wants. Most complaints attempt to tell the plaintiff's story persuasively and make extreme demands for relief in the form of money damages. The federal rules require only that the pleading set forth a statement of the claim showing that the pleader is entitled to relief. There is no requirement that the claim be true.

The judge and the court clerk do not look at complaints to see if they are valid. However, the complaint, and other papers filed later in the case, must be signed by the attorney, who is an officer of the court. That signature is the attorney's personal certification that such papers are well grounded in fact and warranted by a reasonable legal theory. If a pleading is filed in violation of the rule, the judge can punish the attorney and the party the attorney represents. Your attorney may refer to "Rule 11," which provides sanctions for filing papers that are not justified by the facts and the law. Sanctions may be assessed against the attorney who files an improper paper or against the client, and may include a fine or payment of the opponent's attorney's fees.

After your attorney drafts and signs a complaint, incorporating the facts of your story into a legal theory, the complaint is filed with the appropriate court clerk and the filing fee is paid. That starts the lawsuit. The judge is involved at this stage only if you are seeking a temporary restraining order or some other immediate relief.

Service of Process

The clerk issues the summonses to be served on the defendants. This is where the exact identification of the defendants is important. There is a temptation to skimp on service of the summons. Many business defendants will respond voluntarily when they know they have been sued. Some, however, will dodge service.

In a mortgage foreclosure, the lender saved some money by not paying a process server to track down and personally serve the debtor, who was hiding to avoid service. A receiver was appointed to operate the property, an apartment complex. The receiver collected the rents and paid the bills, but held the excess cash flow, paying no interest or principal on the debt. The cash accumulated, offsetting the interest which was accruing. Several years later, the court threw out the case because the service had been bad. By this time the receiver was holding several hundred thousand dollars in positive cash flow, the subject of a whole new lawsuit between the lender and the debtor. Everything about a lawsuit depends on this routine, perfunctory chore of serving the summons.

Not only does the summons have to be served on the right defendant, it must be served within 120 days after the complaint is filed. That is not much time if the defendant decides to hide. From the defendant's perspective, there is a danger that a court will decide that a purported service is sufficient. A careful defendant should always respond when legal papers are delivered, even indirectly.

Motion to Dismiss

As noted in Chap. 10, the defendant has only a short time to respond once service is made. The time, typically 20 days, begins to run as soon as service has been made. Within that time the defendant must select and retain an attorney and deliver to her the information needed to respond. If you are a defendant, assemble the needed information using the service of process control record, Fig. 10-1, and the report to trial attorney, Fig. 10-4.

The defense attorney has one chance, and one chance only, to raise questions about the jurisdiction of the court, the correctness of the service of the papers, whether the proper parties are in the case, and whether a claim is stated against the defendant. Those kinds of issues are brought to a head quickly by filing a motion to dismiss.

A defense attorney may suggest a motion to dismiss on the grounds that the complaint fails to state a claim against the defendant. This is a very technical motion which is difficult to win. Even if the defendant convinces the judge that the complaint is inadequate, the judge will grant the plaintiff some time to correct deficiencies. Such motions are wasted effort if the purpose is to dispose of the case. All that the defendant accomplishes is to educate the plaintiff about how the case needs to be presented. However, the motion may be very useful in testing the opponent's ability and the judge's temper.

On the other hand, a motion to dismiss based on a flaw in the way the papers were served must be made immediately. A good motion to dismiss on grounds of defective service is supported by affidavits from persons with actual knowledge. There is no time to spare in getting the papers drafted, to the knowledgeable person and a notary public for signature, and back to the court within what is left of the 20 days.

The Answer

The defendant responds by admitting or denying each claim. If the defendant does not have enough information, saying so is treated as a denial. The defendant also uses the answer to bring up additional matters which may affect the outcome and to make counterclaims against the plaintiff, to cross-claim against other defendants, or to bring in additional parties with a third-party complaint. The answer is tested by the same standards as the complaint; that is, the attorney who signs it certifies that it has some reasonable basis in law and fact.

The federal rules, and the rules of most states, have reduced the pleading process to merely giving notice that there is some kind of a dispute. In fact, except for jurisdictional issues, if the pleadings are wrong they can be amended to fit whatever the proof turns out to be. However, the pleading process can be used to good advantage to plan a strategy. A true practitioner of the legal craft, after doing some research, will write out a list of facts which, if proven, will decide the case. Using the list of required facts, the available evidence is inventoried. Files are searched for relevant documents. Witnesses are interviewed. The existing proof is identified and preserved. The proof that is not readily at hand is also identified, and a plan is made to obtain it. Some proof will be turned up with further investigation. Some proof will be created by expert witnesses. Some proof will be found in the hands of the adversary by discovery. With a firm idea of what the evidence will be, the lawyer drafts a pleading that makes exactly the claims that will be proven.

The federal courts have a rule that the parties must meet with the judge for a scheduling conference within 120 days of the filing of the complaint. These scheduling "conferences," however, are not really conferences: Federal judges arbitrarily set dates within which the preparation of the case must be complete. That schedule can be changed only by the judge upon a showing of good cause. This setting of deadlines demonstrates the coercive power of the court. Litigation, originally a substitute for trial by combat, soon begins to feel like trial by ordeal.

Discovery

The basic idea of the 1937 federal rules was to avoid the technical game-playing of old-fashioned pleading and get to the facts. This is done with *pretrial discovery*. Each party can obtain information from the other on any matter connected with the subject matter of the lawsuit. This process is intended to reveal all of the relevant facts before trial, supposedly eliminating surprise. The rules of evidence, which govern the admission of evidence to the record considered by the court, do not apply in the discovery process. The scope of discovery is not limited to admissible evidence, but may include anything which might lead to admissible evidence. This has led to a modern form of game-playing, exhaustive discovery.

One monster case involved about 35 lending institutions and a group of transactions that took place over a 2-year period. There were claims of fraud involving a couple of loan brokers. One group of plaintiffs thought that it would be helpful to look at the telephone records of each of the 35 institutions to determine if and when phone calls had been placed to the brokers. So a request was made that the telephone records covering several years be produced for inspection. Some of the institutions had several offices. Each location had local and long-distance telephone bills. The original telephone service invoices had been bound into files with other payable invoices. All of the paid invoices were in boxes in warehouses when the discovery was requested. Extracting the telephone invoices from the files, from the boxes, and from the warehouse, on the chance that proof of a telephone call would be found, was required on the grounds that it was intended to lead to the discovery of admissible evidence. The total cost of the exercise was in excess of $100,000 for attorney fees alone. No one ever found any relevant phone calls.

The telephone records horror story illustrates the waste that drives up the cost of litigation. You cannot control litigation costs without understanding four processes which occur in discovery. First, as the rules intended, the facts which lay behind the parties stories are identified and reduced to evidence that can be carried to the courthouse. While the facts are explored, issues of law are also identified, researched, and often disposed of. The entire process puts the facts and the law before the parties so that they can each judge the merits of their positions and perhaps seek a settlement. As a practical matter, the parties know what the truth is without the need for discovery. The hardest cases to settle are those in which one party is totally in the wrong. The party that is in the wrong keeps fighting to delay the inevitable outcome.

A second essentially wasteful process is the search for a "smoking gun" that does not exist. In this common situation the attorneys are coming up with "what if" questions. In the telephone horror story, the question was "what if" an institution placed numerous long-distance telephone calls to the crooked loan broker around the time that the bad deals were made. Experience indicates that if an attorney digs deep enough and long enough, something will turn up that can be misconstrued to support an otherwise worthless theory. Thus, depositions go on for days in the hope that a witness will become tired and make a mistake that can be hailed into court as the real truth. Papers are picked over in the hope of finding something that cannot be explained.

The third process involves the subtle psychological interplay of the parties and attorneys. In discovery, an attorney wins by developing favorable evidence and by blocking the opponents' efforts to do the same. For example, if your chief engineer can be made out to be a fool in a deposition, the adversary has gained an advantage even if no one ever intended to call the chief engineer as a witness. Alternatively, if your chief executive officer demonstrates honor and integrity in withstanding an abusive deposition, the adversary has wasted resources. These exchanges create momentum for or against either party.

The fourth process that occurs in discovery is the generation of billable hours and attorneys' fees. If enough digging is done, something usually turns up. Clients pay attorneys for doing something. Attorneys often succumb to the temptation to keep on digging, knowing the fee will be paid, regardless of what they are finding. You know the true facts, and you can control discovery costs by telling your attorneys not to look for something you know isn't there.

You can avoid having your resources exhausted by discovery if you have a plan at the beginning of the case. Establish discovery objectives. One set of objectives is to know what the opponent's case is. The second set of objectives is to nail down evidence for use in a motion for summary judgment or at trial. Then go about the business of building your case and create the momentum that will carry you through settlement or trial. When you are making steady progress toward obvious goals, the opponent is losing. It is a good time to settle.

Used efficiently, discovery is a two-edged sword. Precise, direct inquiries reveal to the opponent what you are thinking about the case. Similarly, you can discern what your opponent thinks about his own case from discovery directed at you. Some attorneys attempt to conceal what they are after by serving up vast quantities of inconsequential nonsense, a wasteful technique that won't work with anyone who understands it.

The order in which the various discovery methods can be used is a tactical decision for the trial attorney. In most cases, all can be utilized to good effect.

Interrogatories

Interrogatories are written questions served on the adversary and call for a written response. The usual responses are evasive and intended to reveal as little as possible. Since the responder has plenty of time to pick the written questions apart, interrogatories seldom result in major revelations. The practice of serving hundreds of interrogatories has been stopped by local court rule in most places. The major advantage of interrogatories is low cost. Their most effective use is in getting the adversary to designate targets for other discovery devices.

If you are served with interrogatories, study them carefully; you will find within them much of what your adversary thinks the case is about. This close study must be done by both you and your attorney. You understand the background of the case much better than your attorney does. Go behind the interrogatories to try to discern why each question was asked. For each interrogatory, prepare, as a confidential and privileged communication to your attorney, a response covering why the question was asked, the information that answers the question, who provided the information, and what documents contain the information. An intense effort will be required to get this done and back to your attorney so she can draft and file answers within the time limit. Always serve fully responsive answers and serve them within the time allowed. Failure to respond to interrogatories does little for you and puts you on the defensive with the judge.

In you are a defendant you can take the offensive by serving interrogatories with your answer. At the very start of the case, you have your attorney's attention. This is the time to collaborate in developing a set of interrogatories that will create favorable momentum. With your background knowledge and your attorney's tactical skills, you will be able to build a set of interrogatories that will test the opponent's case.

Document Production

The horror story about telephone records relates to procedure commonly called *document production*. Any party can ask any other party to produce any document, or anything else, for inspection and copying. The documents requested may be narrowly defined—certainly telephone records are a narrow group—and still impose a significant burden in locating and producing them. When broadly defined, the volumes of paper may be unmanageable.

There are two ways to respond to document requests. The "boxcar" response, a reference to the amount of paper needed to fill a railroad boxcar, is to produce the requested documents as they are kept in the usual course of business. In the telephone records example, the party asking for the documents might have been given the keys to the warehouse. If you are confident that there is nothing useful among the documents, the boxcar technique is an effective way to push the opponent's costs up. However, you accept the risk of the opponent's finding something you did not expect. Actually, the boxcar method is usually used in hope that the adversary lawyer will miss the good stuff buried in the garbage. The other response, organizing and labeling the documents to correspond with the categories of the request, is an opportunity for "nitpicking." The nitpicking response interprets the request narrowly so as to exclude the meaningful documents, or filing objections to the request. The object of the nitpicking approach is to keep the opponent from ever seeing any hurtful documents.

Document productions can create misleading evidence. A document viewed in isolation may look like a "smoking gun," but when the smoking gun is put in the context of all of the other documents generated at the same time, it may be seen to be nothing more than an old cigar. Document control is essential to maintain the context, and true meaning, of documents. Your attorney should identify and preserve all relevant evidence, including documents. This is an expensive process that calls for the use of clerks and computer databases. However, an early start will reduce wasted effort and enable a more precise and limited production.

A practical way to reduce the cost of producing documents is to implement a document retention program that ensures the complete and total destruction of every piece of paper that you are not required by state or federal law to retain. This is not protection against the harmful documents. Some loyal and dedicated employee will always save a copy of the most damning piece of paper.

There are two ways to reduce the cost of using document requests offensively. First, each request should be framed with specific and meaningful objectives. The horror story of the telephone bills had a specific objective which was not meaningful. Don't waste time with documents that don't matter. Second, if the documents are going to be produced as they are ordinarily kept, insist that the attorney make a careful study of the documents at that location and copy only those which are likely to be useful. Lazy lawyers copy everything, and never look at any of it.

Examination of Things

The same procedure used with documents may be used with any tangible thing. Often, in a product-liability case, the defendant wants to test the allegedly defective thing. That raises a question about destructive testing that must be worked out by agreement. The rule permits you to inspect and copy, test, or sample the thing. The rule also permits entry onto premises for the purpose of measuring, photographing, etc. Cases involving an injury inside an industrial facility may require the owner to permit a party to come on the site with an expert witness and a photographer. The important thing with such inspections is to watch the inspectors to see exactly what they do, and if they do it properly. It may be an opportunity to acquire information from the adverse expert about his theory and what he is looking for. Of course, you want to make sure that no questions are asked of your employees.

Examination of Persons

A separate rule provides for the physical and mental examination of any person whose physical or mental condition is an issue in the case. This is done in every personal-injury case. The secrets of selecting examining physicians are well understood by personal-injury attorneys.

Depositions

A *deposition* is the examination, under oath, of a party or a witness. The deposition is usually taken down by a certified court reporter, who prepares a written transcript of what was said. Depositions are where most of the information is revealed in discovery, mainly because the witnesses are answering directly and not through an attorney. The process is fairly expensive. The cost of the transcript will be about the same as an attorney's fee for the actual time spent taking the deposition.

For anything except a routine personal-injury case, there is substantial preparation time on both sides. The examiner needs to have in mind what information he is seeking from the witness, and have documents at hand to stimulate the witness's memory. The attorney working with the witness wants to ensure that the witness listens to the questions, answers only the questions asked, and doesn't guess at answers. Early in a complicated case, the examiner will be thorough to the point of being tedious, not being sure of what is important. Even when the examiner knows what he is after, it takes many questions to break down defenses and get the witness into a pattern of responding truthfully and without thinking.

Inexperienced lawyers sometimes defeat themselves by overpreparing. With every document analyzed and indexed, the lawyer may know much more about the case than the witness. But the lawyer does not know what the witness knows. Busy showing off what he does know, the lawyer may not listen to what the witness says, or does not say, and may learn nothing from the witness.

Some witnesses are untruthful and evasive. The former head surgical nurse at a small hospital was subpoenaed for deposition about an accident which occurred during her employment. She was not a defendant. Asked what years she had worked at the hospital, she said that she did not remember. Asked the names of the surgeons with whom she worked, she said that she did not remember. Asked to describe the layout of the surgical suite, she said that she did not recall and perhaps never knew. Asked if a wet package of surgical instruments that looked like it had rust stains was likely to be contaminated, she said that she did not know. Before a jury, such obvious lies would raise questions about who or what she was protecting. At deposition there is no practical remedy for such conduct.

When witnesses are evasive, examiners long-winded and misdirected, or the witness's lawyer obstructive and offensive, the transcript may run on, page after wasteful page. An effective way to control the behavior of witnesses and attorneys in depositions is to have the court reporter record the depositions on videotape as provided by the rules. The parties each receive a copy, which can be used in court.

Requests for Admissions

A party may request that any other party admit the truth of any matter involved in the case, including opinions, facts, the genuineness of documents, or the application of law to fact. If the party refuses to admit and the matter is subsequently proven, the cost, including reasonable attorneys' fees, of proving the matter can be shifted to the party who failed to admit. Clients are rarely willing to admit anything. This is a way to demonstrate to the judge that the other side is being obstructive. Also, the threat of shifting attorney's fees is real.

Discovery Abuse and Sanctions

The legal system we have adapted from England is adversarial. The different claims of the parties are presented by their respective attorneys before a neutral court. This is a contest. Ideally it is a contest of ideas. Each attorney has a duty to make the best possible presentation on behalf of his client. Assuming that the attorneys are of equal ability, the court should be able to choose fairly between the presentations. The advantage of the adversary system is the creativity of arguments on close questions. As each decision is added to the body of law, the law adjusts to changes in the real world.

The trouble with the adversary system is that it encourages contention over issues of no substance. This is a nice way of saying that sometimes lawyers delay, obfuscate, and obstruct the processes of the law. Clients hire attorneys to win. The economic pressures tend to squeeze out the ethics, as described in Chap. 8, including the ethical duties to avoid false or frivolous claims and to expedite litigation.

The process of discovery has simply moved the game-playing and trickery out of the courtroom. In 1990, the American Bar Association reported that 45.1 percent of attorneys believe that discovery is frequently abused, and 50.9 percent believe that it is sometimes abused. Discovery eats up legal fees and wears down clients. Judges do not like to become involved because of the endless and pointless wrangling. Nonetheless, if the obstruction is flagrant, the judge will eventually punish (sanction) somebody by ruling on a motion to compel discovery. The sanction may be by a contempt proceeding, which can lead to jail, or by ruling arbitrarily on all or part of the case.

Used effectively, discovery converts the "real truth" into evidence for all involved to consider. If there is only one "true" set of facts, then discovery should lay out the evidence which will dictate a jury's verdict. The parties can view that evidence and know the likely outcome. Clients sometimes urge a lawsuit to "bring them (the adversary) to the table." Actually, most adversaries take a tougher position when they have to hire an attorney. The mere filing of a complaint and service of a summons, while more than a threat, does not change anything. However, proper discovery forces the parties to face facts.

Discovery lays the foundation for settlement. The litigation process requires that the facts of the real world be converted into evidence that can be presented in the courtroom. A discovery record that demonstrates your ability to prove the facts that will win your case may convince the adversary that you will win at trial. Fear of losing motivates settlement.

Motion for Summary Judgment

It is sometimes possible to dispose of a case, without committing to trial, by a *motion for summary judgment*. This is a presentation to the court that says that there is no genuine dispute over the controlling facts. With no dispute about the facts, there is nothing for a jury to decide. The court can decide the case by applying the law to the undisputed facts. The opposing party will either argue that important facts are in dispute and must be decided by a jury, or perhaps file a cross-motion for summary judgment.

If the discovery process has been used to convert real-world, true facts into evidence, there will be a discovery record that clearly establishes the controlling facts. The record may be clear enough to convince the judge that there is no genuine dispute about the facts. If the facts are favorable to your cause, your motion for summary judgment may be granted. However, an order granting a motion for summary judgment is appealable. Most judges are reluctant to grant a summary judgment except on either overwhelming facts or a default by the loser.

Up to this point there is little involvement of the court in the litigation process. Discovery is between the parties. The court becomes involved only in the event of some misconduct. If the case is not disposed of by settlement or summary judgment, it must be set for trial. You may have thought you wanted a trial. In reality, when the court takes over, you totally surrender control of the outcome. Going to the courthouse means dealing with two threats, your adversary and the judge. They are not allied against you, but either can do you harm. If you are going to trial, you will do much better if you have a polite and respectful relationship with your adversary. If the relationship between the attorneys is acrimonious or bitter, they will have a problem with the judge. The judges demand that the attorneys, as officers of the court, work together to expedite the trial and minimize the court's burden. Whenever you really intend to take a case through trial, keep your lawyer mellow.

Investigation:
  Facts:
    Identify witnesses
    Identify documents and physical evidence
  Law:
    Precedent:
      Binding appellate decisions in same jurisdiction
      Persuasive authority from other jurisdictions
    Legislation:
      Constitutions
      Treaties
      Statutes
      Ordinances
      Regulations

Plaintiff's choices:
  Who to sue (parties)
  Where to sue (jurisdiction and venue)
  State or federal courts with power to decide subject matter
  What claims to plead (complaint or petition, injunction)

Service of summons

Defendant's choices:
  Move to dismiss because court lacks jurisdiction
  Move to dismiss because claims do not justify a legal remedy
  Answer by admitting, denying, or adding facts

Injunction cases — immediate hearing

Scheduling conference

Discovery:
  Processes:
    Develop true facts (efficient)
    Search for "smoking gun" (wasteful)
    Gain psychological advantage
    Employ attorneys (wasteful)
  Methods:
    Interrogatories (low cost)
    Production of documents (moderate cost)
    Examination of persons, places, and things (moderate cost)
    Depositions (high cost)
    Request for admissions (low cost)
    Motions to compel (high cost)
    Sanctions (dangerous)

Motions for summary judgment
  No significant facts in dispute
  Law dictates outcome

Procedure: Preparing for trial.

12
What Happens When You Finally Get to the Courthouse

You have been "taken to court" when a complaint is filed and you have been served with a summons. At first, the court will not be much involved in the lawsuit. There will be a scheduling conference within 120 days of filing the complaint, and rulings on motions to dismiss or for summary judgment. Some judges require periodic status reports to keep the court's docket moving. Asking the judge to rule on discovery problems is dangerous, because many judges routinely impose penalties on one or both parties. Although the case is pending, you are not "at the courthouse" until it is ready for trial.

During the period between the filing of the lawsuit and going to the courthouse for the trial, your attorney should be converting the true facts of the real world into evidence. Putting the truth into the form of evidence requires investigation into what you know, and discovery of what the adversary knows. Without regard to fairness, or importance, the only "truth" that the court will consider is "truth" which can be presented by testimony or stipulation. The time for getting ready ends at the final pretrial conference.

A date for the final pretrial conference is set by the judge at the first scheduling conference, along with dates for the completion of discovery and the filing of motions. In state courts the pretrial conference may be held when a party moves to enter the case on the trial docket, or files a "note of issue and statement of readiness." However it comes about, the holding of the final pretrial conference requires that the attorneys report to the judge that they are ready for trial.

There are four distinct stages in going to the courthouse with a lawsuit. At the pretrial conference, the judge will review a memorandum submitted by the attorneys which lays out what is to happen at the trial, using it to enter a trial order governing every aspect of the trial. The trial begins with the selection of a jury and ends with a verdict which is a decision on the facts. Then the law is applied to the verdict to reach a judgment, which may be appealed. Finally, the judgment is enforced by the sheriff. Beginning at the pretrial conference, the judge will continually try to get the case settled. The pressure from the judge to settle reflects the urgency of other matters pending on the docket.

The Pretrial Conference

The conference with the judge is often a sham. It will lead to either a settlement, ending the case, or a trial order. The judge wants to discuss settlement. The attorneys want to talk about the trial order. The judge is in charge. If no settlement develops, the pretrial memorandum, with any changes made by the judge, becomes the trial order. The preparation of the pretrial memorandum is crucial in that it provides the parties with the opportunity to affect the course the trial will take.

The Pretrial Memorandum

About 6 weeks before the scheduled date of the pretrial conference, you should ask your attorney for a draft of the pretrial memorandum. If no pretrial conference is scheduled, ask your attorney to prepare a draft pretrial memorandum as soon as any party starts the process of setting a trial date. You may be told that local practice does not require a pretrial memorandum. Some courts accomplish the same thing by requiring that the attorneys exchange the information by a certain date. Regardless of local practice, insist that your attorney demonstrate that she is prepared with a pretrial memorandum, or other information exchange, that meets requirements of the trial court or the local federal district court. The purpose of the exercise is to be sure that the right issues are covered at trial and that the judge will let your case be presented.

The usual form of pretrial memorandum is prepared jointly and signed by all attorneys of record. Personal conflicts between the attorneys can cause difficulty here. Disputes among the parties must be accommodated within the overall document. In some jurisdictions, attorneys are required to agree to a master document into which each party inserts its own materials.

A statement of agreed facts or stipulations will dispose of points which might affect the outcome if disputed. These may be basic, such as the existence of a corporation or the residence of a person. Clients are sometimes troubled by stipulations to specific facts, such as the ownership of the car involved in a collision. There is a natural inclination to force your adversary to prove every point. If you insist on proof of a point which is not actually in dispute, you are wasting the court's time.

Each party makes a detailed statement of factual contentions. These are not just arguments. A factual contention is a promise that you will prove what you said, and that if you fail, you should lose. The conflict between the factual contentions defines what the jury has to decide. Argument about what the law is or should be can be mixed in, but the focus is on the facts.

The judge may request or accept questions to ask jurors during the selection process. In a lawsuit involving airplanes, for example, you might want to identify, and exclude, any pilots, to avoid having the jury deliberations dominated by one person claiming expertise. If you are suing a bank, you might want to exclude people who keep their money in that bank. Some judges permit the attorneys to ask the questions, but that practice is becoming rare.

A list of exhibits to be introduced at trial, with the details of the evidence used to verify each item, is commonly required. In commercial cases there may be many document exhibits. Some judges demand that exhibits be bound into a book and numbered before trial. As a practical matter, most documents are covered by stipulations.

A list of witnesses, including experts, who may be called at trial is required, along with a summary of each witness's expected testimony. This is a problem for defendants who do not know what the plaintiff's witnesses will testify to.

At the end of the trial the judge will instruct the jury on the law. Some judges request that proposed instructions be in the trial order to be checked against the evidence presented. In cases where the jury will report the verdict as answers to a series of questions, the trial order will include a proposed verdict form.

Finally, the pretrial memorandum should address any questions that can be decided before trial. Evidence that is misleading or prejudicial may be identified with a specific request that it be excluded. For example, in a suit involving claims of an expelled partner, the court granted a "motion in limine" to bar evidence of illegal drug use by some of the remaining partners.

The preparation of the pretrial memorandum is quite burdensome and tedious. It requires substantial time and is therefore costly. But you cannot get to trial without it. Failure to have it done on time is very harmful to the negotiating position of the party who is tardy. If your trial attorney cannot give you a usable draft of her part of the pretrial memorandum 6 weeks before it is due, you should use that 6 weeks to get her up to speed. Otherwise, she will not be ready to do an effective job for you at trial, or in the settlement negotiations that will continue through the trial.

Why 6 weeks? This is the last chance that you will have to make a strategic change in the trial process. Six weeks is barely enough time in which to serve some interrogatories or requests for admissions, get the responses back, and incorporate the responses into the pretrial memorandum.

The preliminary draft of the trial memorandum should tell you, as a layperson, what the case is about, what the points in dispute are, what you are going to prove, what each witness will testify to, and what exhibits will be introduced. At this early stage, it should logically describe how the case will be presented. An ordinary person, not well educated, should be able to read the memorandum and explain it to you. It should be so simple that the judge will understand it in one reading.

The trial order is used by the judge to set up the mechanics of the trial. In the simple case, the plaintiff presents a case and the defendant responds. In a case with many defendants, cross-claims, counterclaims, and third-party claims, the judge has to decide the order in which issues will be presented and attorneys will examine witnesses.

The Burdens of Proof, Going Forward, and Persuasion

In a "slip-and-fall" case, the defendant, owner of the premises, may claim that the plaintiff's injury was his own fault, caused by the plaintiff's failure to exercise reasonable care. The defendant is saying that the plaintiff should have watched his step. The defendant has the *burden of proof* of such contributory negligence. However, before the defendant has to prove anything, the plaintiff has the *burden of going forward* with proof that the defendant had a duty to the plaintiff to maintain the premises free of the hazard alleged to have caused the slip and fall, and also proof of his own freedom from carelessness causing his injury.

This is mumbo-jumbo of the first order. It means that the plaintiff has to show that he was as careful as a reasonably prudent ordinary man would be in similar circumstances. If the defendant claims that the plaintiff failed to exercise due care, then the defendant's proof has to be stronger than the plaintiffs. In legal jargon, the defendant has the burden of proof of the affirmative defense of contributory negligence. And the burden of proof differs, depending on the type of case: beyond a reasonable doubt for criminal matters; a mere preponderance of the evidence in most civil matters. Such jargon determines the outcome of a case when neither side has overwhelming proof. The judge needs a pretrial memorandum because all this legal mumbo-jumbo is too complicated to figure out in the courtroom while the trial is going on.

The important question is hidden in discussions about who has the burden of proof and the burden of going forward. Juries reach verdicts which determine who gets the money. You need to understand who has the *burden of persuasion*. In personal-injury cases, the plaintiff always has the basic burden of proof and going forward. For example, in a case where a railroad train ran into a car at a grade crossing, killing the husband and crippling a couple of children, the widow had to prove negligence and damages. The real burden, that of persuasion, was on the railroad. The railroad had to persuade the jury that, despite the terrible injuries, no money should be paid to the grieving widow or her children.

The pretrial memorandum, whatever form it takes under the local rules, is the inventory or "bill of materials" from which your case is built. What is not on the list cannot be used. Study the memorandum carefully to see if your attorney understands what the case is about, and what the proof means.

The Judicial Art

Once the trial memorandum has been submitted to the court, the court becomes a major player in the process. The judge will be involved in everything that happens from here on.

Citizens are summoned to jury duty for cases on the docket of a term of court. Jury panels of from 20 to 60 members, from which 12 or 6 will be selected, are held in dreary waiting rooms, then herded into courtrooms where they are selected in a process that is at best degrading. In a metropolitan courthouse, there may be as many as 400 persons called to serve as jurors on the first working day of any month. As a matter of constitutional law, jury panels must be selected in some random manner. All the important people—physicians, lawyers, CPAs, and CEOs— try to get excused. The effect is that jury panels end up being biased toward the lower end of the economic scale. Jurors are paid a pittance, often not enough to cover their parking, but in the aggregate a large item in the court's budget. Judges see juries as costly, and are embarrassed at the amount of time wasted by jurors who are waiting around for something to happen.

The last thing the judge wants to happen is to get a jury panel in and then not have any cases for it to try. That wastes the jury fees, as well as an available courtroom and judge. Judges are just like CEOs when it comes to productivity. Therefore, most judges will schedule many cases for trial on the first day of the term.

The pretrial conference, with its memorandum, was invented to ensure that cases are actually ready for trial. There was once a problem of attorneys asking for continuances on the trial day. Today, the pretrial conference has practically eliminated such requests for continuances, which are rarely granted.

Still, the practice of setting many cases on one day continues. There are many variations. Some courts set seven cases for the first day and perhaps five cases for the second day. If all the cases settle on the first day, perhaps even after the trial starts, jurors can be called back to start cases on the second day. Other courts set all of the cases on the first day, in order of date filed, or likelihood of settlement, or whim, and try them in that order until the month runs out and the jury panel is released. You may be set as the eighth case on the first Monday in the month, held for trial until the last working day in the month, and then find that your case is to be reset at some future court term. During that entire time, the attorney has to stand ready, with witnesses on call.

The reason that judges set so many cases for trial on the same day is that most cases settle, many "on the courthouse steps." Calendars that show 10 or 12 cases on Friday afternoon may shrink to five or six cases by nine o'clock on Monday. As the judge starts to call prospective jurors into the courtroom for the jury selection process, (the questioning of jurors is called *voir dire*), the lawyers ask for a few minutes. An auction is going on. When a price that each attorney can sell to his client has been reached, the case settles. Judges want cases to settle. When such last-minute "caving in" goes on all day, however, all of the cases that were ready for trial may be disposed of without any actual use of the expensive jury. That irritates judges.

The problem of last-minute settlements is now attacked in the pretrial conference. The judge may get directly involved, or refer the parties to another judge who conducts a settlement conference. Court-annexed arbitration, mediation referrals, "summary jury trials," or simple head-knocking are used to force a settlement. At this point, your "settlement posture" had better be well defined and justified by careful consideration of the facts and the law. The courts punish any party that appears stubborn or unreasonable in refusing to settle. The trial order is under consideration, and the court can rule against a recalcitrant party on many points. A well-reasoned settlement posture must be presented to avoid the judge "fixing" the trial against you.

Parties move toward settlement as they become aware of what can and cannot be proven and reevaluate their positions accordingly. Most parties start lawsuits with optimism which gradually erodes as the proof emerges. At the same time, the expense, mostly attorneys' fees, tends to wear down the enthusiasm of the parties.

The most common form of judicial involvement in settlement is the "mandatory settlement conference." This may be informal, but it always involves a requirement that the attorney or other representative for each party appear with "authority" to enter into a settlement agreement. This poses a special problem for attorneys who represent government agencies where there is no one person with real authority. Where the agency's authority can be exercised only by a committee that is subject to audits and controls, the attorneys have sometimes been fined for failure to obtain "authority." With private parties, the judge may insist that the CEO be at court or available by telephone.

The conference begins with the judge asking "What's this case all about?" Usually he will give each attorney a few minutes to lay out the reasons why his client should prevail. Then the questions start. It is soon clear that the judge's first question was only a gambit to get things started, since the judge's familiarity with the court file soon becomes apparent. After the discussions have settled down, the judge may hint to the parties what he thinks the likely outcome of the case will be. Since the judge is going to run the trial, his prophesy tends to be self-fulfilling. The judge will send the attorneys out to talk among themselves, then he will talk to the attorneys one at a time, and then he will get everybody together again. This is a good time for the judge to rule on some pending motions and requests for jury instructions. Sometimes the trial date can be reset for maximum inconvenience to either or both parties. Motions to limit proof or to sanction discovery abuse are sometimes ruled upon in a manner that suggests that failure to settle, well before the jury is empaneled, will have unpleasant consequences. At this point, if your settlement posture is not well founded, it will fall apart.

Some federal court judges have been experimenting with a process that goes by the name "summary jury trial." The court selects six jurors from a panel drawn for a pending term. The jurors are given some instructions, but they are not told that their decision will not be binding. Then each side is given a limited time, usually 1 hour, in which to make a presentation. As a practical matter, there is nothing to prevent attorneys from making arguments that are not supported by evidence, which is a serious flaw. The jury is instructed by the judge on the law and retires to deliberate. After the jury reports its findings, it is discharged. The summary jury is useful in that the parties get to see their attorneys in action. Seeing the live presentation is often a disappointment. The jury findings show how persuasive the attorneys are with jurors drawn from a typical panel in that court. The only purpose of the exercise is to motivate parties to settle.

The Trial

The first day of a major trial is usually taken up with jury selection. Traditionally, trial attorneys used the *voir dire* to establish rapport with the people chosen to hear the case. The attorneys would ask questions and listen to the answers, looking for people who might be sympathetic to their client's cause. In recent years, most federal judges and some state judges have taken over the *voir dire,* not permitting any questioning of jurors by the attorneys. The judge asks the questions suggested by the attorneys, but there is no opportunity to follow up and expose bias or prejudice.

After a period of questioning, the attorneys can reject prospective jurors for cause, usually a fixed opinion about the case or a close relationship with one party. The attorneys also may reject a few prospective jurors without cause, an exercise of intuition. Picking juries is a dying art. With individual attorneys trying so few cases, the limited interplay permitted by the judges, and the secrecy of jury deliberations, it is difficult to gauge whether any particular choice was good or not.

The trial begins with logistics problems. Arrangements must be made to get witnesses to the courthouse at the time they will be called. When a case is on hold waiting for the judge and jury, the witnesses are also on hold. Transportation, food, and lodging must be attended to. Careful attorneys make sure that witnesses do not drink at lunch before testifying. Some witnesses need continuous preparation and conditioning to keep their wits about them when they are on the stand.

The fancy graphics, easels, overhead projectors, big-screen televisions, and computer simulations require transportation, parking, porters to get them into the courthouse and remove them, the proper extension cords, blinds for the windows, and other extraneous paraphernalia that has nothing to do with the business of the law. In many courthouses this process must be repeated at the end and beginning of every trial day. As in any business, ordinary ideas effectively executed will beat great ideas that are never presented.

It is an ancient and honored rule that testifying witnesses are *sequestered*. The purpose of sequestration is to prevent witnesses from hearing each others' testimony. Witnesses will subconsciously adjust their testimony to be consistent with other testimony with which they agree and to contradict more forcefully any testimony with which they disagree. The theory is that the jury will find the truth in the differences of the testimony of witnesses. An exception is made for the actual parties and a single corporate representative sitting with the corporation's attorney.

Attorney performance pays off in the courtroom. Witnesses who have told their whole story and have been looked after and prepared emotionally and factually generally testify accurately.

The Rules of Evidence

The *rules of evidence* are often discussed and rarely understood. The purpose of the rules is to prevent witnesses from making statements that cannot be tested for truthfulness. The basic rule against hearsay is based on the impossibility of asking questions of someone who is not in the court in order to find out what they meant when they said something. Your report of what someone else said is proof that the statement was made, but not that the statement was correct. The basic idea of the rules of evidence is to require a connection between the evidence presented and the real-world truth.

As a practical matter, the rules of evidence require that a witness testify, from direct personal knowledge, to every important point in the presentation of the case. For example, your attorney might want to show that sales increased steadily, month by month, until a competitor marketed a confusingly similar "copycat" product. A graph is a good way to do that. To get the graph into evidence, she will have to prove the monthly sales figures. She might do that by introducing original business records, supported by the testimony of the custodian of the record who can testify that the record entries were made by persons with knowledge in the course of regularly conducted business activity. The evidence of the regular business practice is part of the foundation required to place the graph in evidence. Judges prefer to have parties stipulate to such dull evidence, to speed up the trial and keep the jury's attention.

The rules also limit the form of questions. The information presented to the jury should come from the witness's answers and not the attorney's questions. A "leading" question is easy to recognize: "Was the light red when you first saw it?" The not leading form would be: "What color was the light when you first saw it?" More subtle are questions which assume facts not in evidence: "When did you stop beating your wife?" Judges ordinarily allow broad leeway in the form of questions permitted in order to speed up the proceedings.

The attorney–client privilege discussed in Chap. 8 is part of the law of evidence. Privilege limits what the jury is allowed to consider. Another limitation is the concept of relevance. *Relevant* means having a tendency to make a fact important to the outcome more probable or less probable than it would otherwise be. In other words, does the evidence offered have value in deciding the questions in the case? Offers of compromise made in settlement negotiations, as suggested in Chap. 10, may be excluded from evidence on relevance grounds.

The actual role of the law of evidence is to keep both the attorneys and the judges within reasonable bounds of fairness in the conduct of the trial. The judge has broad discretion in evidence rulings. He can exclude evidence on the rather vague grounds of danger of unfair prejudice, confusion of the issues, misleading, waste of time, undue delay, or repetition. In order to be able to appeal from an evidence ruling, the attorney must immediately "make a record" stating the specific ground of the objection or the exact nature and import of evidence excluded.

The Art of Advocacy

The trial attorney cannot use any help in her most important job, advocacy. Who would suggest that a patient's accountant should be at the shoulder of a brain surgeon and make suggestions as to how the knife should be held, or what brain matter should be cut away? The trial attorneys's position is like the surgeon's. Much of the art of persuasion is subliminal. The attorney's personal credibility is central to the fact finder's determination of issues. Much depends on appearances and style. Different localities seem to call for different styles, but individuals do well in every locality with a wide variety of styles.

The trial attorney is busy, especially if she looks relaxed. She has to listen to the questions for possible objections, listen to the answer for responsiveness, watch the judge and jury for the impact of the evidence, plan her next move, and continuously communicate with the jury by her body language. She must be wary of every thing she has an opportunity to say, because you are bound by her every word, and any concession is the same as absolute proof on the conceded point. If you are sitting with your attorney, she may ask you to avoid distracting her by not talking to her, but only writing her notes.

If you attend a trial as an interested party, you will learn that witnesses are unpredictable. Supposedly neutral witnesses, friends of parties, even police officers, will shade the truth in an attempt to make the case come out the right way. Beyond deliberate lies, witnesses tend to change their testimony when it is presented in court, making it more or less emphatic and definite under the threat of cross-examination. Often, witnesses forget what they previously claimed to know. Witnesses project their emotional state, anger or fear, altering the impact of the words they use.

The attorney must grasp what the jury is absorbing from the witness, and by asking questions, give the witness opportunities to say things that will make the truth obvious. Jurors often comment that they are frustrated because they cannot ask questions and the question they wanted to ask goes unspoken. Such questions may go unasked because they call for inadmissible evidence.

Listening to the adversary drone on with one dull question after another is bad enough, but the attorney must analyze each question to determine if the appropriate answer will be admissible. A question may be objectional because of its form—for example, because it is leading—or because of its content—for example, assuming facts not in evidence—or because it calls for an inadmissible answer—for example, hearsay. The objection is lost if it is not made before the answer is given.

Your attorney also must decide whether or not to make objections. Objections always offend the jury, because it looks as if something is being hidden. Leading questions, otherwise objectional, may speed up testimony and are favored by judges for that reason. Even gross hearsay may be harmless if it is about a point that is not in contention. The mode and method of objecting is a matter of the trial attorney's personal style, and the attorney's feel for the judge's attitude. Most attorneys try to make only those objections the judge will sustain.

Judicial Trial Styles

Whatever the attorney's style is, she must adapt it to the particular judge hearing the case. Judges do not like to hear trials. All trials are boring and inefficient. All judges are impatient, biased against your attorney, and anxious to get on to other things. Judges work only a few hours each day. They start late, break often, and quit early. In reality, this is to keep the jury from exploding. Even with the best coordination, 12 bladders permit only a few working hours each day.

As the trial goes on, the judge will be called upon to handle other matters during the lunch hour and breaks. An efficient and hardworking judge will hear other matters at eight o'clock, have a daily conference with the attorneys at nine o'clock to dispose of developing problems, start hearing evidence at 9:15 and go till midmorning, handle motions in other cases during the break, try the case until lunch, handle other cases or go make a political speech or otherwise utilize the lunch hour, and work the jury through the afternoon with one break. Quitting at about five o'clock lets the jurors go home, while the judge spends an hour or two reading briefs and deciding motions in other cases. On days that the jury works six clock hours, the judge works at least nine. Judges do not like to waste time, or to have their time wasted.

The judge dominates the courtroom. He sits at an elevated bench. His comings and goings are announced by the bailiff. He rules on motions and objections. He decides when breaks may be taken. He wears a black robe, and is permitted to speak directly to the jury and respond to their questions. The jurors trust him, and generally assume that there is a good reason when he is irritable, rude, or unfair.

The Jury Sleeps

Some judges will select juries for several cases early in the term, thus permitting the release of jurors who are called but not chosen. Then the lawyers and the jurors chosen for each case are held on standby, waiting for the judge and his courtroom to become available. The alternative is for jurors to report daily to a holding area from which they are drawn in panels for selection. Either way, by the time the trial starts, the jurors have been inconvenienced and discomforted.

Jurors sleep during trials. Sometimes they are totally unconscious, at other times their minds are simply wandering. Trials are incredibly boring. The attorneys are involved in the testimony, but what the jury sees and hears is people talking. The true value of graphics and demonstrative evidence is in giving jurors something on which to focus. A jury is a group of people thrown together to hear the case, and instructed not to discuss it with each other, or any one else, until all of the evidence is in and they are "charged." The group dynamics are about what you would expect to find on a city bus. Some are bright and articulate, others are slow-witted and dull. Some are stubborn, others are indecisive. Some become interested in the case, others never concern themselves with the facts or the law.

The realities about juries have led trial attorneys to the conclusion that the opening and closing statements of the case are very important in determining the outcome. Also, some attorneys like to use an "expert" witness to give a kind of summary of the evidence in the case under the guise of a factual basis of a hypothetical question. For this use, the expert's ability to present well is more important than his technical skill or knowledge. Attorneys know that evidence must be kept simple. Any theory that is presented to a jury must be clear and simple or it is worthless.

When the evidence is all in, and the attorneys have given their final arguments, the judge *charges* the jury by reading the *instructions*. The instructions are statements of propositions of law. Jury instructions are almost unintelligible, difficult even for attorneys trained in the law to understand. The attorneys and judges have labored over the instructions to ensure that they state the law correctly and are supported by evidence in the record. In some jurisdictions, judges comment on the evidence. That means the judge tells the jury what the court thinks the answer ought to be.

The jury then retires to deliberate. Juries do not decide who is telling the truth, or if a product is defective, or what a person really intended. Juries decide who wins the case. The technical issues may have a truth of their own, but the jury, by definition, decides how the case comes out.

In a medical malpractice case, an expert took the stand and with great confidence stated a conclusion that was not supported by the facts or medical theory. Medical terms have intricate sounds and precise definitions. The opposing attorney had studied carefully, consulting his own experts and reading the current medical literature. Under cross-examination, the attorney forced the expert to accept all of the published articles that contradicted him, and acknowledge the facts pointing to an opposite conclusion. Throughout, the expert smiled and spoke with a warm, resonant voice. All of the technical esoterica went right over the jury's head. The attorney, engaged in a battle of wits with the expert, lost touch with the jury and lost the case.

For a long or complicated trial, you might hire a "shadow jury." A shadow jury is a small group, perhaps three or four persons, selected to match the psychological profile of the actual jury. They sit in the courtroom and listen to the case. During breaks and in the evenings, the shadow jury tells the trial attorney what is unclear and what questions are developing in their thinking. This is not a new technique. Trials have always attracted spectators from whom clever lawyers have always sought feedback. This is especially useful if your trial attorney has had little experience with the local jurors.

Verdicts, Judgments, and Appeals

The jury's verdict may be a single decision of who wins and how much, or it may be answers to a series of questions, written out on a jury verdict form, depending on the judge's instructions. The verdict returned by the jury is not the judgment of the court. After the jury has been discharged, the judge will hear motions for a "judgment notwithstanding the verdict" and then formally enter the judgment of the court.

When a judgment is entered against you, there are several decisions to be made quickly. You can accept the judgment, or you can seek redress on appeal.

If you lose at trial, a decision must be made about your legal representation. The practice of law at the appellate level is a specialty with absolute time limits and obscure rules. An appellate specialist can be found by regular outside counsel or another attorney using networks or electronic databases. Get a specialist quickly, but do not fire your trial attorney. Have the appellate specialist supervise the trial attorney through the filing of the notice of appeal and designation of the record. Then, remove the trial attorney from that case. A trial attorney handling an appeal is defending and justifying his tactics and performance. Cold objectivity is required for appellate success.

If you want appellate review, you must decide if the existing record covers the necessary points. Within 10 days a motion for a new trial may be used to get new material before the court. However, such a motion limits the appeal to matters raised in the motion. A notice of appeal does not have to specify the grounds for appeal, and you have 30 days to prepare it.

The appellant must tell the court what points are to be considered on appeal. The other side may cross-appeal and raise additional issues. Then the side making the appeal must tell the trial court clerk what makes up the record to be sent to the appellate court, with the other side free to add anything that is left out. The appellant usually must pay in advance for a transcript of the testimony and proceedings. The record, including the transcript, must be completed and forwarded by the court's clerical staff within a time limit or the appeal will be dismissed. Getting the court's clerks to move promptly is a challenge in itself.

If the record is completed on time and submitted, the parties have the opportunity to write legal briefs to explain to the appellate court why the process in the trial court did not conform to existing law or why the law should be changed. These briefs are first read by law clerks employed by the court, who prepare an analysis on which judges seem to rely. The judges decide whether or not they will hear oral argument, something that occurs in fewer and fewer cases as caseloads increase. The decision of the appellate court is rendered in the form of an opinion, which is published if it is deemed to elaborate or change the law.

In some courts, appeals linger on for years. In the quickest courts, expect at least 15 months for the appeal to the intermediate court, and about as long for each further appeal.

When a judgment is entered in your favor, you need to collect the money. An appeal does not itself stop the collection process. The enforcement of a judgment is ordinarily "stayed" when the party taking an appeal posts a bond. After an appeal, the bond makes collection straightforward. If there is no bond, collection of the judgment requires a reconversion of the legal matter to a real-world reality.

Enforcing the Judgment

The court's final judgment, by itself, does nothing. Obtaining the judgment only begins the process of enforcement. The judgment must be properly documented, a simple but essential procedure that may be overlooked. The judgment is enforced by the sheriff acting under an *execution,* which is authority to seize assets and sell them. The sheriff will be glad to help, the office being supported in part by the poundage fees earned, but will expend no effort to find assets. A judgment filed in a county where the judgment debtor owns real estate creates a lien.

Collecting any money requires that assets be located so the sheriff can be directed to sell them, and the judgment can be filed in the counties where the debtor owns real estate. The judgment debtor can be called into court and examined under oath about assets. Lying can be punished as contempt of court or as the crime of perjury. Few debtors spend time in jail for concealing assets.

Practically speaking, judgments can be collected from debtors who have net assets you can locate and seize. The "deep pocket" is important to attorneys not because of the depth of the pocket, but because of the contents. An insurance policy is such an asset. Most insurance companies will fight bitterly over coverage, the obligation to pay, even after defending the lawsuit. Even if they are held liable, insurers may hold onto the money beyond any reasonable processing period. However, unless they go out of business first, insurers do eventually pay up. Successful business concerns will also pay judgments to avoid being put out of operation.

Typical of uncollectible judgments is the case of an elderly woman who was injured in a "slip-and-fall" incident at a health spa. The liability was based on allowing soapy water to accumulate on the floor at the entrance to the shower room. The case was defended at trial by an attorney retained by the insurer. A jury awarded several thousand dollars. The insurance company was placed in receivership by the state authorities, having no substantial assets. This claim, like many others, was put on the list to be paid if any assets turned up. The spa went out of business, having sold its membership list. The building was leased. The equipment was covered by the bank's lien. Unpaid taxes took the next priority.

The debtor who is willing to sacrifice all to a "scorched earth" policy can frustrate judgment creditors. A real estate developer, having been through more than one boom-and-bust cycle, adopted practices that have permitted him to continue functioning despite millions of dollars in judgments against him, many owned by the FDIC. Throughout the cycle, the cash that comes out of the business is spent, or given to his spouse or his children's trust. All taxes are paid in full, the IRS being a ruthless collector. The expensive car and fancy office furnishings are leased. The prestigious architects, engineers, planning consultants, and appraisers are paid lavishly and in full, as is the loyal secretary. He distributes cash and tax benefits to favored limited partners, keeping them out of the bad deals. What he owns himself is either exempt from execution, or of such a personal nature, clothing and the like, that its value at a sheriff's sale is less than the cost of gathering it up for auction. When boom times return, his consultants, loyal secretary, and favored partners are happy to work with him again.

Often individual debtors use the time gained by defending the lawsuit to place their assets beyond reach. Every state reserves some assets as exempt. Cash can be expended on pleasures or education. Attorneys, of course, have to be paid. When you come to collect the judgment, bankruptcy beckons.

Corporate debtors also frustrate creditors. While the lawsuit is pending, the cash is drained. New, leased equipment is obtained and old equipment is liquidated. The building is mortgaged to its full value. Vendors are reminded to perfect purchase money security interests, and the banker is given a lien on everything else. The only net value is in the customer list and the operating know-how. When you show up to collect, the bankruptcy court protects continuing operations with a reorganization under Chapter 11 of the bankruptcy code. As an unsecured creditor, you will be paid, if at all, only on a par with other unsecured creditors. If the creditors force a liquidation of the corporation, under Chapter 7 of the bankruptcy code, the owner may still be able to start again with the customer list and the know-how.

Winning a total victory at the courthouse may hold little actual reward. That legal victory may mean nothing in the real world, where circumstances continue to change throughout the time taken for litigation to grind out a legal solution. Delay, distraction of management, disruption of relationships, defamation of your reputation, and disclosure of your business affairs have to be added to the out-of-pocket dollars in weighing the costs of litigation against the real-world truth that judgment day is not payday.

1. Pretrial memorandum, 6 week lead time
   List:
      Agreed facts (stipulations)
      Exhibits (documents and things)
      Witnesses (substance of testimony)
   Explain:
      Factual contentions
      Requested questions for jurors (*voir dire*)
      Requested instructions to jurors
      Evidence to be excluded (motion *in limine*)

2. Settlement conferences with court
   State basis of settlement posture
   Resist pressure to make concessions
   Send representative with authority to settle.

3. Logistics
   Deliver equipment and material to courtroom:
   Have witnesses ready:
      Attorney has heard witnesses' entire story
      Attorney has prepared witnesses factually
      Attorney has prepared witnesses psychologically
      Witnesses know when and where to appear
      Witnesses provided with parking, meals, housing
      Witnesses kept occupied

4. Trial proceedings
   Jury selection (*voir dire*)
   Opening statements
   Examination of witnesses:
      Direct, then cross-examination
      Objections
      Do not distract your attorney.
   Closing statements
   Jury instructions and deliberation
   Verdict

5. Judgment and appeal
   Motion for new trial if record inadequate
   Notice of appeal within absolute time limit
   Preparation of record for appellate court
   Briefs
   Oral argument
   Decision and mandate

6. Execution of judgment:
   Locate assets for sheriff's execution
   Bankruptcy may prevent collection.

Procedure: Trial practice.

13
Getting Off the Litigation Merry-Go-Round: Alternative Dispute Resolution

You only end up in court on a business deal when you have failed. It was either a bad deal in the first place, or someone is trying to welsh, or something basic to the deal has changed. In court, you are saying, in effect, "Judge, I am not up to running this business, so you do it for me." Similarly, with a personal-injury claim, failure to settle means that someone is saying: "Judge, I don't understand the facts, explain them to me."

How and Why of Alternative Dispute Resolution

Litigation, the filing of a lawsuit, is a calling upon the power of the state to enforce private rights. The sovereign's force is mighty, and its use against some of the sovereign's subjects for the benefit of other subjects is hemmed in and limited by the procedures and burdens of the law. It is safeguards, and their excessive use by lawyers, that make the law so tiresome, expensive, and slow. Without the safeguards, naked power would be swift to mete out what seemed to be justice to those who controlled the power. You might like to have that power at your command, but you would not much care for being subject to it. There must be safeguards in a system that depends on the consent of the governed. The burden of the safeguards can be avoided by using other methods to settle disputes. You will have more resources available for your real business, if you can get your disputes settled fairly.

As the 1980s came to a close, the leaders of the organized bar began to tout "alternative dispute resolution." They recognized that the legal profession is beginning to price itself, and its clients, out of the market. American businesspeople cannot bear the costs of the legal system and still remain competitive in a world economy. The cost of litigation must be reduced, and the business community must find other ways to get things done. Actually, the state's power is applied only in those very few cases when a case is tried, a verdict rendered, and a judgment entered. In cases that are settled, the state's power is used only as a threat or goad to drive the parties to resolve their differences between or among themselves.

Alternative dispute resolution(ADR) techniques include negotiation, conciliation, mediation, minitrials, and nonbinding arbitration. Mandatory settlement conferences, mandatory court-annexed nonbinding arbitration, and summary jury trials are actually devices used by judges to coerce settlements in pending litigation. Binding arbitration is a system that short-circuits the litigation process but relies on the power of the state for enforcement.

Binding Arbitration

Binding arbitration commonly means arbitration according to the rules and procedures of an organization such as the American Arbitration Association. The role of the arbitration organization is to provide a set of rules, and a panel of arbitrators, for a small fee. An agreement to arbitrate must either specify a complete set of rules and a method for selecting the arbitrator, or refer to an established arbitration organization.

Arbitration has an ancient history. It was rediscovered by reformers in the early part of the twentieth century. It is a contract by which the parties agree to select someone to whom they give the power to decide their disputes. Like any other contract, it can be breached. A party can refuse to submit to the arbitration or can refuse to abide by the decision. The performing party may then sue. The lawsuit enforces the arbitrator's decision without rehashing the underlying dispute. Some courts were offended by the idea that parties would agree to seek justice elsewhere and refused to enforce arbitration agreements. This was overcome at both the state and federal levels by statutes which provide that, where there is a valid arbitration agreement, the arbitrator's decision must be adopted and enforced by the court except in extraordinary circumstances.

There are some problems with arbitration. The quality of the panels of prospective arbitrators is not consistent. Where arbitration is used frequently—in labor relations and the construction industry, for example—the quality of the panels reflects the wisdom born of experience. In geographic areas where arbitration is uncommon or for new or unique cases, there are difficulties in finding arbitrators with experience and a track record. Arbitrators are expected to rely on their own knowledge and expertise. Expertise gained by working in an industry usually comes with a bias. Arbitration shortens the process, limiting the development of the factual background and the legal implications. There is no appeal from the arbitrators' decision except for misconduct. Arbitrators have a tendency to split the differences between the parties, imposing compromises, especially with numbers. These considerations have lead many businesspeople and most lawyers to avoid binding arbitration.

When arbitration is imposed in one-sided transactions—residential home sales contracts and securities brokerage agreements, for example—they seem to be very advantageous to the side doing the imposing. It is rarely to your advantage to accept an arbitration clause proposed by a party with more power than you. The arbitration clause prevents you from using an attorney to shift the power in the transaction.

In industries where binding arbitration between equally powerful parties is established as the common practice, it works well. It is most effective where disputes are expected at the time the contract is formed, prompt resolution is required, the parties have a continuing relationship, and the subject matter of the disputes is unlikely to put either party out of business. The statutes under which arbitration awards are enforced have intricate technicalities in which a misstep may cause the loss of any benefits. Arbitration results may be unsatisfactory where the applicable law is unsettled, the pertinent facts disputed, the survival of either party is at stake, or the relative strengths of the parties are out of balance.

Arbitration is best seen as a form of short-circuited litigation in which you give up the right to a judge and jury, and appellate review, in exchange for low cost and speed. The technical requirements for enforcing arbitration awards require that it be handled as carefully as any other litigation process.

Alternatives to Litigation

Difficulties come up in the real world. You may work out the dispute, surrender, or resort to violence. Litigation is yet another option. ADR is the current buzzword for methodical approaches to helping parties reach an agreement which settles the dispute.

The court process is imperfect. Many court decisions are made for the wrong reasons and reach the wrong result. When a case turns on a technical or scientific question, which is common in product-liability cases, the jury is deciding science, not understanding science. The very concept of "cause" in the legal system becomes "proximate cause," a form of circular reasoning that leaves the outcome of the case to the common sense of the jury. Where the issue turns on who is telling the truth, the most accomplished liar often wins. Judges and jurors are sometimes prejudiced in ways they do not themselves understand. Leaving the case to the judge and jury is an admission by businesspeople that the judge and jury in their ignorance know better than the businesspeople what is right.

There are more reasons than simple disdain for the legal system for businesspeople to settle their differences. The costs of litigation are often disproportionate to the values in dispute. The expenses measured in dollars are substantial, particularly when the lawyers are unwilling or unable to stipulate to the truth of routine matters. Not counted in dollars are the effects of distraction of management, disruption of relationships, defamation of the company, disclosure of confidential matters, and delay, discussed in Chap. 18. Many disputes arise from misunderstandings and mistakes which, if litigated, may ripen into bad precedent that will have a lingering effect.

The power of the state is most needed when you are dealing with a crook or a deadbeat. Some people do not pay and do not intend to pay. Even then, you may net more money by accepting less than you are owed, especially if it comes from a third party. Even deadbeats will pay you something to get you off their back.

If one party to the transaction is powerless, he or she may need to invoke the power of the state. For example, the injured victim of a defective product has little negotiating power short of a jury verdict, especially as new legal rights are evolving. A total failure of communications, something that happens in corporations where messages do not get through to the top management, is sometimes overcome only with the service of a summons. In such situations, litigation may be necessary to create an environment in which the parties can work out their differences. It is in this context that the lawyers speak of alternative dispute resolution.

Putting ADR into Agreements

The concepts of ADR can be incorporated in agreements to create an environment in which disputes are settled. International transactions are conducted successfully without any sovereign power standing by to enforce rights. This is possible because of the honor of the individuals, and their memories. If you choose to do business with crooks and cheats, you ought not to complain when they do not perform.

Beyond honor, however, certain principles guide the formation of workable agreements. Disputes arise out of misunderstandings, compounded by disappointment and anger at the unpleasant surprise. Every assumption that is not made is a dispute avoided. Every question answered before the deal is closed does not have to be asked afterward. Lawyers look for such questions.

In an ordinary transaction, when lawyers negotiate and bargain on every point, they are called "deal killers." In reality, the lawyers are killing the bad deals. Doing business with a "good old boy" whose "word is his bond" is an invitation to a misunderstanding and loss. Lawyers produce good contracts in three ways: by ensuring that there is an actual agreement that can be performed on both sides; by ensuring that the agreement is broad enough so that when the unexpected occurs the parties can work out a fair sharing of the burdens or benefits; and by writing it all down so clearly that there can be no misunderstanding.

Make your lawyer effective. Get her into the deal from the beginning. Keep your lawyer out of the role of advocate by using her as a coach. Before starting the negotiations, ask your lawyer what she thinks you need. As the deal develops, consult constantly. Some lawyers develop negotiating skills that can be very useful; others will ruin everything every time. Some parties fear lawyers, either because they feel incompetent themselves or because they are afraid the lawyers will upset their scheme to cheat you. Most parties will call in their lawyer if they see your lawyer is present. So use some discretion in actually bringing your lawyer to the table. The lawyer's best role is understanding the big picture and counseling you about your potential needs and interests.

Before the deal is set, have your lawyer start drafting the agreement. Use the drafts in the negotiations, modifying as you go. When the writing is complete and accepted by each party, sign it. If you make a deal and then turn it over to the lawyers to work out the details, the lawyers assume an advocacy role and seek to gain an advantage on your behalf. That way you start having disputes before the deal is even signed. If you get the deal written up and then give it to your lawyer to look over, all he can do is check the spelling and grammar, tell you what the papers say, and recommend that you sign (unlikely) or not sign. Anything else requires that the deal be changed. Good advice at that point merely starts disputes.

Every contract should define clearly and explicitly the duties and obligations of the parties. Contracts can also incorporate dispute-resolution tools. An example is a provision that payments will be made upon completion and acceptance of various stages of a project. If the work is unsatisfactory, payment can be withheld until the problem is resolved, balancing the risk of non-completion with the risk of non-payment. Another example is a percentage retention from progress payments pending satisfactory completion. Or, the contract may set up a panel of managers, who are not directly involved, to review contract discrepancies. That way, people with decision-making power are involved before the problems ripen into disputes and before emotions and resources are committed to positions. The use of third-party institutions to disburse funds (banks) or to hold finished goods (warehousers), guarantees and letters of credit, and transfers of technology or data are other typical examples of what amount to exchanging hostages to ensure performance. Such protocols equalize the relative power of the parties so that they can work out their differences together, without the intervention of the state.

In a contract where both parties face unknown risks, a provision for mediation should be considered. Providing for mediation in contracts avoids the risk that the suggestion of its use will be taken as a sign of weakness after a problem has developed. A mediation provision may require the completion of mediation as a condition precedent to the enforcement of the contract by legal process, specifying the procedures to be followed. Of course, that will delay a party seeking to enforce the contract and benefit a party seeking delay.

Advantages of ADR

Litigation offers a narrow range of simple solutions to a broad range of complex problems. Business disputes arise in the real world, with its endless variety of people, places, and things. The legal world is an abstraction, grossly simplified. The real world has the intricacy and detail of a view from a tall building, the legal world is by comparison like a comic strip in the Sunday newspaper. The legal world offers only simple remedies, principally the award of money damages, or occasionally an order that someone do or stop doing a specific act. Between themselves, the parties have much more flexibility in "setting things right."

That the parties can work out settlements far superior to any court-imposed remedy is illustrated by a "take-or-pay" case. An electric utility company refused to accept or pay for quantities of coal that it had contracted to purchase over a long term. The contract price seemed unfairly high in a falling market. The coal mine had been opened in reliance on that contract. A court's only remedy for breach of contract is to award money damages. An amount of money damages sufficient to cover the cash-flow requirements of the investment in the coal mine would have bankrupted the utility company. The seller accepted a lower price and slower deliveries over a longer term, which protected the investment in the coal mine.

Litigation is adversarial and often bitter. The truthfulness of each witness is questioned. The fact of a lawsuit is itself an accusation of dishonesty. Customers are hard to find, and a customer relationship is a valuable business asset. A lawsuit will destroy such a relationship. Resolving a dispute by an agreement between the parties offers as least a hope of ending the problem without ending the relationship.

Litigation takes place in a public forum. Occasionally a judge will attempt to "seal" a file to protect its confidentiality, but judges have no authority to do so. Testimony is given in open court, which the public may attend. Being involved in a lawsuit is not good for your general reputation, even if you have no secrets to reveal. Reaching an agreement keeps a dispute a private matter, between the parties.

Litigation is uncertain. The courts deliberately maintain uncertainty about the outcome of litigation. On its face, this practice is to avoid prejudging a case, before all the evidence has been heard. The parties incur 75 to 80 percent of their cost before the pretrial conference, while the court has expended very little time. Presenting the case to the jury imposes relatively little additional cost on the parties, but a relatively large additional burden on the court. The court is highly motivated to keep the outcome in doubt as a way of inducing settlements.

Litigation is expensive. When the parties reach an agreement, spending on legal fees should end. Litigation is the long way to a solution. Negotiation, conciliation, mediation, and minitrials are shortcuts to the ultimate termination of litigation, that point where all parties conform to a common understanding of reality, whether under the sheriff's compulsion or voluntary acceptance.

When ADR Is Effective

Unfortunately, the flexibility, friendliness, privacy, certainty, and low cost of alternative dispute resolution cannot always be realized. It works only when certain factors are present.

Good faith is absolutely necessary for ADR techniques to lead to a genuine solution. An adversary engaged in a program of asset hiding and dilatory practices is only playing for time. A debtor who could pay, but refuses, offers little potential for working things out. Where the claim involves criminal conduct, fear of prosecution may chill any settlement. However, a vendor or customer, despite appearing to have cheated you, may be willing to seek a solution in good faith. The bad conduct may have been motivated by an understandable mistake.

The ability of both parties to benefit is necessary to any ADR process. A company which is essentially defunct, where the officers are struggling to keep the payroll going so that they can collect a few more checks, has little incentive to transfer assets in satisfaction of a debt to you. Similarly, when a claimant's only hope is to hit the jackpot with his claim against you, there is little incentive to accept any offer you would consider reasonable, a common situation in punitive damages cases.

Some disputes arise from genuine conflict over what the law should be, quite apart from any emotional commitment of the parties. Such cases may require an appellate court opinion to establish precedent needed by the parties.

All the necessary parties to the dispute must be involved. Sometimes a necessary party is absent or incompetent, leaving litigation as the only means to force participation in the process. There can be no dispute resolution without communication. After the lawsuit gets under way, trial attorneys generally state that any offer to negotiate is a sign of weakness that will harden the resolve of the adversary. There is no reason to cut off communication with the adversary in business litigation. On the contrary, if you talk regularly to your adversary, about the lawsuit and other business matters, the problem of opening discussions is avoided. Of course, everything you say can and will be used against you, so avoid saying anything controversial. Ignore a refusal to talk based on the advice of an attorney. No matter, just keep trying. Actually, offers to open settlement discussions are usually a sign of strength, unless you have locked yourself into a demand for "unconditional surrender."

Applying ADR Methods

The failure of ADR to resolve all disputes can be attributed to errors in its application. The vast majority of disputes are worked out without the intervention of law or lawyers. Of those few disputes that become lawsuits, 95 percent settle. The successful application of ADR methods avoids costs. The sooner a settlement is reached, the more you save. As a client, you want to choose the ADR method that best serves your circumstances.

Enhanced Negotiation

Millions of problems are routinely solved by businesspeople through negotiation. When the ordinary negotiation process is working, there is no need for litigation. Problems that are out of the ordinary call for "enhanced" negotiation. The enhancement comes from introducing more people into the process and deliberately using negotiation techniques. The added people may be the trial attorneys, if a lawsuit has already been filed, or may be a higher level of management or in-house lawyers if litigation is merely threatened. Typical negotiating techniques include use of an agenda, issue and interest identification, formation of multiple solutions, and commitment to accept the best available solution.

In any such negotiation, there must be prior agreement that what happens in the sessions will not be deemed evidence of anything or a waiver of any right. If the lawsuit has been filed, the agreement must be incorporated in a court order entered by agreement of the parties. Conduct or statements made in compromise negotiations are not admissible in evidence under Rule 408 of the Federal Rules of Evidence and counterparts in most states. However, facts disclosed can and will be proven by other means. For example, if the boiler blew up, mentioning in settlement negotiations that the engineer told you that he had wired the safety valve shut will lead to a question in a deposition that elicits that same information. If there is a question of intent, a statement that you discussed something with your lawyer will lead to questions about what you told your lawyer, in your subsequent deposition, unless you have protected yourself against an implied waiver of the attorney–client privilege. If there is no lawsuit underway, the necessary agreement can be incorporated in the letter setting up the time and place of the meeting.

The persons who participate in such negotiations should avoid a "victory" orientation. The initial objective should be to find out what the parties actually disagree about, both factual and legal issues, and what each party thinks it wants. However, it may not be possible to get to those issues right away. Most trial attorneys are driven by their instincts to refuse to agree to anything suggested by the adversary. It is a reliable instinct that costs clients lots of money. Personalities are always a factor. Initially, there must be agreement on something, perhaps as simple as a place for a meeting. A fixed agenda will keep the discussion away from subjects that will generate hard feelings. As the parties develop the means to reach minor agreements, increasingly difficult issues can be addressed.

Conciliation

Negotiations are effective only if you can get them started. Conciliation is a way to "bring them to the table." A *conciliator* is a neutral third party who invites the disputants to a neutral meeting place. In the meeting, the conciliator helps the flow of communication. If the conciliator's wisdom and judgment are respected by the parties, they may avoid exaggeration and emotion in talking to each other. If the conciliator is patient, tolerant, open minded, and amiable, those qualities may be mimicked by the parties long enough to get the process launched.

In a dispute between a vendor and a purchaser, a supplier to the vendor or a customer to the purchaser might be a potential conciliator. The most likely prospects are people with a general desire to see the dispute settled but who are indifferent as to the outcome. If you have confidence in the good faith of the other party but cannot get negotiations started, you may be able to induce a third party to help. The conciliator has no need to get into the substance of the dispute. You may be able to find someone willing to serve in such a limited role.

Mediation

A more structured approach to negotiation is the use of *mediation*. Mediation may be distinguished from conciliation by the more active role taken by the mediator or "neutral." A mediator will provide feedback, direct the course of discussions, evaluate the merits of propositions, and suggest solutions. The term *mediation* suggests an element of persuasion and evaluation beyond what a conciliator is asked to do.

In the old days, when there were fewer lawyers and they all had to work together on one case after another, attorneys often functioned jointly as mediators. Retaining an air of professional objectivity, the attorneys could work out a just and fair outcome, consistent with the law, and persuade their clients to accept it. Before the era of time billing, working things out was the only way to make money. With larger numbers of lawyers, especially in big cities, time billing made being a difficult or tough negotiator more profitable. Many lawyers have abandoned the mediation role.

If there is no mediation provision in the contract, someone must propose the idea. Is the suggestion of mediation a sign of weakness? Timing is important. Perhaps such a suggestion early in the dispute implies less because the parties are less committed to their positions. It is important to point out to opposing attorneys that the parties retain total control of the mediation process and can always withdraw.

Once agreement to mediate has been reached, a mediator must be chosen and the ground rules established. The most effective mediator will have expertise in the process. Briefly, the process is conciliation, then negotiation, and finally commitment to a specific agreement, which is written down. Trained mediators will convert subjective demands into objective interests, dampen emotions, suggest solutions, and otherwise attempt to lead the parties to agreement. The mediator must be able to obtain the trust of the parties, particularly regarding neutrality and confidentiality.

Not every individual who is acceptable to the parties will make a good mediator. The basic skills of a mediator are psychological. As a go-between, the mediator has to decide just how the positions of the parties will be presented. Just as we hope that a mediator will make relations between the parties better, we need to fear that the mediator can make things worse by an unfortunate selection of points to emphasize. Mediation is a skill that requires training to develop an inborn talent.

There are several ways to locate qualified mediators. The American Bar Association publishes a list of sources of mediation services. Some states have enacted statutes which provide for mediation services ancillary to the court system. The state-supported systems are just gaining funding as the 1990s begin. The American Arbitration Association has formal rules for mediation of various types of disputes and panels of mediators available to serve. A development of the late 1980s was the emergence of commercial mediation services.

Successful mediation seems to require five things. The parties have to pay the mediator up front, so that the mediator has no stake in the outcome and neutrality is protected. The parties have to have a good-faith desire to reach an agreed resolution of the dispute. This is not a commitment to take any deal, but rather a commitment to accept a reasonable deal. The participants in the process must have authority to make a deal. If all of the authority is held back at headquarters, an accepted agreement may go cold before it is finalized. The participants must commit sufficient time to the process. An announcement at the beginning of a 10 a.m. mediation session that one participant must catch a 2 p.m. airplane is almost a guarantee of a wasted day. Finally, the mediator must be entrusted with control of the process, particularly with deciding if an impasse has been reached and scheduling further meetings.

The advantage of mediation is that it leads to agreement on the outcome. A successful mediation does not lead to a victory for one party over a defeated adversary. Neither party should feel "stung" or "burned" or otherwise oppressed. The possibility of the parties continuing to do business on mutually agreeable terms is enhanced. If the mediator urges one party to make concessions or give up unrealistic demands, agreement is reached by the acceptance of pragmatic possibilities. The disadvantage of mediation is that either party may seek to improve his position by "hanging tough," refusing concession, and attempting to wear down the adversary.

Minitrials

A recently developed alternative that deals with the tough-guy approach is commonly called "rent-a-judge"; it is also referred to as a *minitrial*. This is a form of mediation. In practice, a mediator, a neutral judge, is employed to conduct the process and to render a decision as to the probable outcome. Like arbitration and mediation, it requires agreement of the parties. The agreement can come at any time, even as late as the close of discovery. Be forewarned, however, that the agreement must be quite elaborate, as there are many details. The Center for Public Resources (366 Madison Avenue, New York, NY 10017) has workbooks and other materials that will be useful in putting together an agreement.

The agreement may provide for discovery within existing litigation, the issues to be handled, the selection and payment of the neutral judge, the representatives of the parties who will attend, the settlement authority of the representatives, a schedule, procedural details, preservation of confidentiality, and allocation of costs. Cost allocation is important, because this procedure is not cheap. The judge must be an individual with substantial legal skills and wisdom. Retired judges are a popular choice, but keep in mind that not all judges are equal. The fees charged by the judge will probably be based on the time involved at the highest hourly rate charged by attorneys in that part of the country.

The parties present their cases to the judge. Sitting with the judge are a senior executive from each party. The presentation may include briefs, argument, graphics, and live witnesses, just as it would in the courtroom. The evidence is abbreviated, and the judge must insist that the argument stay within the limits of what can be proven. When the presentation is complete, the judge and the senior executives retire to negotiate. If they do not reach agreement, the judge may make definite suggestions, based on the evidence and the law, as to how the case will come out. This is hard-fisted mediation, with elements of persuasion and compromise, intended to disabuse the parties of any illusions. The party who negotiates by being tough sometimes gets a shock.

The minitrial process leads to settlements because a senior executive of each party sees the case presented. Each side puts forth its best explanation of why it should win. The defects in each case are obvious. When each senior executive sees how weak his own company's case appears, he is more receptive to a fair evaluation of the other side's position. Senior executives tend to be unimpressed by the attorneys' presentations, and to share that view with each other. The senior executives, although on opposite sides of the dispute, easily find common cause against the attorneys. It is a short step to using their settlement authority to rid themselves of the attorneys.

When ADR Fails

If negotiation, conciliation, mediation, and a minitrial do not work, the parties will find themselves at the courthouse. The judges will help the settlement process along with mandatory settlement conferences, compelling attendance by a representative with authority to settle. This is mediation with coercion. The courts use mandatory nonbinding arbitration and summary jury trials to show the parties how the case may come out. There is no subtlety about the pressure to settle on the eve of trial.

The progression from negotiation to conciliation to mediation to minitrial to court-mandated settlement procedures and finally to trial is a progression of loss of control by the parties. Alternative dispute resolution is a way to regain control. ADR reduces all costs, especially legal fees. You will probably have to insist that your attorneys use these techniques.

In situations where:	The dispute may be resolved by:
The parties are still in contact but disagreement exists.	Negotiating in good faith with an open mind.
A disagreement is interfering with the relationship of the parties.	Enhancing negotiations by using an agenda, agreeing that discussions are not evidence, and avoiding a "victory" orientation.
The parties are no longer talking.	A third-party conciliator may reestablish contact, create an atmosphere of shared respect, and motivate an effort to settle differences.
The parties are not able to understand one another.	An active, neutral, third-party mediator may, by providing feedback, directing the discussions, evaluating arguments, and suggesting solutions, help the parties find terms of agreement with which they can live. The participants must compensate the mediator regardless of the outcome, have authority to reach agreement, commit sufficient time, agree to act in good faith, and let the mediator control the process.
One or both parties has assumed a "tough," uncompromising stance.	A minitrial, in which a neutral judge supervises presentation of each party's case to a panel consisting of representatives of top management from each side, may be attempted to produce a settlement. A minitrial can be held at any time with a detailed agreement and at high cost.
On the eve of trial the parties have still failed to work out a settlement.	A judicially supervised process, perhaps with conferences, a summary jury trial, or nonbinding arbitration, informs parties of the real merits of the case. Unreasonableness tends to influence the judge's conduct of trial.
The power of the state is needed to enforce a legal right, or a principle of law must be established.	A trial, judgment, and execution, with high cost, high risk, limited remedies, and complete loss of control by the parties, may resolve the dispute, although enforcement of the final decision may be frustrated by bankruptcy or fraud.

Procedure: Resolving disputes.

14
Budgets: Control of Costs and More

Traditionally, businesspeople have turned legal matters over to their lawyers and paid the bills. As legal bills have escalated, however, many sophisticated clients have attempted to use budgets to control costs. Most law firms will be happy to give you a budget if you ask. Budgets are a good selling tool. A "low-ball" figure helps bring in new business. A high figure conditions an already committed client to pay a high fee.

You can make a legal budget more than an estimate of costs, which can be ignored as the case develops. A budget can be a valuable tool for analyzing a case, developing a strategy, and maintaining control. Those benefits come from becoming and remaining involved in the budgeting process.

Insisting on a budget is a way of getting action. Attorneys, particularly when defending litigation, tend to react. Preparing a budget is a way for you to seize control of the case, creating a strategy which can be carried out with the available resources. As the case proceeds, the budget becomes a gauge of how well you are doing. In your hands, a budget is not merely a way to negotiate a lower fee, but a way to increase the value of legal services.

Budgets as Decision-Making Tools

When you decide to get the lawyer involved, things are apt to be tense. Whether she has been called in as a technician to get the facts right, as an advocate to shift the power balance, or as counsel to look for hidden traps, you are spending money because you need help. You must have confidence in your lawyers in order to follow their advice. Unfortunately, lawyers have a bias in favor of "legal" solutions, which are good for their business but which may not be good for yours.

In the heat of the moment, an attorney may recommend litigation, or a vigorous defense, to vindicate your rights. It is hard for you or your employees to criticize such a recommendation. You hired counsel for just such advice. After the lawsuit gets underway, unpleasant facts are discovered. As the years pass, costs escalate. Eventually, costs may force a settlement, often on terms no better than what was available when the case was started. By the time the case is closed, your attention is focused on new problems. Your dissatisfaction with the outcome is deflected by blaming "our litigious society," the courts, and lawyers in general.

A formal budget puts objectivity into decisions about legal matters at the beginning. At the start, you need to know what it is going to take to finish, both in fees paid out and in in-house resources. An objective budget protects you from excess influence by your attorney, and permits input from your other advisors and managers.

Budgets are useful for managing any legal matter. Litigation is used to illustrate the process because it presents a common set of tasks to be completed and involves the court in addition to the adversary. With nonlitigation matters, a budget helps decide if legal services will be cost effective. A budget for a single transaction—for example, issuing securities—may help you decide whether or not to proceed. Similarly, a budget for a long-term project, such as a trademark-protection program or a lobbying effort, may justify an effort when benefit is weighed against cost.

Litigation Risk Management

You have to make decisions in the operation of your business with less than perfect information. New products are developed, crops are planted, factories are built, oil and gas wells are drilled without knowledge of what the costs will be, or how the market will value the effort. The art of management is making good decisions without all the information. This is called business judgment. Refusing to exercise this judgment, waiting for all of the information and refusing to take any risk, is paralysis. The market rewards careful risk taking. Early planting accepts the risk of frost in the hope of a higher price for being first to market.

With the advent of hourly billing, attorneys have no incentive to suggest that clients accept any risk. Instead, attorneys do everything they can think of in preparing a case, and charge the clients for it. When representing a corporate client, attorneys have little basis for assuming that anyone is authorized to accept risk. Intending to leave no stone unturned, every task, no matter how pointless or futile, is dutifully completed. The budget process requires an explicit justification of each task so that you can decide if the benefit outweighs the expense.

Most cases start with a flurry of activity and high monthly bills. As long as you pay the bills promptly, the activity level will remain high, without regard to the usefulness of the work being done. Defense attorneys often file a motion to dismiss. That requires the drafting of a brief and argument before the court. If the defense motion wins, the plaintiff merely has to amend its pleading. Usually, the whole exercise is nothing but expensive paper shuffling. The problem is that your attorney may use up all of your resources before you get to the important part of the case. With a budget, you can decide what need not be done, and conserve assets for what must be done.

Bluffing is for poker. Attorneys get rich calling bluffs. You may be tempted to file a lawsuit to see what kind of an offer it brings. Usually, the response to a summons is an answer, a counterclaim, a request for production of documents, and interrogatories. Litigation is no place for bluffing. When you are involved in a lawsuit, there are some things that you must do. The secret is to do everything that is necessary, and nothing that is not necessary. The budget is a plan to use in deciding what is necessary and what is not.

Causes and Meaning of Budget Variances

Lawyers are reluctant to project the costs of litigation. At the beginning the evidence is unknown. The tactics of the adversary and the requirements of the court may push costs up. A figure high enough to cover all contingencies may scare you away. The projection of litigation costs is more art than accounting.

In any given case, a single lawyer can drive every one else's costs up by simply doing things that require a response. Dilatory tactics are officially discouraged, sometimes punished, and commonly used. In Louisiana practice, there is even a formal "dilatory plea." Worse than delaying, many prominent law firms brag about playing "hardball." This is slang for agreeing to nothing and fighting over every point. Hardball includes disrupting depositions by inserting improper objections and arguing with the examiner both to obstruct the discovery and to run up the cost of the transcript.

Some clients encourage hardball tactics. It makes them feel tough. Taking a tough stance may be justified as defending a principle or industry practice. For example, an investment banker or securities broker might defend efforts by an investor to shift a loss, already incurred, back to the broker or banker. More often, parties use such tactics to delay. When the market prices of natural gas fell in the early 1980s, pipeline companies owed huge sums to gas producers. They did not pay. By delaying the court processes, they were able to pressure the producers into compromise. Debtors fight mortgage foreclosures, skimming the cash flow during the delay and then seeking protection in bankruptcy.

Court-imposed procedures may also needlessly increase costs. In one case, a federal judge repeatedly ordered attorneys, none of whom was located nearer than New York, to come to a Philadelphia courthouse for settlement conferences. The clients had to bear the time and travel costs. Most judges are concerned with managing their calendar, trying to control delay. Judges impose deadlines, and require reports such as the pretrial memorandum. Even if a case is moving toward settlement, some judges, especially in the federal courts, punish lawyers severely if such reports are not filed when they are due.

An experienced practitioner should be able to predict accurately the cost of routine litigation such as collections, foreclosures, and motor vehicle negligence defenses. If the actual cost is out of line with the prediction, either the case is not really routine or there is a problem with the representation. What might look like a simple foreclosure is not routine if, for example, the mortgage has the wrong description of the collateral. If the lender cannot calculate accurately the amount due, or account for payments received, the representation problem may be on the client's side. In routine cases, however, deviations from a budget usually indicate problems with the lawyer and a need for corrective action.

Budgets are less accurate in nonroutine cases. Variances from projections call for explanation of the causes and implications. There is always a reason and perhaps an excuse, but what you need to know is whether the cost variances mean that assumptions on which you have relied are wrong. If an adversary refuses to admit an essential fact, perhaps timely delivery, and you have no actual proof of when delivery occurred, the problem may show up in increased discovery cost as your attorney searches for the required evidence. If no evidence of timely delivery is found, an adjustment in your settlement posture may be wise.

A Simple Budget for a Routine Case

You want to know two things about any case: What is it going to cost, and how long will it take? In Chap. 4 it was suggested that you send a litigation cost estimate form (Fig. 4-4) to attorneys you are thinking of hiring. The format includes a statement that no independent investigation has been done and that the fees will be based on hourly rates. This simple form may serve as an adequate budget for a routine case.

Your use of the litigation cost estimate is a way to test the attorney's attitude toward controlling costs. A prompt, complete response gives you a basis for discussing the requirements of the case and deciding whether the attorney is compatible. Optimistically low figures may be suggested in the hope of getting your business, so do not rely on the estimate in choosing an attorney.

This simple estimate is designed to ensure value, not to control cost. You control costs of routine cases by looking at the bills. Listening carefully to an attorney's explanation of why an estimate differs from other estimates, or actual experience, helps you judge the attorney's competence.

Complex Case Budgets

You can use the budget to assemble the information needed for the critical decisions that must be made early in a case. The budget requires the development of a strategy or theme to guide decisions about what actions will be necessary or useful. With the work planned, staffing, fees and other costs, and the time that will elapse during the suit can be projected.

The budgeting process is not a beauty contest. Architects, advertising agencies, and other providers of creative services often submit elaborate proposals in a design competition. Usually only the originator can turn the creative concept into a finished project. Legal theories lack artistic uniqueness. Valid legal theories are adopted and implemented by judges. A theory developed and disclosed to the extent necessary to be useful in budgeting can be executed by any journeyman attorney. Few attorneys will make that creative effort without having been retained.

The selection process identifies the lead attorney you are hiring to represent you. You may also identify a junior partner or senior associate, often referred to as the "second chair." The active position at the attorney's table in a courtroom is at the corner. The assistant sits in the next or "second" chair. The budget process forces both the lead, and the "second chair," to pay intense attention to your case. That way, you and the "second chair" get the benefit of the wisdom of the lead attorney you have selected.

A plaintiff's budget should be completed before the lawsuit is filed. Pay your attorneys to draft the pleading and prepare a budget before making the final decision to sue. The pleading may be exactly what you expected, but an accurate budget may give you second thoughts. The benefits of the lawsuit may not justify the cost. Or you may be dissatisfied with the attorney's ability to project the cost. It is better to find out before you are committed that the costs will be overwhelming, or that your attorney cannot perform a simple budget analysis.

A defendant must file a responsive pleading before there is time to prepare a budget. Ordinarily the budget should be done before any scheduling conference with the judge. The Federal Rules of Civil Procedure require the court to hold a scheduling conference within 120 days after the filing of the complaint. The judge may simply dictate a schedule with deadlines. If you have a complex case, the deadlines will create a problem. With a budget completed, you have a basis for advising the court of the time the case requires.

Survey the Law and the Facts

Within the limits of the time available, the facts relevant to the lawsuit should be assembled before the budget is prepared. In business disputes there are usually documents that tell most of the story. Such documents should be inventoried, and copies forwarded to the attorney. There is also time for brief interviews of any fact witnesses who can be identified. The attorney needs to have some idea what facts are undisputed or established by readily available evidence so that some judgments can be made about evidence that must be developed by discovery or with experts.

The attorney also needs to survey the applicable law. This may require some research. The objective is to define what factors will determine the outcome of the case and what further research will be required. This is an informal process which may never be reduced to writing. With this preliminary study of the whole case, the attorney can make a general prediction of how the case should go, if the system works right. The attorney's job is to see that the system works right.

Determine the Limits of Your Resources

If you run out of money before the case is over, it may not matter whether you win or lose. Spending more than your net cash flow and reserves will soon put you out of business. You may be able get through some tough spots by slow-paying your attorney. When a case is close to trial, judges will not permit an attorney to withdraw or grant a continuance, so your attorney will probably be compelled to present the case even if she is not paid. If you lose, you are out of business. If you win, the legal bill is just another account payable. Attorneys are in business; they know that the chances of being paid after the fact are slim.

When you are close to the edge of bankruptcy, the best approach is to keep your attorney's account paid current and in full. However, don't let her do anything that is not absolutely required by the court.

A profitable business with a healthy cash flow and adequate reserves still has limits to the resources it can make available for legal matters. In pursuing a claim, the limit is probably the total value that is likely to be collectible. An unsecured claim against a debtor being liquidated under

Chapter 7 of the Bankruptcy Code has only a small value. It is certainly worth the postage to file the claim, if only to justify the write-off to the Internal Revenue Service. If your claim is seriously disputed, cut its value in half. Then decide what part of that half you are willing to pay your attorney. As to claims against you, estimate their fair value and figure on paying no more than half for a successful defense. If you expect to pay something, limit fees to half of the difference between what you might pay and the fair value. Don't ever put any such calculation in writing, ever, anyplace. It is all discoverable.

For a business that is not on the edge, the real limit of the resources available should be related to the value of benefit to the business that may result from the services. If an important principle is at stake, you might pay much more than the actual amount of money involved. For a one-time nuisance deal it may be cheaper to pay off than to argue. As you begin the budgeting process, you should have a figure in mind.

Let Your Attorney Know Your Goals

Your attorney needs to know what you wish to accomplish by the litigation. Defendants usually want a complete victory and recovery of any attorneys' fees or other expenses incurred. Plaintiffs desire complete vindication and to impress on the adversary the foolishness of ever having challenged the claim. Such objectives can be refined. When defending a new product in a product-liability action, the goal may be to win and establish precedent. In defending an old product, the goal may be to control damages. In a commercial case, you may seek a workable compromise that permits both parties to survive. In a suit over product licensing, resolution before the market disappears may be each party's goal.

Clients frequently complain that attorneys do not understand the problem or the business from which it arises. In a business matter, you need to teach your attorney something about your business so that she will understand what you are after. Judges and jurors do not understand the problem, or the business, either. The very heart of advocacy is teaching. The best attorneys learn the truth and then teach it. The process starts with defining your objectives.

Attorneys do not like to make predictions early in a case because it may put them at odds with the client. You don't want to hear that your case is a loser. This is the justification for visiting the attorneys before hiring them. The attorney must know your real objective. You need the attorney's honest evaluation. With a clear statement of your goals, and the attorney's evaluation, an acceptable outcome, a kind of preliminary settlement posture, can be stated. Both you and your attorney must commit to working toward it. If you are unable to accept anything short of a smashing victory, that may be the only acceptable goal.

Facts Become a Theme

A few facts will control the outcome of your lawsuit. Every case comes down to a few fact questions which can be decided by a jury. Most of what is proven in the courtroom is just background material, not really in dispute. The background gives meaning to the few sharply disputed facts that determine the outcome. Identifying and defining those facts requires wisdom, judgment, and knowledge of the law. With the benefit of the pleadings, a preliminary investigation, and a survey of the applicable law, a competent attorney can determine what the issues of the case are, and can tell you the likely outcome. That likely outcome and your goals define an acceptable outcome.

The few facts which must be proven to achieve an acceptable outcome make up the strategy, or theme, of your case. A plaintiff must prove a case to win. A defendant can win by preventing the plaintiff from proving a required fact, or by proving an additional fact that nullifies the plaintiff's case. The truth which you intend to prove about each critical fact should be written out as a complete sentence. These sentences form the theme or strategy of your case. You may modify the theme as the case develops, but keep it simple. Enter the theme at the top of the *task list* shown as Fig. 14-1.

A Budget Format

The budget starts with a list of tasks. Figure 14-1 is a list of tasks that are commonly performed in complex business litigation, arranged vertically in the order in which they are done. Figure 14-1 also shows the various cash expenditures that can be expected. The list goes all the way through an appeal, just as the case will if it is not settled.

Refining and elaborating this list in light of what is known about your case will create the framework for your budget. You and your attorney must both contribute. For example, on the second page of Fig. 14-1, there are four deposition lists, for adversaries, nonparties, third parties, and experts. The preparation of your own witnesses is an item on page 3. You need to complete the list with descriptions or actual names. The sales manager, engineer, and accountant of the adversary might be listed by title, and the salespeople by name. Think through all of the people who might be deposed. Do the same thing with documents. You know where your documents are. Describe how you will acquire all of the adversary's documents. Include conferring and reporting as tasks so that provision is made for talking to your adversary and keeping you informed, burdens which are usually underestimated.

Add to the list any tasks suggested by the rules and forms used by the court in which the case is pending. Also add any tasks suggested by your

Budgets: Control of Costs and More 221

	Task	Contribution to theme	Time cost	Cash cost	Due date
	Task List				
	Theme:				
	Task imposed by:				
	Plaintiff (P)				
	Defendant (D)				
	Codefendant (Co-D)				
	Third-party defendant (3rd)				
	Court (Ct)				
	Investigation				
	Internal interviews				
	Internal document search				
	Follow-up interviews				
	Identification and indexing of documents				
	Copying				
	Research of law				
	Draft pleading				
	Draft motion to dismiss				
Ct	File pleading				
	Effect service				
	Remove to federal court				
Ct	Scheduling conference				
	Lift bankruptcy stay				
	Multidistrict panel consolidation				
	Join new parties				
	Amend pleadings				
	Conferences and reports				
	Travel expense and disbursements for pleading				
	Interrogatories				
	30(B)(6) Deposition				
	Selection and retention of expert witnesses and consultants				

Figure 14-1. The *task list* provides the framework for the litigation budget.

Task	Contribution to theme	Time cost	Cash cost	Due date
Location and assignment of in-house expert consultants				
Response to interrogatories				
Request for documents				
Response to document request				
Copying and indexing of documents produced				
Adversary depositions, list:				
Nonparty depositions, list:				
Third-party depositions, list:				
Expert depositions, list:				
Preparation of witnesses for deposition, list:				
Transcript fees, electronic media				
Expert witness fees				
Copying expenses				
Travel expense for discovery				
Requests for admissions				
Response to admission requests				
Discovery motions				
Conferences and reports				
Ct Arbitration, court-annexed				
Motion for summary judgment				
Ct Settlement conference				
Ct Draft pretrial order				
Ct Exhibit list				

Figure 14-1. *(Continued)*

Budgets: Control of Costs and More   **223**

Task	Contribution to theme	Time cost	Cash cost	Due date
Ct Witness list				
Ct Contentions				
Voir dire questions				
Complete discovery				
Ct Requests for charge or jury instructions				
Final dispositive motions				
Jury selection studies				
Stipulations				
Motions *in limine*				
Trial briefs				
Expert hypothetical				
Final pretrial order				
Report of settlement discussion				
Courtroom graphics				
Ct Pretrial conference				
Conferences and reports				
Jury selection				
Opening statements				
Plaintiff's case in chief				
Defendant's case				
Plaintiff's rebuttal				
Closing argument				
Jury charge				
Ct Verdict forms or proposed findings of fact and conclusions of law				
Motion for new trial				
Notice of appeal				
Transmittal of record				
Preparation of briefs and submission				
Oral argument				

Figure 14-1. (*Continued*)

trial attorney. The list will not be perfect, but strive for completeness. The actual performance of these tasks will overlap, and the exact order may be changed for tactical reasons. An approximate order is adequate.

Each of the tasks is done to meet someone's requirement. Classify each task according to the party requiring its performance. Some tasks are required by the court and must be performed. Tasks required by a codefendant may be done informally to save time and effort. It is a matter for negotiation. Figure 14-1 provides for entering this classification in the left-most column.

Each task should be examined to determine its contribution to establishing your theme for the case. Many of the tasks on the list are neither necessary nor helpful. Here the lead trial attorney should exercise considered judgment. The contribution of each task should be written in just a few words. Later on, the justification may disappear and the task can be eliminated. There is real potential for cutting costs here, without loss of value. Avoid doing tasks that do not help establish the theme of your case. If the task is imposed by the court, there is no choice. If the task is imposed by the adversary, there may be some cost benefit in asking the court to intervene.

Large law firms, with many associates to keep busy, may recommend that every task be completed. There is risk of a surprise if any task is left undone. There are very few real surprises to clients. The attorney's reluctance to skip a task is understandable. You may sue for malpractice if something important is missed. A well-informed client can make the decision to take the risk of missing something. If you are willing to take the time to review each task with the lead trial attorney, much pointless effort can be avoided with little risk.

The date for completion of each task should be estimated when the budget is prepared. If the court enters a scheduling order, the budget should be modified to reflect every task and date in the scheduling order. The due dates should be before any absolute deadlines.

The column headed "Cash cost" is for the out-of-pocket expenses incurred as the case progresses. Court costs for filing papers and having them delivered are usually nominal. The cost of stenographic transcripts of depositions runs in excess of $500 per day. Expert witnesses will charge for their time. They may have to conduct a study or do experiments before knowing if their testimony is useful. Travel is also very expensive, especially if you are paying the lawyer's hourly rate while she is riding an airplane.

Attorneys generally underestimate the time costs. The reason is that they are self-centered. Most of the important tasks involve the contributions of several people. An accurate estimate picks up all of the time of each person.

Figure 14-2, the time cost extension, adds five columns to Fig. 14-1.

	Time Cost Extension					
	Hours used					
Task	Lawyer	Attorney	Counsel	Clerk/paralegal	Client	Time cost
Deposition of von Slugger	5.0	11.0	0.5	4.0	16	36.5

Figure 14-2. The *time cost extension*, used for each item on the task list, collects all of the time expended on the task.

The reason is that you will be charged different hourly rates for the services of different individuals in most law firms. Three rates for lawyers should be enough, corresponding roughly to three kinds of service—counsel, attorney, and lawyer—and the relative status of each. The clerk/paralegal classification will be used for people employed to search for and copy documents and do other tasks supervised by a lawyer. Often neglected, but never unimportant, is the cost of your own time.

A typical task is the deposition of an employee, Mr. von Slugger from Chap. 9. His deposition will be taken by the adversary, so there is no choice. Before the deposition, a paralegal will use up 4 hours to collect all the documents sent to, or from, Mr. von Slugger or referring to him. A lawyer who is familiar with the file may take 2 hours to prepare a memo of what questions Mr. von Slugger is likely to be asked, why they are important, and how the documents may be relevant. The attorney may spend 4 hours getting Mr. von Slugger ready for the deposition, and 7 hours at the deposition itself. Mr. von Slugger himself will spend 2 full days, including travel, amounting to 16 hours. Afterwards, the lawyer may use 3 hours to review the transcript, forward it to von Slugger, and dictate a summary. The counsel may expect to spend about 30 minutes reading the summary. The time cost of the simple deposition adds up to 36½ hours.

If you are using a computerized spreadsheet, you might want to set up the cost extension with a separate group of five columns for each hourly rate: time; cumulative time; hourly rate; dollars (time multiplied by hourly rate); cumulative dollars. In addition, you can have columns for: time all classes; cumulative time all classes; dollars all classes; cumulative dollars all classes. This illustrates the biggest problem with budgets: The details can overwhelm the purpose.

For a quick estimate, you can add up the cash costs to obtain a sum of money needed for disbursements. Adding the time cost column will give you a total number of hours. Multiply the number of hours by the hourly rate charged to obtain an estimated cost of services. The total of the disbursements and the cost of services will approximate what the whole lawsuit will cost you.

You also need to know how long the case will take. When the court has entered a scheduling order, many of the interim dates will be set. The actual trial date depends on the court docket. The trial attorney can tell you how long after the final pretrial conference the actual trial might commence. If the court does not impose time limits, you can use a further extension of the task list, illustrated by Fig. 14-3, schedule extension.

The first sample entry is Mr. Von Slugger's deposition. The second sample entry represents the indexing of documents produced by the adversary and copied. An estimate of time to do the job is based on assumptions made by the trial lawyer. The time shown for the deposition runs from the notice to the filing of the transcript. The time for looking at documents is 35 days from when they are produced. The job cannot start until the documents are actually produced. The job cannot be finished until the court decides any motion to compel discovery. This is a typical application of critical-path management for those who are familiar with that technique. Litigation does not have the orderly logic of a construction project, where the hole has to be dug before the cement can be poured. Litigation can, and usually does, proceed willy-nilly. If you put enough people to work on the case, all of the tasks could be completed in about 60 days. Much of the craft of the trial lawyer is in choosing which task to do next, based on estimates of the adversary's weaknesses.

The fewer people who work on your case, the better. Each additional person working on the case has a learning curve to climb. With more people there is more time spent talking. The time cost within any given

Schedule Extension					
Event required to start	Time used (hours)	Time elapsed (days)	Finish event	Target complete	Deadline date
Notice of deposition	36.5	35	File transcript	Aug. 30	Sept. 12
Production of adversary documents	500	35	Decision on motion to compel	June 30	Sept. 12

Figure 14-3. The *schedule extension* shows when the task can be started and how much time will elapse until completion.

limits determines how many people are needed. Apart from the actual trial, unless a case will require more than 500 hours in a six-month period, no more than two attorneys should be working on it. A case that needs more than 1500 hours in a six-month period should be staffed by at least three attorneys. The claim that junior partners and associates work at lower hourly rates ignores the cost of explaining to them what they are supposed to do.

This budget format gives you an estimate of how much a case might cost and some sense of how long it might take. Not addressed are such things as customer relations, business reputation, and financial reporting requirements, each in itself a significant burden of being involved in litigation. Most internal costs are ignored. Major litigation distracts management from concentrating on the business. Searching for and copying documents disrupts the departments involved. Investigation fosters a sense of insecurity, a concern on the part of employees that they may not be believed. When making decisions, such nonfinancial costs are as real as the copying bill.

Using the Budget

The completed budget may seem to be somewhat of a disappointment. The numbers are not precise, the time estimates are crude. That accurately reflects the litigation process. The great benefit of making up a budget is that you get a plan. Starting with the beginning of the case, the lead trial attorney's creativity and imagination are focused on your problem. A theme, and a sense of purpose, emerge. There is action to be taken, in furtherance of your objectives. You have some control.

The budget is a tool for shaping your case. It is not the case, or the underlying dispute. Don't fixate on your budget and ignore what the adversary is doing to you. Most of the value is extracted from the budget process simply by thinking through the tasks and why each is being done.

Litigation is a competitive endeavor. Quick responses and flexibility are needed to do well. A budget should never be allowed to drive or limit the attorney's conduct of the lawsuit. Excessive detail leads to rigidity. When expectations are not met, there is reason to reconsider assumptions and revise objectives. Find out why the variances occur, and make adjustments.

As the evidence develops and you become familiar with your attorneys, rely more on their advice and lay the budget aside. It has served its principal purpose by getting your case off to a good start. As the body of evidence grows, control of the outcome shifts away from the parties and abstract law increasingly influences the outcome.

The budget will have continued use. As the case proceeds, and attorneys' efforts are closely studied, as described in Chaps. 15 and 16, you may consider if tasks, when completed, do actually contribute to establishing your theme as predicted. Large variances from the budget indicate errors in evaluating the case, good reason to reevaluate your settlement posture. When the matter is finally resolved, the budget variances are a sound basis for evaluating the results obtained.

The use of a spreadsheet program run on an ordinary office computer is probably the best way to put together the budget described. You hire attorneys as advocates, not computer whizzes. Many lawyers use computers and know a lot about them. Of course, malpractice lawyers know a lot about surgery, but you wouldn't want one to remove your appendix. If you want to do this on a computer, use your own in-house computer expert to set it up, unless the lawyer has a tried-and-tested application ready to go.

A budget is like a road map. It is useful for orientation and planning before you start the trip, it will help you find the most direct route to your intended destination, and it will help you stay on track. But the road map does not dictate the route; you can always detour to avoid unexpected obstacles or take advantage of scenery if the weather is nice. And the best road map, by itself, will not move you a single inch toward the intended destination.

1. Select an attorney who is willing to work with a budget.

    Test the attorney's ability to commit to cost, time, and staffing with Fig. 4-4, the litigation cost estimate.
    Base your selection on ability, not low bid.

2. Develop a budget with the attorney selected and retained.

    If you are the plaintiff, budget before suing.
    If you are the defendant, budget before the scheduling conference.
    Identify the lead attorney, and any helpers.
    Survey the law and the facts.
    Determine your objectives:
        Tell your attorney your goals.
        Establish a settlement posture.
    Determine how much you can spend:
        The amount at stake in the case
        The benefits of the case
        Your ability to provide cash flow
    Define the theme of your case.

3. List each task to be completed:

    Who requires the task?
        Court
        Adversary
        You
    How does the task contribute to the theme of your case?
    How much money will the task require?
    How much time will elapse in completing the task?
    Who will perform the task?

4. Consider causes of budget variances:

    Unusual demands by the judge
    Adversary efforts to exhaust your resources
    Your misconception about what the case is about
    Your attorney's errors in predicting
    The failure of expected evidence to develop

5. Consider adjustments to budget variances:

    Reduce costs by deleting tasks and accepting risk.
    Change your settlement posture.
    Replace or help your attorney.

6. When a satisfactory relationship has been established with your attorney and a satisfactory course has been set for the conduct of the case, lay the budget aside for later use in evaluating results.

Procedure: Budgeting for legal projects.

15
How to Read Your Lawyer's Bill

The one complete and candid report that your lawyer wants to send you is the bill. This simple truth is the key to controlling and directing outside attorneys.

Why Lawyers Bill by the Hour

Talking about fees, especially when the relationship is first being formed, may seem difficult or embarrassing. If you are just bargaining for lower hourly rates, the sense is that you don't think the lawyer is worth as much as she is asking. The lawyer may agree to discount the rate, expecting to make it up by working more slowly, or just padding the bill. Focus the discussion on how the lawyer will be paid. You want to pay her. She wants to be paid. That way, you and the lawyer are on the same side. To accomplish that mutual goal, you each must share an understanding of what the job is, what will be paid for, the procedure for getting paid, and only then what the hourly rate will be. The retainer agreement is used to specify the details of this shared understanding. You should insist on a retainer letter for every case or major project, even with your regular outside counsel. Use the retainer agreements to establish the billing procedure. The lawyer will use the procedure to get paid. The same procedure enables you to keep track of what the lawyer is doing.

In the good old days, when carbon paper was in common use, lawyers would work on a matter until it was completed. Then an invoice would be sent that looked like Fig. 15-1.

Before the 1970s, lawyers did not ordinarily keep detailed time

How to Read Your Lawyer's Bill   **231**

```
From:   Law Offices of John G. Smith
        120 Main Street
        Oneida, New York 13421

To:     XYZ Corporation
        P.O. Box ABC
        Oneida, New York 13421
        ─────────────────────────────────────
        For services rendered:

        Jones case:                $110.00
        due on receipt
        Thank You
```

Figure 15-1. In the good old days, a lawyer's bill told you how much to pay, and little else.

records. Most did not even know how. At the end of the case, the lawyer would look at the amount involved, the outcome, the pocketbook of the client, and charge as much as he thought he could collect. Lawyers did not make much money that way. Too much time would be spent on small cases. Clients would complain, and simply not pay bills. Most lawyers felt that they could make a better income handling matters where the fees could be calculated as a percentage of the value involved, such as real estate transactions or the probate of estates. The local bar associations did not think that the antitrust laws applied to the professions, so there was no trouble with misunderstandings about what the percentages were. By the mid-1960s, antitrust enforcement was directed at price fixing by the professions. At the same time, competition from title insurance companies and mortgage brokers began to squeeze the profits out of routine real estate transactions.

The larger law firms in big cities had found that keeping track of the time expended was a good way to determine the cost of services provided to corporate clients. Tracking cost by recording time was important in setting fees where the work was done by associates who were hardly known to the billing partner. This hourly billing seemed to be the answer to lawyers' financial distress. Early studies showed that clients were more likely to pay if they thought the lawyer had worked hard. What better way to show how hard the lawyer worked than to show all of the hours, or rather tenths of hours, that had been devoted to the client's cause? And best of all, if lawyers wanted to increase their income, all that was needed was an increase in rates, or hours. And there lay the trap.

Lawyers have found that even if clients might balk at high hourly rates, the clients have no idea of the number of hours needed to complete the work properly. There is no limit to the amount of hours that can be billed. The discovery provisions of the Federal Rules of Civil Procedure permit, even encourage, exhaustive investigation with no regard for relevance. Law firms can increase income by hiring associates and keeping them busy producing billable hours. Turning the billable hour into income requires sending the bill to the client. The detailed billing is the lawyer's key to the client's treasury. In the hands of someone who knows how to read it, the detailed billing is also the key to effective management.

Lawyers don't enjoy keeping detailed time records. The requirement that every act be written down is a distraction even after it becomes a habit. The billing entry can take more time than doing the job. Reading the incoming mail is an example. A time entry must be made for each letter, even if the letter is merely read and sent to the file. It may take an hour to look at 30 letters relating to 30 different files. Looking up 30 billing numbers and writing 30 descriptions is the only way to get paid for the hour. With a minimum billing unit of one-tenth, a job that should take 1 hour actually takes 2 hours and generates bills to clients totaling 3 hours.

Keeping time records is a constant nuisance. Each time entry must be made contemporaneously. Going back over the day, or several days, to reconstruct time expended substitutes creativity for data. That is why imposing hourly timekeeping requirements on salaried in-house lawyers is usually counterproductive.

Despite the burden, hourly billings are the standard method of charging legal fees to business clients. Some lawyers or law firms may tell you that they are not set up to keep such records and prepare detailed bills. Three hundred dollars will buy excellent timekeeping software that will run on personal computers available for less than $1500.00. Vendors are happy to rent complete systems, hardware and software, for under $200 per month. A lawyer who is unable or unwilling to comply with this type of billing requirement may have other important shortcomings. Insist on receiving the detailed time records regardless of how the fee is to be determined.

Billing Format

The more frequent billings are, the more effectively they can be used to maintain control. Monthly bills are appropriate for most cases and for regular outside counsel. In major or complex cases, it is a good idea to be billed twice a month or every 2 weeks. Quarterly billings are too far

How to Read Your Lawyer's Bill   **233**

apart to use to catch deteriorating situations. Specify the billing period in the retainer letter. More frequent billings lead you to pay more often and sooner, which increases the cost of the money used. If that is a concern, negotiate a prompt-payment discount, perhaps a 1 percent discount for payments remitted within 10 days of the billing. Of course, with a shorter billing cycle, a smaller fee deposit adequately protects the law firm.

The retainer letter is where you also specify the information to be included in the bill. The items suggested here can be easily accommodated by the common timekeeping and billing systems.

When a single law firm does a variety of work for a client, separate bills should be rendered for each matter. Ordinarily, each lawsuit is a separate matter, but sometimes more than one suit may arise from a single transaction. An example is a real estate foreclosure, where the foreclosure occurs in state court, but the deficiency judgment may be dealt with by the bankruptcy court. The entire situation could be treated as one matter, a single indebtedness, or two matters, the foreclosure of collateral and the bankruptcy claim. For internal cost allocation purposes, you might want regular outside counsel to render separate bills for various departments or topics—for example, personnel, credit, and shipping. The client's accounting system and convenience should dictate when the lawyer opens another billing file.

Figure 15-2 is the detail portion of a fictitious legal bill. It was generated on typical timekeeping software to illustrate some of the points you might consider when reviewing your attorney's bills. In the following text, the dates in parentheses (01/10) indicate the illustrative entries.

The date that the work is done and the name or initials of the person who does the work is part of each entry. Aside from being required by the logic of most timekeeping systems, that data gives insight into what is really happening to the file. Is the work all being done on the last day before it is due? Is the work being done on weekends and holidays? Are the more experienced attorneys doing any of the work?

Most important is a statement of exactly what was done in each instance that time was charged to the matter. This should be in full text, with no codes. Each entry began as a note made by the lawyer on the original time record, hand written, dictated, or keyed directly into the computer. Persons communicated with, by phone or face to face, should be named (10/02/98). The issue should be specified in all entries for research (10/03/98). If a deposition is being summarized, the deponent's name and connection with the case should be shown (10/04/98). Study and analysis of discovery documents should show which documents, perhaps by source (10/05/98).

The ultimate entry is the time charged. Often this is measured in quarters or tenths of an hour. When you have a choice, tenths are better

HEDGLON, ALLAN & SLAYTON
301 N.W. 63rd Street, Suite 700
Oklahoma City, Oklahoma 73116
(405) 555-8127
Federal Employer's ID No. 12-3456789

Invoice No. 12693

Page: 1

10/10/98

TO: Crush Cart Company
21 N. West Street
Waukegan, Illinois 60085

		HRS/ RATE	AMOUNT
10/02/98 #1167	PTR/C11 Office conference, R. von Slugger re: engineering change notice procedure during 1987–88, documentation of reasons, required approvals, assignment of steering box to project engineer. *John Doe Claim	1.40 150.00	$210.00
10/03/98 #1168	EYA/C12 Research re: admissibility of evidence of action taken to identify and correct claimed defect accident. *John Doe Claim	2.70 100.00	$270.00
10/04/98 #1169	WGA/C1 Summarize deposition transcript, Sam Slick, golf pro and operator of golf cart concession, source golf carts, maintenance program, rented to Doe who he did not know before, Doe seemed Ok, Golf cart normal, accident reported in early afternoon, found Doe under cart at bottom of slope, turned cart back on wheels, it seemed ok except batteries dry, Doe had not obviously drunk, Doe hurt, called ambulance, good witness for plaintiff. *John Doe Claim	3.20 125.00	$400.00

Figure 15-2. The detail generated by modern timekeeping and billing software is a candid, complete report on your case.

Crush Cart Continued   Page:2

		HRS/RATE	AMOUNT
10/05/98 #1170	EYA/C12 Review Income tax returns of Claim John Doe for Years 1994, 95 96 97. *John Doe Claim	1.20 100.00	$120.00
10/06/98 #1171	EYA/C12 Telephone Dr. Jones office re: completion of report of exam of Doe. *John Doe Claim	0.30 150.00	$ 45.00
10/07/98 #1172	WGA/C1 Telephone Ed's Photo shop re: blow-ups of accident site, Telephone Dr. Jones office to see if report ready for pick up. Telephone Fred's Golf cart Supply to see if rental cart available for testing, Telephone Joe's Golf cart supply to see if cart available for testing, Telephone Crush Cart Co. to see if cart available, or if any old test have been done. Telephone adversary to set date for von Slugger deposition. Telephone from Fred's no cart will be available. *John Doe Claim.	2.10 125.00	$262.50
10/08/98 #1173	TJB/C11 Conference, at courthouse, with adverse attorney Smith, Doe is very depressed, will not recover soon, wants about $1,500,000 suggested $15K more appropriate for soft tissue and psychic injury only, Smith will get back. *John Doe Claim	0.60 150.00	$ 90.00
10/09/98 #1174	WGA/C1 Deposition of Doctor Blackwell, Plaintiff's treating psychiatrist, patient has post traumatic stress disorder, manifested by severe and profound depression which is totally disabling and destroys the very essence of life. Doctor well qualified and makes an excellent witness. *John Doe Claim	4.70 125.00	$587.50

Figure 15-2. (*Continued*)

Crush Cart Continued			Page:3
		HRS/RATE	AMOUNT
10/10/98 #1175	PTR/C11 Conference with EYA and WGA regarding graphic presentation of vehicle dynamics evidence with client's expert von Slugger, and his explanation of the missing records. *John Doe Claim	1.70 150.00	$255.00
10/10/98 #1176	EYA/C12 Conference with PTR, WGY re: employee testimony of changes in design. *John Doe Claim	1.80 100.00	$180.00
10/10/98 #1177	WGA/C1 Conference with PTR,EYA regarding admissibility of destruction of documents and need to find other expert witness. *John doe Claim	1.50 125.00	$187.50
10/11/98 #1179	EYA/C12 Conference with WGA regarding prior design changes as proof of defect. *John Doe Claim	1.90 100.00	$190.00
10/11/98 #1178	WGA/C1 Conference with EYA regarding relevance of evidence of prior design changes in defective product. *John Doe Claim	1.70 125.00	$212.50
10/12/98 #1180	EDG/C12 Research, relevance of evidence *John Doe Claim	3.60 100.00	$360.00
10/13/98 #1181	EYA/C12 Called Bill French, Judge's clerk, asked if Motion to Compel granted, No decision yet, maybe end of next week. *John Doe Claim	0.40 100.00	$ 40.00
10/14/98 #1182	WDG/C12 Review file *John Doe Claim	0.30 100.00	$ 30.00

Figure 15-2. (Continued)

How to Read Your Lawyer's Bill **237**

Crush Cart Continued		Page:4
DESCRIPTION	HRS/ RATE	AMOUNT
TOTAL BILLABLE TIME CHARGES	29.10	
TOTAL BILLABLE COST		$ 0.00
TOTAL NEW CHARGES		$3,440.00
NEW BALANCE		
New current month		$3,440.00
TOTAL NEW BALANCE		$3,440.00

Figure 15-2. (*Continued*)

for you. As a practical matter, there will be a minimum entry, which reflects the fact that it takes some time to focus on any matter. Expect to be charged at least one-quarter or three-tenths for any phone call, no matter how brief (10/06/98). But four or more phone calls on one matter within an hour of clock time should not result in charges totaling more than an hour (10/07/98). The reality of time records is that many small bits may add up to more than a full day.

Using Your Lawyer's Bill to Manage the Case

To be an effective management tool, the bills have to come frequently, at least every month. A timekeeping system in which entries are made promptly will easily produce a draft of the bill within two working days of the end of the billing period. The lawyer may need a day or two to clean up the first printout. The time is well spent if it is used to clarify what was done. You ought not be billed for the lawyer's time in making out his own bill without a prior explicit agreement. The final revised and corrected bill should be in the mail to you within a week after the month closes.

Pay the lawyer's bill immediately upon receipt. Take the discount if one has been negotiated. Do not hold the payment pending approval. Establishing a pattern of prompt payment creates a negotiating position that will you help resolve any difficulties which may arise. Use the retainer agreement to expressly reserve the right to audit and review the bill after payment and provide for subsequent adjustments.

The hourly detail portion of the bill, Fig. 15-2, is your primary progress report. Do three things with the bill: process it for payment, keep it as a historical record, and analyze it. Some accounts payable systems require that the original bill be used for routings and approvals required for payment. There is a risk that some courts will hold that a bill routed for payment is not a privileged document because it is seen by accounts payable clerks and others not normally privy to confidential information. That problem is avoided by using a summary page or invoice, of which Fig. 15-3 is an example, and detaching the detail. The billing detail is retained in the confidential files and never sent to the accounts payable department.

HEDGLON, ALLAN & SLAYTON
301 N.W. 63rd Street, Suite 700
Oklahoma City, Oklahoma 73116
(405) 555-8127

Federal Employer's ID No. 12-3456789

Invoice No. 12693

TO: Crush Cart Company
     21 N. West Street
     Waukegan, IL 60085

October 31, 1998

For professional services rendered:

In connection with:

Claim of John Doe
Our file 3542-0405

Paula T. Ripper	4.0 hours @ $150
Edgar Y. Answorth	8.0 hours @ $100
William G. Associate	13.2 hours @ $125
Warren D. Goode	3.9 hours @ $100

Total fee for services:	$3,440.00
Disbursements	$NONE
Total due this invoice:	$3,440,00
Past due	$NONE
Total now due:	$3,440.00

Due upon receipt. Thank you.

Figure 15-3. The summary invoice, without the detail, may be processed for payment.

Your Lawyer's Bill as History

Keep one copy of the bill, both the invoice and the detail, in a cost file for each case or matter. All of the dollar costs of the matter should be accumulated in the cost file, including internal costs such as employee time, travel, and copies. The legal bills break down into fees for professional services, the lawyers' operating expenses, and costs and disbursements.

Fees for professional services include time charges for paralegals, data-entry clerks, investigators, and process servers, as well as partners and associates. Where such support staff are utilized, their efforts should increase the efficiency or the impact of the lawyers' work. The professional services portion of the bill is easy to recognize because it is calculated by multiplying time expended by hourly rates.

The lawyers' operating expenses include travel and entertainment, copying, postage, and long-distance telephone. Some firms will also charge for use of databases such as WESTLAW, Lexis, or Dialogue. In some law firms the copy machine or other expense item becomes a profit center. If that is the case, you may want to insist that specific controls be adopted for those items. The best control is to require that such items be charged at actual cost. It is usual, and probably better, to send a major copying project out to a copy shop than to pay 23 cents per page to have the work done by a secretary. The law firm will tell you that 23 cents is justified by the labor cost of the secretary. If your case will require heavy copying, or other such nonprofessional services, make a specific arrangement to avoid excessive markup. Travel expense is a special problem. The easiest thing is to reimburse only the amount provided by your own company policy for employee travel.

When lawyers refer to "costs," they usually mean the amount of money that will be added by the court to the judgment. This includes filing fees, daily witness fees, and sometimes court reporters' fees. Filing and witness fees are usually nominal and advanced by the lawyer. Other disbursements, especially for expert witnesses and transcripts of depositions, often run to tens of thousands of dollars. Paying the expert, court reporter, or other vendor directly often promotes harmonious relations with the lawyer and her firm. Consider such direct payment whenever a single disbursement will run to more than a thousand dollars. An advantage in paying experts directly is that you may have use for their services in the future.

You should keep a complete cost file mainly because law firms do not do this kind of clerical work very well. If you ask a typical law firm to give you a total cost summary at the end of a case, it is a major project for them, and a substantial expense for you. Also, you have information about your internal costs that the lawyers don't have.

A complete cost file gives you an accurate and readily accessible history of everything that happened in the case and the total dollar cost incurred. When facing settlement decisions on the eve of trial, you will want to know how much was spent on the case. That is a knowable bit of information which should not control a settlement decision, but which seems to give litigants some comfort. Later, you may use cost information to evaluate results.

The cash outlays required in modern litigation are substantial. In certain limited situations, the court is authorized by legislation to shift the winner's litigation expense onto the loser. The opportunity to apply for an award of litigation expenses comes suddenly, at the end of trial. You want to be ready with complete figures.

Using the Bill to Detect Problems

When a lawyer does a bad job, the client suffers the consequences. Close study of the lawyers' billing detail will reveal most problems as they develop. Quick corrective action often prevents any permanent harm. "Quick" means without delay. This analysis of billings should be done immediately upon receipt of the bill. Make a copy of the bill to use solely for that purpose. Do not put off looking at the bill until the payment has been processed.

The billing detail is analyzed for several things. Who is doing the work? What are they doing? Are tasks being completed, or are the attorneys just spinning their wheels? Are the completed tasks making the expected contribution to establishing the facts or legal theories which make up the theme developed when the budget was prepared?

Attorneys' work fits into a few classifications: learning, analyzing, communicating, executing, advocating. *Learning* includes both researching the law in the library and studying the facts by talking to people and looking at documents, places, and objects. *Analyzing* means doing something with the material learned to give it meaning and impact. *Communicating* includes returning your phone calls, but more important, putting the fruits of the analysis into a form that can be used to obtain the desired results. *Executing* means doing the job, sometimes drafting documents, or taking a deposition. *Advocating* is a special kind of communicating, implying persuasion in the presence of opposition. The attorneys' bill should have enough detail so you can figure out which of these kinds of work each item is. Most work that does not fit one of these classifications contributes little or nothing to accomplishing your objectives.

Who is doing the work on the case? Presumably, you selected a partner at a law firm for her personal ability. Summarizing a deposition transcript is probably a job for a junior associate or even a paralegal. Attending the pretrial conferences is appropriate for the lead trial attorney, the partner you hired to do your case. Is an associate skillful enough to take the adverse doctor's deposition (10/09)? If six months' billings show no participation by that lead attorney, you may be getting the best strategic efforts of an associate with one year or less of experience. Reading the bills will tell you who is running your case. Expect to pay for some communication time within the firm between the lead attorney and her associates (10/10/98). However, conferences among junior associates are merely the blind leading the blind (10/11/98).

The summary that shows the total time charged by each person, Fig. 15-3, is a big help in keeping track of who is working on the case. When unfamiliar names appear on the bill, you may want to address the cost of bringing such new people "up to speed" (10/14/98). Research on a specific and narrow point of law can sometimes be done by a person who knows nothing about the case (10/12/98). But ordinarily a researcher has to know what the case is about in order to know which issues to discard and which to follow up on. The cost of acquiring that knowledge is charged to you somewhere.

A more serious problem is identified when one associate after another seems to take over the file. You are paying the cost of the time spent while each one learns about the case. Worse, such passing of the file from one associate to another means that no one wants to do your work and no partner is looking after your interests.

The amount of time charged in each instance indicates more than just raw time. If the time is charged for a telephone call, the bill should say who was called, what was discussed, and any results. In the example at 10/13/98, the call was not worthless. Some knowledge was gained of the status of the case. The time represents thinking about the call, dialing, exchanging information, and writing it down. This is communicating time. It often comes in small bits, such as three- or four-tenths of an hour.

Except for communications, where the individual cannot control the other party, billing for many small bits of time indicates inefficiency. Incoming mail may call for a decision to act on it or merely file it, perhaps some analysis. But otherwise, the time it takes to focus on a matter suggests that chunks of less than an hour are used poorly. This is especially true where junior associates are charging 0.3 hour to "review file" (10/14). It means either that they are looking for something to do so they can make their monthly billing requirement, or that they are doing the copying and filing because they have no secretary.

Larger amounts of time should relate to identifiable projects within the case. Typical projects might be the drafting of a motion for summary judgment, producing requested documents, or taking a group of depositions. Each project should move to completion, with a tangible result. Some work never seems to get finished, or produce results. In one instance, a Washington firm with special expertise was retained by the government to investigate a fraud at a particular institution. The fraud involved the churning of futures accounts by a broker. The investigation started in March. By mid-summer the client had made a decision to proceed with a lawsuit. Monthly bills came in through the autumn, winter, and into spring. Over a period of six months, more than 135 hours were charged to "drafting complaint." This was in addition to adequate time charged for investigation and analysis. At the end of the sixth month, a copy of the "draft complaint" was requested. It did not come. Over a period of several more months, increasingly assertive requests were made for the elusive complaint. Finally, with the balmy breezes of the following June, a document arrived, reflecting perhaps two days work. As a business client, if you are billed for a draft complaint, you should expect to see a draft complaint.

When you have bills for several periods in hand, you can look at the projects or tasks which have been done and get some sense of how much is being accomplished. For example, a motion to dismiss which is not granted contributes nothing to accomplishing your objectives. You should be able to look at each completed task and evaluate it as helpful, neutral, or worthless. Put the misdirected or unnecessary effort in the worthless category. There is always some waste motion in litigation, but it should be less than half. Also, with several bills in hand, you can begin to compare results, both in dollars expended and time elapsed, with the budgets or estimates developed at the beginning of the matter.

Look at the relationship between time billed and disbursements. Large payments to experts should be accompanied by attorney time spent learning how to use what the experts are producing. An attorney may buy and read a transcript instead of attending a deposition. In a simple case, the attorney may attend a deposition to see how a witness presents, and then rely only on notes as to what the witness said. Asking the attorney to explain how and why disbursements relate to time charges will help you communicate.

There is a story hidden in the fictitious bill, Fig. 15-2. Read it closely. The entries at 10/02, 10/03, 10/10, and 10/11 each relate to changes in design and the apparent absence of some expected documentation. These indicate a developing risk that a jury will believe that vital evidence has been destroyed or concealed. If von Slugger has hidden some evidence, you need to know it now, as it may affect your settlement posture. Your attorneys may hesitate to question him, or to tell you of the problem. By watching the bills, you will know when to intervene and straighten out the confusion, or get the case settled before it gets worse.

Use with Caution

Close analysis of legal bills can become micromanagement. If the attorney was carefully selected, she should have the expertise and dedication to do a good job with no supervision at all. That is what it means to be a professional. Close and frequent analysis of the bills will make you aware of every activity and decision. Such awareness can lead to a degree of involvement which blurs responsibility. Or it can lead to nitpicking and fault finding that blunts initiative. Either limits the value of the legal services.

The close analysis technique may also tempt you to try to beat down the amount of the legal bills. It is easy to complain when you are charged for research on issues that are later deemed not to be relevant, for phone calls that are not completed, or for depositions of witnesses who turn out to know nothing. The reality is that in contested matters, sometimes the only way to find out what works is to try some things that don't.

When close analysis of the bills leads to micromanagement or efforts to squeeze the fees, attorneys quickly learn to edit all useful information out of the detail descriptions. This unhappy result can be avoided if you limit your use of what you learn by analyzing the bills to correcting serious problems. Rely on the systems described in the next chapter for your routine interaction with the attorneys.

1. Billing requirements:

    Bill sent within 10 days of end of billing period
    Billing period 1 month or less
    Separate bill for each matter
    Summary invoice to process for payment, including:
       Hourly rate and time expended by each attorney
       Total fee for each attorney
       Total expenses and disbursements
       Total amount due on that invoice
    Statement of detail of work:
       Date each service performed
       Initials of person doing work
       Description of work performed and with whom
       Time expended doing the work described

2. Read billing detail as a whole, and each entry, and note:

    As to the lead attorney you selected:
       Quantity of time devoted to your matter
       Legal work she does herself
       Her supervision of subordinates
       Her contribution to strategy and key decisions
    As to the tasks being worked on:
       Contribution to the theme of the case
       Progress toward completion of the task
       Work product you have received that incorporates the tasks
    As to each time entry:
       If, for tasks involving learning, analyzing, or executing, enough time, more than ½ hour, is spent to accomplish something significant
       If frequent charging of small amounts of time indicates work done as filler during slow days
    If the file is being passed from associate to associate
    If you are paying associates to talk to each other
    If there are any persons you cannot identify working on your case
    Attorney's utilization of experts and your employees

3. Classify the tasks reflecting work in successive billings as worthless, neutral, or helpful in accomplishing your objectives.

4. Look for indications of unusual or unexpected problems with evidence or people in the detailed descriptions of the work.

Procedure: Reading a Legal Bill.

16
Systems That Keep You in Touch with Your Attorney and Your Case

You set the tone of your relationship with your attorney at the beginning. A systematic approach to selecting and retaining attorneys is a clear and direct statement of what you want. An active follow-up keeps things moving in the right direction.

Studying your attorney's bills is an effective way of detecting problems as they develop. When you retain a lawyer for some jobs, such as drafting a contract, perfecting a security interest, or applying for a license, you expect it to be completed before you get a bill. You may never see a bill at all if the attorney is paid by an insurer. Discussions in reaction to billings always seem to imply criticism and concern about costs. While the bills are the best way to protect yourself against problems, here are eight ways to create opportunities to react to your attorney with positive input.

Periodic Visitations

The most experienced users of trial attorneys are insurance companies. Traditionally, before the modern marvels of communications, the insurance company claims manager would periodically ride the circuit, visiting each of his local trial attorneys and going over the cases which that attorney was handling. The attorney and the claims manager came to understand each other, and the cases, so the attorney could act effectively on behalf of the company. Get out of your nice, warm, comfortable office and visit your attorney at her office. You want to observe the attorney in her operating environment, and have your impact there.

The visit is not a social call. Attorneys, especially trial attorneys, are self-directed and expect to dominate most relationships. Careful preparation is necessary. Take an agenda, written is better, and your own file with you. Go over the file. If the matter is a lawsuit, the attorney should be telling you what will have to be proven, what evidence will prove those points, and what steps she is taking to identify the witnesses and exhibits and get them ready to be taken to the courthouse. Direct the conversation toward the budget and schedule, if there is one. When the right tone is set, establish goals and deadlines and extract commitments to meet them, just as you would with any employee or contractor. Within such a framework, the attorney should be telling you what her "feel" for the case is, so you can be formulating a realistic settlement posture.

It is best to make at least three visits: when the budget is prepared, at the midpoint of discovery, and before the pretrial memorandum is submitted. These visits should be made by the person charged with managing the case, usually the person who signed the retainer agreement and approves payment of the bill. Conferences between the attorney and witnesses don't count as visits. The visit should end with both the attorney and your representative knowing what they are going to do next.

Copies of Everything

It is easy to instruct your attorney to send you copies of everything. Most of what happens in a legal matter involves something written on paper. Just receiving all the paper does not give you any information unless someone reads it, understands it, and files it. You may not have space to store all of the paper, much less time to read it.

Attorneys have a practical problem with requests for copies of everything. It is easy to send you copies of papers prepared by your attorney. It is more difficult to copy and forward papers which are received. Some things, such as correspondence regarding dates for depositions, are unimportant. The extra step of copying and sending on to the client everything received seems to burden attorneys, perhaps because it is not reflected by an hourly billing system. Some items are rarely copied. Casual notes made during phone conversations or meetings, interim research notes, and copies of research material have little information value when removed from the context in which they are created.

To use a "copy everything" system, tell the lawyer, in the retainer agreement, to send you copies of: everything filed, by any party, with the court and the court's orders; all correspondence, including correspondence with your own employees involved in the case; research memoranda; reports of experts and investigators; discovery requests and responses; deposition transcripts and summaries; and indexes to materials produced for inspection. In a simple case the material can be filed in the order in which it is received. You should study all these copies to see what action may be called for and to match the work product with the descriptions of work in the billing detail.

The practical problem is finding time to read, understand, and file the volume of paper that comes from a request for copies of everything. Insurance companies employ analysts for this purpose. If you have a steady flow of cases that follow consistent patterns, such as collections, foreclosures, or personal injury, you might train someone for that function. An analyst need not be a lawyer or even have formal training as a paralegal. The analyst promptly and carefully reads all of the papers received. The important points are added to a summary along with supplemental information. The papers are maintained in orderly files. The analyst will soon become familiar with common patterns and be able to bring discrepancies to the attention of the person responsible for decisions about the matter.

The "monster" case requires special consideration in requesting copies. Some cases—for example, "Superfund," toxic tort, securities fraud, and product-liability claims—may involve hundreds of parties. The court may force your trial attorneys to work through a committee or liaison counsel. As a single party, you may be little more than a bystander. The volume of paper generated in such a case, perhaps several hundred pages every week for years, may overwhelm your in-house ability to digest it. At the end of one such case, 67 cartons of file were shipped to the client for long-term storage, the attorney keeping only a skeleton file of two cartons. In such cases, you should ask your attorney to send you copies of all court orders, any pleadings and discovery materials filed on your behalf, and selected items of particular interest. The time lapse between when your lawyer receives material and when she forwards it to you will reveal how closely she is watching the case. If you are getting only "selected" copies, a regular report of the significance of all documents received will show if your lawyer read and understood each item before she filed it.

Receiving and understanding this information creates an opportunity for you to take an active role in the direction of the case. Read the copies and react. Tell your attorney how you interpret developments. You know the dynamics of the marketplace, the histories of the players, and the relevant science or art. This is your opportunity to use your time, not your attorney's time, to bring your special knowledge to bear on the problem. The benefit of getting copies comes when you share that special knowledge with your attorneys.

Relying on copies has dangers. Asking your attorney to send copies of everything may cause a misunderstanding about who is responsible for communications. Sending you a copy of something is not the same as telling you about it. Proper interpretation may require an understanding of local procedures or background information. You may miss the significance of things you receive. Also, what is really important about a matter may be conversations and observations that are never written down. A lawyer retained as a lobbyist concerning a pending legislative matter may see and talk to many people, but write little of importance. There is nothing to copy. Finally, copies are just copies. You may put off reading them until it is too late to act.

Discretionary Reports

When you are comfortable with a particular attorney, you might simply rely on her professional judgment about keeping you informed. If you adopt such a passive approach, get the reports in writing. Legal matters go on for a long time. A written report will remain in your file to remind you of what happened and to protect the attorney from your malpractice claim.

You assert minimal control by asking the attorney write a report whenever a significant event occurs. By writing, the attorney can put what is important into a letter while it is fresh in her mind. The dictating machine is always available; you may be hard to reach by phone. The formality of a letter keeps the focus on what is important and preserves details; the spontaneity of a phone call may distract either of you from the main message. Of course, when you have to make decisions there is no substitute for an immediate, direct exchange of views and information.

Periodic Reports

The difficulty with regular, periodic reports is that nothing may be happening when the report is due. The attorney will just update the last report. You cannot tell what has changed unless you compare successive reports.

It is a small step from asking for periodic reports to creating a form. When you have numerous similar cases, as in collections or workers' compensation matters, it is convenient to keep track of the cases on a computer, perhaps with a relational database. Soon the system dictates what information is asked for, and limits what can be reported. Law